Rural America's Pathways to College and Career

Steps for Student Success and School Improvement

Rick Dalton

NEW YORK AND LONDON

First published 2021
by Routledge
52 Vanderbilt Avenue, New York, NY 10017

and by Routledge
2 Park Square, Milton Park, Abingdon, Oxon OX14 4RN

Routledge is an imprint of the Taylor & Francis Group, an informa business

Library of Congress Cataloging-in-Publication Data
Names: Dalton, Rick, author.
Title: Rural America's pathways to college and career:
steps for student success and school improvement / Rick Dalton.
Identifiers: LCCN 2020047788 (print) | LCCN 2020047789 (ebook) |
ISBN 9780367528508 (hardback) | ISBN 9780367530433 (paperback) |
ISBN 9781003080268 (ebook)
Subjects: LCSH: Education, Rural–United States. |
School improvement programs–United States. |
Academic achievement–United States. |
School-to-work transition–United States.
Classification: LCC LC5146 .D35 2021 (print) |
LCC LC5146 (ebook) | DDC 370.9173/4–dc23
LC record available at https://lccn.loc.gov/2020047788
LC ebook record available at https://lccn.loc.gov/2020047789

ISBN: 978-0-367-52850-8 (hbk)
ISBN: 978-0-367-53043-3 (pbk)
ISBN: 978-1-003-08026-8 (ebk)

Typeset in Optima
by Newgen Publishing UK

Rural America's Pathways to College and Career

This book provides solutions to the vexing educational challenges that rural communities face and serves as a how-to guide for building college and career readiness within rural schools.

Rural America's Pathways to College and Career shares practical tips that can be used by educators and community members to transform rural schools, help students develop essential skills, locate and train college- and career-ready advisors, establish business partnerships, build college readiness, leverage technology, build interest in science, technology, engineering and math (STEM) careers, and understand how to pay for college.

Based on research and drawing on best practice and poignant stories, Dalton shares examples of success and challenges from interviews conducted with over 200 individuals who have participated in programs across the country. By helping rural youth learn about the opportunities available and by providing them with the support they need to succeed, this book serves as an actionable guide to helping students in rural schools attain postsecondary school success.

Rick Dalton is President and CEO of CFES (College for Every Student) Brilliant Pathways and has spent the last 35 years expanding opportunities in higher education for economically disadvantaged youth. He has written more than 200 articles and op-eds on college access and success.

Other Eye On Education Books Available from Routledge

(www.routledge.com/eyeoneducation)

A Guide to Impactful Teacher Evaluations: Let's Finally Get It Right!
Joseph O. Rodgers

A Guide to Early College and Dual Enrollment Programs: Designing and Implementing Programs for Student Achievement
Russ Olwell

The Strategy Playbook for Educational Leaders: Principles and Processes
Isobel Stevenson and Jennie Weiner

Unpacking Your Learning Targets: Aligning Student Learning to Standards
Sean McWherter

Strategic Talent Leadership for Educators: A Practical Toolkit
Amy A. Holcombe

Becoming a Transformative Leader: A Guide to Creating Equitable Schools
Carolyn M. Shields

Bringing Innovative Practices to Your School: Lessons from International Schools
Jayson W. Richardson

Working with Students Who Have Anxiety: Creative Connections and Practical Strategies
Beverley H. Johns, Donalyn Heise, and Adrienne D. Hunter

Implicit Bias in Schools: A Practitioner's Guide
Gina Laura Gullo, Kelly Capatosto, and Cheryl Staats

Leadership in America's Best Urban Schools
Joseph F. Johnson, Jr, Cynthia L. Uline, and Lynne G. Perez

Leading Learning for ELL Students: Strategies for Success
Catherine Beck and Heidi Pace

Contents

Preface

I began studying rural schools in 1983. That year, I was working in the admissions office at Middlebury College when I was asked to join three other researchers on a team that would lead the National College Counseling Project (NCCP). With support and financial sponsorship from the National Association for College Admission Counseling (NACAC), we conducted a three-year study on who goes to college and why. It was the most extensive research ever done on the topic, and the findings were published in the book *Frontiers of Possibility* in 1986.

Following the publication of *Frontiers,* we were asked to test our theory on how to turn around schools and change life trajectories in two rural Florida Panhandle communities. We developed the Gulf County Project that created significant gains in academic performance and in the number of students attending college. The success of that rural program changed my life trajectory. After being a part of transforming lives, I wanted to do that work full-time. So, in 1990, I left Middlebury College and founded CFES (College for Every Student) Brilliant Pathways, an organization that has helped 100,000 youth from low-income households go to college and become ready for the workplace.

As I reflect on my experiences, I realize how much of my own life has been defined by rural communities. Beginning at age five, I spent ten summers on the shores of Lake Champlain in bucolic Willsboro, New York, the community I returned to ten years ago to live full-time.

Although I was born and raised in the suburbs of western Massachusetts, I've been pulled to rural communities my entire life. I attended Colgate University in the pastoral Chenango Valley of New York State. After college, I headed to the most rural part of Connecticut to teach high school, and eight years later, I signed on at Middlebury College in Vermont, the country's most rural state. During my first few years at Middlebury, I lived in the mountain town of Ripton, where I headed the school board.

Years later, I find solace tending my fruit trees, small vineyard, and blueberry bushes, and working the soil in my vegetable garden. I love connecting with my neighbors at the post office, talking with the owners at the Village Market, and laughing with friends at the Essex Inn. I see beauty and harmony and possibilities in rural America. That's why I'm so disturbed by the crisis that is facing rural communities.

Jobs are fleeing, poverty rates are high, there is an opioid epidemic, and too many young people are being pushed out of small towns to realize their dreams and to achieve economic sustainability. As I look out my kitchen window across the lake to Vermont, I see solutions in that state's plan to increase the number of postsecondary degrees and credentials for its working-age citizens. Vermont realizes that for its rural communities to be vibrant, they need to be economically viable—and that requires more residents with higher education training and skills. More than forty other states have come to the same conclusion, and they've set goals for increased numbers of postsecondary degrees. But standing in the way, among other obstacles, is a distrustful relationship between rural America and higher education.

I realize that the answer is complex and requires lots of solutions but helping the next generation become college and career ready is a great place to start. Everyone has an important role to play in making this work. This book provides practical steps that parents, teachers, educational leaders, and community members can use to help build incubators of college and career readiness in rural schools and communities across America. If we can contribute to the turning around of rural communities, students won't have to leave. And we will ensure that rural America finds its own brilliant pathway.

Overview of Chapters

Chapter 1 outlines why rural America's schools and communities are falling behind their urban and suburban counterparts. The chapter also tells the story of CFES Brilliant Pathways' evolution since its founding in 1991 and how college and career readiness strategies can help turn around rural communities and their economies.

Chapter 2 tells the story of a K–12 rural school that resurrected itself from the ashes to become a model that, because of its success, is being analyzed by researchers from institutions such as the Harvard Graduate School of Education and the University at Albany. The chapter provides steps that were integral in the school's transformation.

Chapter 3 provides an overview of the Essential Skills™ that were identified by CFES (College for Every Student) in their most successful scholars—those who graduate from college on time and attain well-paying jobs that move them and their families out of poverty. The six Essential Skills—goal setting, teamwork, leadership, networking, perseverance, and agility—helped the students succeed in college and beyond. This chapter defines each skill and provides activities that can be used to help students develop these skills.

Chapter 4 discusses how college- and career-readiness counselors can provide needed support to rural students. Young people, especially those who are unfamiliar with higher education, need advice and support as they move toward college and career readiness. All students need advisors who are able and available to help them meet admission and financial aid deadlines, understand how to pay for college, complete applications, find internships and job-shadowing opportunities, and navigate the realm of college- and career-readiness challenges. This chapter outlines the importance of training college, community, and business personnel, as well as educators and staff in schools and provides information on how to train these individuals.

Chapter 5 highlights the important role community partners can play in helping students understand the workforce pathway. Since there are generally so few businesses located in rural communities, it can be difficult to identify prospective local partners, especially in industry sectors that are positioned to flourish in the next decades. Despite these obstacles, CFES has developed hundreds of highly successful business partnerships for its rural schools that accelerate college and career readiness. This chapter looks at how these partnerships provide mentors, internships, speakers for college- and career-readiness events, apprenticeships, and job-shadowing opportunities. Corporations including Ernst & Young, MetLife, and Southwest Airlines have partnered with rural schools across the United States through CFES.

Chapter 6 looks at what it means to be college ready and provides strategies to help rural students prepare for college life. CFES has set up more than 500 school–college partnerships in its history, and the most successful schools have been found to have robust higher education partnerships, whether with four-year universities or community colleges. Schools and colleges need help launching and maintaining these partnerships. Chapter 6 highlights successful partnerships between colleges and rural schools, and defines college readiness and shares special strategies to help rural students attain college readiness.

Chapter 7 discusses the importance of technology in leveraging opportunities and providing access to information in rural communities. The COVID-19 pandemic exposed our country's digital divide. A lack of high-speed internet and other attendant technologies greatly affects rural economies. Despite this challenge, some rural schools are finding ways to leverage technology to overcome cost, distance, and other obstacles. Technology has the potential to shorten the distance between communities and colleges, which will greatly benefit rural students. This chapter shares ways to leverage technology to ameliorate this situation and ultimately enhance college and career readiness.

Chapter 8 examines what keeps rural students from graduating college. Each year more than 500,000 rural students drop out of college. Graduation rates are lower for rural kids than for their urban and suburban peers because rural students have less exposure to diversity and less support from their home communities, where there are likely to be far fewer people with college degrees. This chapter shares strategies that colleges and college- and career-readiness advisors are implementing to ensure that rural students graduate, as well as what young people and their families can do to ensure greater likelihood of on-time degree attainment.

Chapter 9 examines the importance of science, technology, engineering and math (STEM) education and the challenges rural students face. In the United States, low-income students are ten times less likely to attain a STEM degree than their high-income peers. Given that the majority of the new, high-paying jobs in our country will be in STEM, it's crucial that we fix this broken pipeline and include more low-income students, especially those from rural communities, who are woefully underrepresented in the STEM workplace. This is critical because STEM jobs are the future. This chapter looks at how CFES is addressing these issues by providing hands-on activities for rural students to build STEM awareness, interest, and readiness.

Chapter 10 provides helpful information for students on understanding the cost of college and how to pay for it. The cost of college has increased significantly in the last decade. Not surprisingly, cost is now the greatest obstacle preventing young people from pursuing college. For students from rural America, cost is an even greater deterrent. Chapter 10 shares strategies for paying for college that will benefit students, their families, and their schools. While the most important strategy is to stay informed and meet deadlines, residents of rural communities across America are also creating their own innovative scholarship programs that are helping thousands of students attain college degrees and transform lives.

Acknowledgments

Rural America's Pathways to College and Career would not be possible without the support of dozens of colleagues, students and friends. At CFES (College for Every Student) Brilliant Pathways, Natan Arrazate, Rose Breen, Claire Carson, Karen Judge, Stephanie Senclair, Tara Smith, and Manny Tejeda provided technical support. My CFES colleague, Jon Reidel, wrote Chapter 7. Scott Thomas, Dean at the University of Vermont, wrote a sidebar in Chapter 4.

Ken Aaron, Jen Roberts, Kelly Hofschneider, Felicia Lee, and Katie Shepherd provided editorial support.

Thanks to the education stars from Crown Point Central School—Shari Brannock, Drew Malone, Tara Spaulding, Mitch St Pierre, Kristen Thorpe—for sharing their remarkable stories.

Richard Childers, Andrew Crain, Pete Emerson, John Fortune, Dreama Gentry, Chris Green, Gary Kuch, Dan Mannix, Judy May, Andrea McDonald, John McDonald, Dave Morell, Brogan Morton, Don Outing and dozens of others shared their pathway stories and wisdom.

Rural America Today

Rural Schools: A Hidden Crisis

Thirty years ago, any serious conversation about troubled schools in America would have evoked—accurately—an image of crumbling, underfunded inner-city schools and the underserved students struggling to learn in them. Conventional wisdom would have said the good schools were those supported by affluent taxpayers in the suburbs or rural schools (see Box 1.1 for a definition of "rural"), which, while lacking the wealth and resources of their suburban counterparts, boasted tight-knit, proud communities and students who were fiercely loved and supported by their families and neighbors.

But the situation is different today. While urban schools continue to face serious challenges, it is rural schools and communities that are now in crisis. Urbanization and economic shifts have drained rural economies and populations, leaving those remaining in rural communities with few financial resources or professional opportunities. Poverty and addiction have become part of the rural landscape. As a result, rural schools now struggle to attract qualified teachers or provide the resources needed to prepare their students to face the larger world. In particular, college readiness is a serious challenge for rural students, who face daunting obstacles—both financial and social—in attempting to pursue higher education.

While the challenges of rural schools have attracted relatively little public attention, they are every bit as urgent as those faced by urban schools. Rural communities desperately need creative new ways to support and grow their economies, and an educated population is

Box 1.1 Defining "Rural"

According to the United States Census Bureau, rural communities are defined as those places that are not urban and are less dense, with a sparse population (Ratcliffe et al., 2016). At CFES, we think of rural as communities with fewer than 15,000 residents. Other rural indicators include no broadband and the presence of a Dollar General store, which is becoming a symbol of rural poverty and isolation.

critical for making this happen. The talents of rural youth are all too often wasted in dead-end, unskilled jobs; a cure for cancer or solution to climate change may well be developed by a young person from a logging town in Oregon or a farming hamlet in Vermont if he or she only receives the necessary support and guidance to make it to, and through, college.

This book addresses the challenges and triumphs of rural schools and presents action steps that communities, families, and educators can take to support them and their students. The recommendations and strategies in this book are informed by my over 40 years of experience as an admissions director, researcher, and president of an educational nonprofit, CFES (College for Every Student) Brilliant Pathways.

This chapter provides the context for the rest of the book. I start with an overview of the challenges faced by rural communities, how they impact education, and why they matter. Next, I present a short introduction to my research and recommendations—in collaboration with other respected educators—on rural schools and improving college readiness. I then share the results of our first attempts to put the findings of our research into practice in rural schools and the evolution of our model for college readiness and support for schools.

While at times it might seem that the problems of rural schools and communities are insurmountable, rural America has many stories of hope and resiliency. Exciting ideas have emerged from rural communities—from simple but inspiring actions by intrepid teachers to young people returning after college to build tech startups in their communities. It is my hope that these stories will spark readers—whether educators, parents, or concerned community members—to contribute their own knowledge, resources, and creativity to help make college and career possible for every student.

 The Canary in the Coal Mine

Rural youth face a unique constellation of obstacles to higher education. I began to recognize these as I became actively involved in helping schools foster college readiness. Over and over, I saw instances where rural youth were losing ground. In 2005, I met Fred, a then 9th grade student at a small rural school in the Adirondacks. Fred participated in college readiness programs offered by CFES, the predecessor to CFES Brilliant Pathways. He was beaming and eager for any opportunity CFES offered. In 10th grade, he participated in the annual CFES New York City exchange, where eight rural students spent the day at a CFES school in the Bronx, toured Columbia and Fordham Universities, and took in cultural sites around the city. In his 9th and 10th grade years, Fred visited a half dozen colleges in New York and New England and participated in peer mentoring and workshops to develop what CFES calls the Essential Skills™.

As Fred grew older, however, he lost that bright-eyed look. Halfway through his 11th grade year, he stopped coming to leadership meetings and participating in CFES activities. Fred didn't want to go to college. He didn't even apply. His parents didn't see it as a necessity. "We didn't go, and you don't need to be better than us," they told him. Today, Fred works sporadically, picking up a catering job here and there. He still lives with his sister in the house where they grew up.

I spoke to Gail, a teacher who works in a rural community, about Fred not applying to college. "Not every student needs college," she told me. "My son didn't go. And he's got a truck that's paid for and a boat and a house." I realized then that we needed to change our approach to thinking about and preparing for a college education.

These challenges are why CFES came to Essex, New York. We wanted to be part of the solution. So in 2010, CFES moved across Lake Champlain from Vermont to the Adirondacks, from rural to very rural. We brought jobs to a rural community and attention to college and career readiness. We spread awareness to the obstacles that rural children, families, and their communities face. Living in a town of 600 residents, I now see those challenges every day.

Rural youth like Fred are more likely than their urban peers to drink alcohol, vape, and engage in other at-risk behaviors. Rural adults are more likely to suffer from obesity, mental health issues, diabetes, cancer, and opioid addiction. The number of people living in rural communities is dropping daily. One third of the people living in rural communities don't have broadband internet service, and jobs are leaving rural areas at an accelerating rate (Kight & Bartz, 2019).

Idle Men in Their Prime

I don't have to read *The New York Times* to know about the prevalence of jobless men in their prime working years or the despair in declining rural areas (Krugman, 2019). I can walk across the street to talk with Steve and Randy, both of whom are healthy and in their 50s. Neither of these men have worked a day in the last 20 years—well, except Steve, who had a gig removing asbestos for a few weeks. He was caught illegally dumping asbestos, and that's the reason he spent two years in prison. The prevalence of men like Steve and Randy, healthy but not working, is an indicator of challenges in rural America.

Clean Air, No Traffic—and No Future?

Despite the challenges mentioned above, I also know that most rural Americans are resilient, value their family roots and history, have a commitment to their communities, and love the natural environment that encompasses their day-to-day existence. Rural areas also benefit from stronger social ties and unique forms of social capital, often benefiting from more intimate school and community contexts (Byun et al., 2012; McNamee, 2019). I live in one of the most beautiful natural areas anywhere. The air's clean, and there's no traffic. If I ask my neighbor Steve to help me get my lawn tractor out of the mud, he'll say yes and smile while he's helping.

Despite the beauty and tranquility, our rural communities face big economic obstacles and other problems that impact the choices rural children make on their trajectory toward college and careers.

Rural Poverty and the Loss of Skilled Workers

Since educational attainment is highly correlated with measures of regional economic prosperity, rural counties with the lowest levels of educational attainment face higher poverty, unemployment, and population loss (United States Department of Agriculture Economic Research Service, 2017).

Limited jobs and an unskilled workforce also result in poverty in rural America, poverty that is wider and deeper than in urban America. Sixty-four percent of rural counties have high rates of child poverty, compared to 47% of urban counties, and 13% of children under six years of age in rural communities experience severe financial difficulty, whereas 10% of young children living in urban areas experience deep poverty. From childhood to adulthood, poverty is more persistent and more likely to last for generations in rural areas (Lavalley, 2018).

Major urban centers are magnets for economic growth. They offer large markets, specialized suppliers, large pools of skilled workers, and the exchange of information that comes from face-to-face contact (Duranton & Puga, 2003). As jobs in agriculture, manufacturing, and mining disappear from rural areas, the urban-rural divide widens. Even though millions of jobs have been created in the last decade, these new jobs have been located primarily in major cities, leaving small-town America far behind.

In most rural places, there isn't easy access to education past high school, which usually means there isn't a highly trained workforce. This, in turn, discourages technology businesses and those in other growing fields from coming to town. As David Jesse wrote in a *Detroit Free Press* article, "[This] means not many jobs that pay well, which means poverty, which means it's harder for people to have money for college, which means … well, the circle just continues" (Jesse, 2019).

Because of these economic shifts, college-educated people are leaving small towns for urban areas, deepening an educational and political divide that is increasingly coming to define our country (Waddell, 2019).

The decisions that young people on the edge of adulthood make about whether to stay or leave home have profound implications for the future of rural America. Rural students who pursue degrees at residential, four-year colleges and universities are significantly less likely to return to their home communities, especially if they acquired educational loans. This creates a perplexing situation for local educators, who are often measured by how many of their students ultimately enroll in college. At the same time, local government officials are desperate to keep young people in their communities as older residents pass away. The picture is bleak for rural America, where, in any given year, more than 6% of America's rural bachelor's degree holders migrate to a metropolitan area (Carr & Kefalas, 2010).

Back in 1940, when just 5% of Americans possessed a college education, degreed teachers, physicians, and business owners were scattered across small towns and cities fairly evenly. By 1970, only 5 percentage points separated the most highly educated regions in the United States from the least highly educated regions. By 2000, the regional education gap had more than doubled, to 13 percentage points (Carr & Kefalas, 2010). The youth exodus benefits the destination cities and hurts the regions from which migrants flee. For every current thriving metropolis, there are dozens of rural brain-drain areas where economic growth has stalled (Carr & Kefalas, 2010).

The Case of Ticonderoga, New York

Ticonderoga is a small village in upstate New York where John McDonald grew up. After graduating from the local high school, McDonald headed off to Washington and Lee University in Virginia. McDonald came back to his community about ten years after finishing college, where he served as Ticonderoga's Superintendent of Schools for 20 years.

Recently, McDonald looked at where Ticonderoga's top students ended up living after college. "In the last quarter century, only one valedictorian or salutatorian has returned to Ticonderoga," he said. "On a similar note, fewer than 10% of the top ten students in each class are still in Ticonderoga during that same period of time."

The problem, says McDonald, "is we don't have sustainable jobs that can support people coming home. Living here is a choice, and not everyone that grows up in Ticonderoga wants to come back. It is a big world, and people need to make life choices. Nevertheless, those that want to return don't have that option."

The 10/10 Phenomenon

Ticonderoga isn't the only community facing such problems. Over the last dozen years, 75% of the top ten students at Vermont's Vergennes Union High School (24 miles south of Burlington) went to college and didn't return to their hometown. On the other hand, 85% of the bottom ten students in the class stayed in Vergennes.

What the Most Important Numbers Say

It's easy to be fooled by looking at educational performance statistics for rural students. On many state and national tests, including the National Assessment of Educational Progress (NAEP), rural students score better than their urban peers. Likewise, high school graduation rates are practically the same (84% in rural areas versus 83% in urban areas), while urban kids go to college at only a slightly higher rate (62 versus 59%) than their rural counterparts (Marcus & Krupnick, 2017).

However, when it comes to college retention, rural students fall far behind. The most troubling education statistic for rural America is the fact that of all rural residents between the ages of 18–24, just 29% are enrolled in college. On the other hand, 49% of urban residents in the same age group are pursuing higher education (Krupnick, 2018). This means that urban youth aged 18–24 are a staggering 68% more likely to be enrolled in college than their rural peers.

Isolation

Most rural students live in communities where there are few colleges nearby, thus constraining educational opportunities. The root cause of inequality in many communities is the simple fact that no accessible college is located nearby. The farther a young person lives from a college, the less likely they are to attend. Those living more than 50 miles away are far less likely to pursue a postsecondary degree. Where students go to college depends largely on where they live (Hillman & Weichman, 2016).

In the Adirondack Region of New York, where CFES Brilliant Pathways is headquartered, the primary roads are well maintained, but the winding secondary roads are in poor condition. Many Adirondack students live on unpaved roads that are barely passable during the heavy snowfalls of the winter months. Some students spend two hours per day travelling to and from school, and many residents travel more than 25 miles to the nearest grocery store. Rural students are also isolated by limited access to internet connectivity. Today, rural America is 15 times less likely to have broadband access than their urban counterparts (Federal Communications Commission, 2020).

Rural America's Distrustful Relationship with Higher Education

Despite the correlation between education and jobs, rural America is distrustful of postsecondary education. Rural residents see college costs as unchecked and college degrees as pushing young people out of their hometowns. This has conspired to make rural residents wary of higher education, which helps explain why only 33% of rural dwellers believe that a four-year degree is worthwhile, compared to 52% of urban dwellers. Forty-three percent of those with a high school diploma or less—from both rural and urban communities—see a four-year degree as worthwhile.

Forty percent of rural white fathers think their children will grow up with a lower standard of living than they enjoyed, compared to 23% of urban fathers. Fewer rural white men believe college is worthwhile; 71% believe college can provide their children with necessary skills, compared to 82% of white urban men and 84% of suburban white men (Morin, 2016). For rural Black, Latinx, and Native populations, far more research is needed to fully understand the barriers related to college access but recent studies suggest that these populations are among the most disadvantaged in terms of college-going support (Cabrera, Lopez, & Sáenz, 2012; Means et al., 2016).

The Shrinking Teacher Pipeline

Rural teachers are older and less likely to have a master's degree, and rural schools have more difficulty filling vacancies, especially in science, technology, engineering and math (STEM) positions. "Fifteen years ago, we had 42 people apply for a history teacher position," said the Superintendent of Willsboro Central School. "Last year, we had a hard time filling the position."

The rural Van Horn (Texas) school district has dealt with the teacher pipeline challenge by providing housing for its teachers. "We offer teacher housing for single teachers and teachers with families as part of our recruiting strategy," said School Counseling Head Sondra McCoy. "Not having a Wal-Mart is a challenge for attracting teachers who have lived in larger cities. It helps that we have a high population of teachers that grew up and graduated from here. We refer to that as 'grow your own'."

Analyzing America's College Readiness Trends

Through the National College Counseling Project (NCCP), introduced in the Preface, we surveyed 2,200 schools, from a randomly selected group that included 10% of America's high schools. Our findings were supported by state-of-the-art research at the University of Vermont. The results confirmed a direct correlation between family income and whether a student went to college. It also revealed a disturbing phenomenon: Those who needed the most help in the college readiness process received the least. This reality has only gotten worse since the study was first conducted in 1985.

The research also identified schools that were beating the odds by sending large proportions of low-income students to college, some from rural communities and others from urban areas. We asked volunteer educators to act as field researchers and nominate schools that were doing an exemplary job at helping their students become college ready. In our third year of the study, the NCCP Directors visited 13 of those exemplary schools to gather details about how they helped their students achieve college readiness. Those schools were rural and urban, high and low income, and small and large. Serving a range of ethnic populations, these schools were spread across America—from the borders of Canada and Mexico to the Black Belt of Alabama, the woods of Maine, and the barrios of Los Angeles.

Nascent Strategies for College Readiness

In the final phase, our study identified strategies shared by schools that produced high percentages of college-ready students. These guiding principles became the inspiration for what would become the theory behind CFES Brilliant Pathways, the organization I lead today. Whether rural or urban, we found that each of these exemplary schools:

- enlisted educators throughout the building,
- helped students and families understand *early* how to pay for college,
- involved families,
- promoted student achievement,
- partnered with colleges and businesses, and
- robustly celebrated higher education (Holmes et al., 1986).

College Readiness: Theory Becomes Practice

After the President of Rollins College read about our three-year study in *Frontiers of Possibility*, he shared it with the Jessie Ball duPont Fund. The foundation later awarded us a three-year grant to test our theory on what makes an exemplary school. In 1987, we began working in rural Gulf County, Florida.

By the end of the project, in 1990, Gulf County showed significant gains (see Box 1.2), including the highest test scores for Black students in the state, improvements in grades and behavior, and a growing student awareness of the opportunities available beyond high school. Ted Fiske, former education editor at *The New York Times*, described the Florida program as a:

> heartwarming story of people. It is a story of young people who were led to shed their blinders and reach for the academic stars. It is the story of dedicated teachers and administrators—the kind that can be found in all schools—who simply needed new tools and of families empowered to have aspirations that previously they dared not entertain.
>
> (Dalton & Erdmann, 1990)

Box 1.2 Measurable Results: Gulf County Project

	1987	1990
Average daily attendance	92%	96%
Dropout rate	3.4%	1.8%
Graduation rate	90.5%	98.1%
Postsecondary participation	50%	80%

Box 1.3 Walter Wilder: I'll Do What It Takes

"Come on in, men. I'm glad you're here." With white hair, brown eyes, and a burly build, Wilder looked more like an ex-tackle than a former professional center fielder. Elected by voters rather than appointed by a school board, Wilder showed us why he appealed to the electorate: He's direct, compassionate, and savvy. Our mission was to discuss the project blueprint. Wilder quickly grasped our plan and pledged his support. "I'll do what it takes to see that these kids get every chance possible."

(Dalton & Erdmann, 1990).

Gulf County's success had much to do with leadership throughout the district. Superintendent Walter Wilder in particular saw the value of raising student aspirations and achievement, and he realized that lessons learned by the NCCP could benefit his students, their families, and ultimately his community. Where many leaders saw a threat, Wilder saw an opportunity. He loved his community and wanted the best for his students. Box 1.3 provides an example of Wilder's approach during our first meeting with him.

The Project's Second Iteration

Following the success of the Gulf County Project, the Jessie Ball duPont Fund asked David Erdmann and I to develop another three-year initiative. Called

Partners for Educational Excellence, this seven-state program centered on nine high school–college partnerships: Colleges worked with high schools to provide resources, training, and mentoring to promote college readiness. By the time that project ended, every school in the program posted double-digit gains in the rates of students who had graduated and gone on to college.

College Readiness Strategies Learned from Two Research Projects

From the Gulf County and Partners for Educational Excellence projects, we took away the following critical lessons for success, which we are continuing to expand and build on in our current work with CFES Brilliant Pathways:

- build a team of educators, parents, and community members,
- enlist mentors and tap into college students,
- get students to visit several college campuses,
- involve students in service activities,
- expose high school students to college students with similar backgrounds, and
- help students and families understand how to pay for college early.

See Box 1.4 for a list of the partnerships developed by Partners for Educational Excellence.

Reflection and Learning

In 1986, the same year we began working in the two Florida Panhandle high schools, I took a sabbatical from Middlebury to begin a doctorate at the Harvard Graduate School of Education. My experience at Harvard gave me the opportunity to combine academic study with hands-on work in the Florida Panhandle and to grapple with questions about opportunity and equity. If college is a ladder to opportunity, how do we build a better

Box 1.4 Power of Partnerships

Agnes Scott College ↔ Pickens County High School (GA)

Ancilla College ↔ Knox Community High School (IN)

Arkansas College ↔ Cave City High School (AR)

Chipola College ↔ Marianna High School (FL)

Converse College ↔ James F. Byrnes High School (SC)

LaGrange College ↔ Villa Rica High School (GA)

Mississippi Valley State University ↔ Greenwood High School (MS)

Rollins College ↔ Maynard Evans High School (FL)

Xavier University of Louisiana (LA) ↔ Warren Easton High School

ladder? How do we get more students, especially those from low-income backgrounds, to climb that ladder?

That year of traveling back and forth between Cambridge and the Panhandle changed my own professional pathway. In Port St. Joe and Wewahitchka, I saw firsthand the power of ordinary people doing extraordinary things. I saw how educators supported by sound practice can change life trajectories. All of this supported the ideas I was studying and the change theory I was developing back at Harvard.

Upon my return to Middlebury, I spoke with College President Olin Robison about the need to increase the number of students of color at our college. Robison realized Middlebury couldn't achieve the greatness he envisioned without diversity, and he gave me the opportunity to lead efforts to recruit and retain more students of color. I developed a strategy and a program, and was given a budget to increase diversity.

I created a partnership between Middlebury College and DeWitt Clinton High School in the Bronx and established three diversity task forces: One in Boston, one in New York City, and one in Washington, D.C. The task forces included educators, philanthropists, and leaders such as Ron Brown, an alumnus of Middlebury College who went on to become Secretary of Commerce in the Clinton administration. The initiatives and strategies we developed tripled the number of Latinx and

Black students at Middlebury by the time I left in 1991 to start CFES Brilliant Pathways.

Change, Whether Urban or Rural, Requires Leadership

While Middlebury's diversity efforts targeted urban communities, the two projects financed by the Jessie Ball duPont Fund focused on rural schools, and the NCCP examined both rural and urban schools across America. There were obvious differences between urban and rural schools: Rural schools were smaller and less ethnically diverse, and, although we saw varying levels of effective leadership in both rural and urban schools, it was easier 30 years ago to create change and increase the number of college-ready students in rural schools than in urban ones. In 1990, residents of tight-knit rural communities were more trusting of higher education than they are today and would rally around a program that promised a better future for their children. Today, effective change in rural communities requires even more impactful leadership—which means leading communities toward change through mentoring and role models, and offering the information and resources needed to make higher education feel attainable and beneficial. The CFES Brilliant Pathways model, developed from our previous research and experience, offers a blueprint for providing such leadership (see Box 1.5).

CFES Comes to Schools in Central New York

Shortly after the NCCP morphed into the nonprofit called Foundation for Excellent Schools, or FES (which later became CFES Brilliant Pathways), we received our first grant from the Clark Foundation. We could thank Gulf County Superintendent Walter Wilder for that, as he met and sold the project to the Executive Director of the Foundation, Joe Cruickshank. In July of 1991, CFES began working in central New York State with the Leatherstocking cluster (the region named after James Fenimore

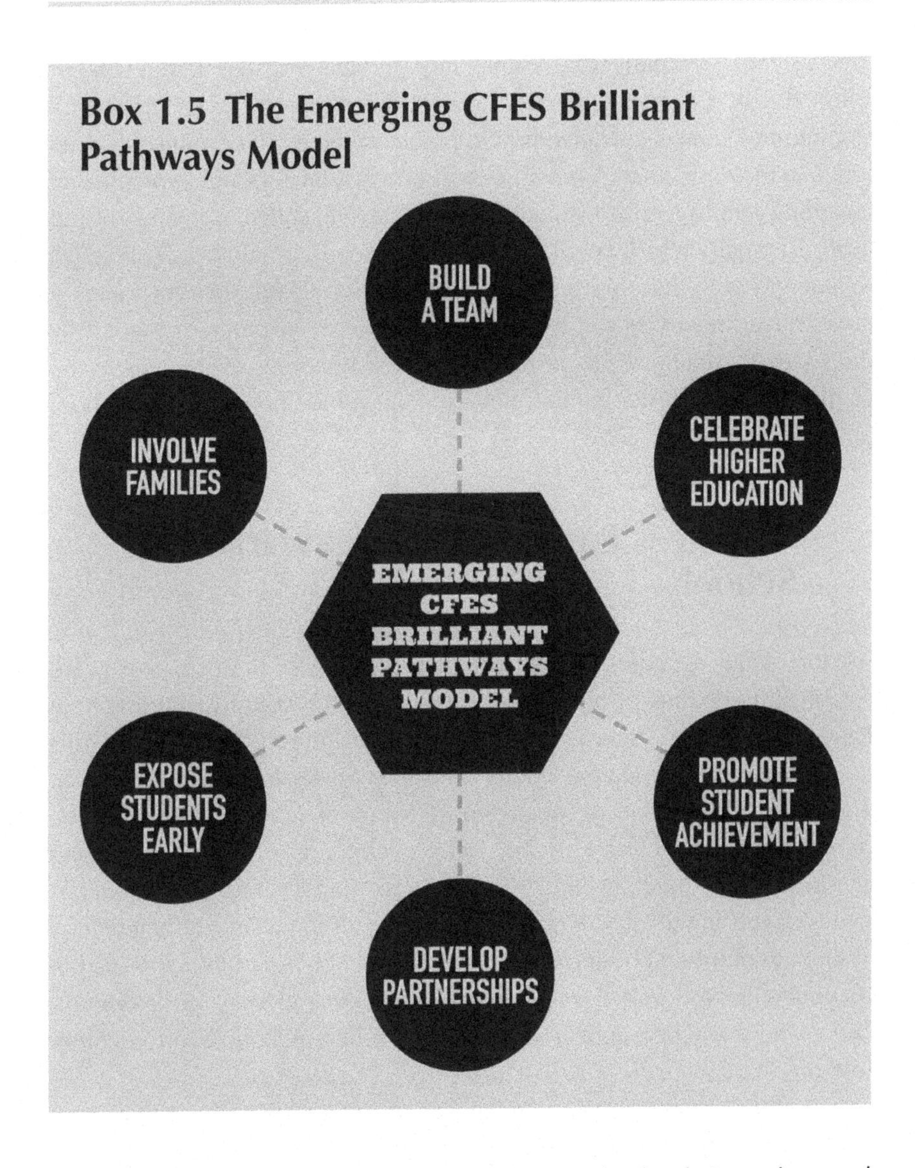

Cooper's books, *Leatherstocking Tales*) of 11 rural schools in and around Cooperstown. The rural consortium, like the Gulf County schools, had outstanding leaders. They had vision, cared deeply about students, and were good team leaders.

The Leatherstocking cluster embraced strategies that I learned in our Gulf County and Partners for Educational Excellence programs. The cluster rallied a dozen regional college partners to provide opportunities for their students and educators. Elementary students and their families spent a full day at Colgate University, and students toured Herkimer County Community College, where they sat in on biology classes and enjoyed lunch in the dining hall. Several schools adopted a Gulf County practice of awarding purple cards to students who achieved academic success or put forth exemplary effort. Local merchants provided discounts at their stores to students with these purple cards. The most powerful force for building college readiness was the long-standing scholarship program funded by the Clark Foundation. This program provided hundreds of students in the Leatherstocking cluster with money for college based on their high school grade point average (GPA).

Change is Possible: A Look at Urban Schools

As the CFES Leatherstocking program began to flourish, we were establishing dozens of other rural sites across the country. International Paper supported ten schools in communities where they had paper mills in Alabama, Pennsylvania, South Carolina, Mississippi, and Louisiana. The Freeman Foundation supported 50 Vermont schools. But while the number of rural schools in the CFES network was expanding, urban schools were struggling. In 1991, Jonathan Kozol's *Savage Inequalities* exposed the inner city as mired in poverty, despair, and hopelessness. That view of urban communities caused the CFES Board to advise us not to work with New York City schools. "You'll get tangled up in the bureaucracy, and you'll end up wasting valuable resources," one board member told me.

In 2000, when the Board finally agreed to let CFES work with a small group of schools in Boston, New York City, and Washington, D.C., we met outstanding educators, as well as students who were not only readying themselves for college but ensuring that their peers were ready too. In 2005, Shameka, a senior at Wadleigh Secondary School in Harlem, took the lead in an initiative that propelled every member of her class to apply to college. The first in her family to complete high school, Shameka graduated from St. John's University with a 3.9 GPA and then went on to Weill Cornell Medicine.

The 100 Percent Campaign: Urban Scholars Raise the Bar

As a CFES Scholar (a student participating in the CFES program at their school), Shameka became a leader at Wadleigh. "I learned some very important things from a CFES student leadership summit," she said. "I learned the importance of listening and putting other people first as key leadership ingredients."

Shameka not only shared what she learned but also inspired other students to take control of their own destinies and put college in their future. Shameka and seven other CFES Scholars formed a team called Da Committee to give structure and meaning to their mission, under the theme "Believing in Achieving."

Using the resources and opportunities available through CFES, Shameka and other members of Da Committee worked to get their peers on track toward college. They served as mentors and assisted peers in all aspects of the college application process. This effort, which began in 2006, became known as the 100 Percent Campaign. In 2016, members of the classes of 2007 and 2008 returned to Wadleigh to help students in grades 11 and 12 become college ready. "Eight of us split the class, each helping a dozen peers find schools, fill out applications, and write personal statements," Shameka said. "It was a long and hard task, but we were dedicated."

The result? Every CFES Scholar in the 12th grade applied and was accepted to college. "One hundred percent college acceptance was amazing," Shameka said. "We showed the school that we could actually set a goal and complete it with little help from advisors. This may not sound like much to the average person, but to students in our neighborhood, it's like a fairy tale."

Under Shameka's leadership, Da Committee also planned and facilitated the first CFES New York City student leadership summit, bringing together hundreds of their peers from Wadleigh and other CFES schools in Harlem, Brooklyn, and the Bronx (Dalton & St. John, 2017).

Across the Lake: A Beacon

In Essex, we look across Lake Champlain at the state with the nation's highest percentage of rural residents: Vermont. Like other rural states, a large percentage of Vermont high schoolers earn diplomas, but far fewer pursue college, and many of those who do earn degrees leave the state. This has caused Vermont leaders to project a shortfall of 132,000 job-ready workers in the next few years. In response, Vermont has an ambitious goal to increase the number of citizens with postsecondary degrees from 60% to 70%. The need is similar in other states, but Vermonters are taking action by recognizing the problem and endorsing a solution.

The Case for College

Like Vermont, almost every state has set attainment goals. Local and regional economies depend on having a critical mass of citizens with degrees, and individuals themselves need degrees. As a recent *Harvard Magazine* article explained, "Getting ahead—or getting by—is increasingly difficult in the United States without a college degree" (Duggan, 2020).

Those who don't go to college earn, on average, half what their college-educated peers will make. This is happening at a time when almost all of the 21st-century jobs that pay a living wage require a college education—not necessarily a bachelor's but an associate degree or postsecondary certificate.

Consider the fact that a young person with a bachelor's degree will out-earn the high school grad by $1 million over the course of a lifetime. College grads are healthier, live longer, and contribute more civically. This is why CFES has spent three decades helping young people become college-ready. We know it's challenging, especially in rural settings. Yet, at the time of writing, CFES Brilliant Pathways has worked with 400 rural schools in 35 states, over a period of 30 years, helping 30,000 low-income rural students move down the path to college. Between 2005 and 2020, 92% of the 200 rural schools that CFES has worked with have seen their student populations drop, some by more than 60%. These plunges in enrollment cause budget cuts and a scarcity of new programs, opportunities, and teachers.

This book provides solutions to the vexing challenges that rural communities face because merely recognizing the problem doesn't necessarily shed any light on how to solve it. As Vermont's Lieutenant Governor, David Zuckerman, said, "We know where we need to go, we just don't know how to get there. We don't know how to move the needle to 70%."

Box 1.6 The CFES Model that Emerged

Mentoring: CFES builds school-based mentoring programs with community members, college students, teachers, and/or peers. Every CFES Scholar works with a mentor who can share first-hand experiences and help overcome challenges to becoming college- and career-ready.

Pathways: CFES builds a college- and career-readiness culture by exposing students to postsecondary options and helping students understand the types of careers they can pursue and what it takes to attain them.

Essential Skills™: Students need more than academic and job skills to be successful in a world of exponential change. These Essential Skills are an intrinsic part of that process: Goal setting, teamwork, leadership, networking, perseverance, and agility.

This book shows rural regions like Vermont exactly how to move the needle. It is a how-to guide for building college and career readiness for rural communities, schools, and students. See Box 1.6 for an outline of the CFES model.

Closing the Divide: Cause for Optimism

We Need to Pay Attention to Rural Students, Rural Schools, and Rural Communities

The problems we see in rural education have taken years to develop. What's more, because rural districts are small, their problems tend to go unnoticed, but, collectively, these problems affect millions: One half of the school districts, one third of the schools, and one fifth of the students in the United States are located in rural areas (Lavalley, 2018). If we continue to ignore rural America, we are ignoring a quarter of the population, putting the entire nation at risk. This neglect will harm all of us who call America home, not just our rural communities and residents.

Reviving rural America is an enormous but doable task that must be done one community at a time. The rebirth of rural America will require 21st-century jobs and a skilled workforce. All of this depends on a pipeline filled with college- and career-ready youth.

Government and business leaders are recognizing the correlation between workforce needs and postsecondary attainment. Like Vermont, almost every state has set postsecondary and workforce readiness goals to strengthen their economies. California, for example, plans to help an additional 1.5 million residents attain college degrees by 2030.

Matt Dunne of the Center on Rural Innovation, a nonprofit that is building a network of rural innovation hubs across America to help revive struggling small towns, touts the advantages that rural communities offer: Affordable real estate, hardworking people, and increasingly prevalent high-speed internet access (Anarde & Dunne, 2019). In addition to an educational pipeline that can produce the next college- and career-ready generation, Dunne and others look to create strong digital economies that will allow small towns to thrive.

Beacons of hope can be found in rural communities throughout America. One such town, Crown Point, sits on the western shores of Lake Champlain in New York State. Crown Point Central School is led by ordinary people who are doing extraordinary things, leaders whose approach is based on high expectations, trust, and respect. These leaders believe that their formula can transform other struggling rural schools.

Instead of following the current system, which concentrates resources in too few places and leaves talent on the sidelines, we should learn from small towns engaging in regional economic development strategies that will ensure the promise of the modern era is shared more evenly across the country. As we'll see in the next chapter, Crown Point is doing just that—and their experience is a guide for other places to follow.

Conclusion

Chapter 1 exposes how rural schools are being left behind while their urban counterparts are gaining. Indicators of the widening gap are deeper poverty in small towns than cities; a brain drain, where high-achieving kids are leaving rural America; and other challenges, including isolation and a shortage of teachers. While higher education can help solve some of these maladies, rural communities have an inherent distrust of college, a condition that academia has, in part, brought upon itself with costs that have increased sixfold between 1990 and 2020.

All of these forces have created a cumulative disadvantage (Giudici & Pallas, 2014), where small and persistent equity gaps add up to a substantial outcome differential over time.

This chapter also tells the story of how CFES evolved from a three-year, national research venture on college readiness and strategies for promoting it to a pilot project whose findings and theories were tested in the Florida Panhandle before finally going on to become a nonprofit organization. Today, CFES has evolved into CFES Brilliant Pathways, which continues to work with rural schools to help them prepare their students to change their communities and their world.

References

Anarde, S., & Dunne, M. (2019). Speak your piece: What's possible in rural America? Plenty. Daily Yonder. www.dailyyonder.com/speak-piece-whats-possible-rural-america-plenty/2019/03/25/

Byun, S. Y., Meece, J. L., Irvin, M. J., & Hutchins, B. C. (2012). The role of social capital in educational aspirations of rural youth. *Rural Sociology, 77*(3), 355–379.

Cabrera, N. L., López, P. D., & Sáenz, V. B. (2012). *Ganas*: From the individual to the community, and the potential for improving college going in the "land that Texas forgot." *Journal of Latinos and Education, 11*(4), 232–246.

Carr, P. J., & Kefalas, M. J. (2010). *Hollowing out the middle: The rural brain drain and what it means for America*. Beacon Press.

Dalton, R. & Erdmann, D. G. (1990). *The chance to dream: A community success story*. Plan for Social Excellence, Inc.

Dalton, R., & St. John, E. (2017). *College for every student: A practitioner's guide to building college and career readiness*. Routledge, Taylor & Francis Group.

Duggan, C. (2020). Could college be free? *Harvard Magazine*. https://harvardmagazine.com/2020/01/free-college-deming

Duranton, G., & Puga, D. (2003). *Micro-foundations of urban agglomeration economies*. National Bureau of Economic Research.

Federal Communications Commission. (2020). *Inquiry concerning deployment of advanced telecommunications capability to all Americans in a reasonable and timely fashion*. (Report No. FCC-20-50). www.fcc.gov/document/new-fcc-report-shows-digital-divide-continuing-close-0

Giudici, F. & Pallas, A. (2014). *Social origins and post-high school institutional pathways: A cumulative dis/advantage approach*. Teachers College, Columbia University.

Hillman, N., & Weichman, T. (2016). *Geography shapes equity and opportunity in higher education*. American Council of Education.

Holmes, D., Dalton, R., Erdmann, D., & Roberts, A. (1986). *Frontiers of possibility: Report of the National College Counseling Project*. University of Vermont, Instructional Development Center.

Jesse, D. (2019). College, a way out of poverty, is a distant dream in much of rural Michigan. Detroit Free Press. www.freep.com/in-depth/news/education/2019/10/16/college-rural-michigan-poverty/3836576002/

Kight, S. W., & Bartz, J. W. (2019). The rural America death spiral. Axios. www.axios.com/the-rural-america-death-spiral-7c177126-638f-4270-8987-59ab8bf76faa.html

Krugman, P. (2019). Getting real about rural America. The New York Times. www.nytimes.com/2019/03/18/opinion/rural-america-economic-decline.html

Krupnick, M. (2018). The students who don't believe college is an option. The Atlantic. www.theatlantic.com/education/archive/2018/01/the-students-who-dont-believe-college-is-an-option/550715/

Lavalley, M. (2018). *Out of the loop: Rural education in the US*. Center for Public Education.

Marcus, J., & Krupnick, M. (2017). The high school grads least likely in America to go to college? Rural ones. The Hechinger Report. https://hechingerreport.org/high-schoolgrads-least-likely-america-go-college-ruralones/

McNamee, T. (2019). Social capital in the rural United States and its impact on educational attainment. In Bartee, R. D. & George, P. L. (Eds.), *Contemporary Perspectives on Social Capital in Educational Contexts*, (pp. 201–219). Information Age Publishing, Inc.

Means, D. R., Clayton, A. B., Conzelmann, J. G., Baynes, P., & Umbach, P. D. (2016). Bounded aspirations: Rural, African American high school students and college access. *The Review of Higher Education, 39*(4), 543–569.

Morin, R. (2016). Behind Trump's win in rural white America. Pew Research Center. www.pewresearch.org/fact-tank/2016/11/17/behind-trumps-win-in-rural-white-america-women-joined-men-in-backing-him/

Ratcliffe M., Burd C., Holder K., Fields A. (2016). Defining Rural at the U.S. Census Bureau, ACSGEO-1. United States Census Bureau, Washington, D.C.

United States Department of Agriculture Economic Research Service. (2017). Rural education at a glance, 2017 edition. United States Department of Agriculture. www.ers.usda.gov/webdocs/publications/83078/eib-171.pdf?v=42830

Waddell, K. (2019). Student debt is depleting rural America. Axios. www.axios.com/student-debt-urban-rural-divide-4418ba84-257c-4790-804c-efd40756c0a4.html

2 Building Successful Rural Schools
Beating the Odds

A Little School That Could

State Route 22 meanders north from the Bronx to the Canadian border on the eastern edge of New York State. Take a two-hour drive south from Montreal, and you'll wind through Crown Point, which sits on the western shores of Lake Champlain and today has a population of 2,000, roughly unchanged from two centuries ago. Because of its location on the narrows of the lake, Crown Point, once the water highway between New York City and Montreal, played a prominent role in the Revolutionary War. The remains of Fort Crown Point, built in 1759 during the French and Indian War by British and Provincial troops, can be seen from the road as you travel east to the bridge that connects Crown Point to Vermont.

Vermonters began creating a permanent settlement in what would become present-day Crown Point in 1800. The first school was opened soon after in 1805 with an inaugural class of five students in a small store that provided supplies to pioneers. Other schools followed, with educators from Vermont traveling to these schools to teach. Many Vermonters first crossed the lake to clear land, plant crops, and begin building homes for their families. A ferry eventually connected Crown Point with the Green Mountain State, and by the 1820s, industries such as lumbering and mercantile operations followed. The Penfield ore bed was discovered soon after and was later transformed into the Irondale complex. By 1873, a railroad linked the iron towns of Hammondville and Irondale in Crown Point to the rail lines north and south.

By the mid-19th century, Crown Point was a thriving industrialized community with fine homes and wealthy, educated individuals, including doctors, lawyers, business owners, and educators who attended a local academy for teachers. Prosperity was abundant.

Sadly, this was not to last. By the turn of the century, the iron mines showed signs of overuse and were eventually phased out. Agriculture decreased, businesses closed, and wealthy residents moved elsewhere. Crown Point struggled to replace these jobs as the United States transitioned from an industrialized, agriculture-based economy into a digital and service-based economy. It was a devastating decline, but not one capable of breaking the backs—or spirits—of its resilient residents.

Today, if you drive through Crown Point toward Ticonderoga, another Revolutionary War site, you pass a diner, a gas station/deli, and a fuel company. In many ways, it's quintessential small-town America, populated by people whose families have lived there for centuries. Some people graduate high school and never come back, others never leave, and some return after a time away.

By the start of the 21st century, a group of local leaders decided that if their beloved town was going to thrive, quality education was going to have to be the catalyst. Tucked away on the eastern side of town sits Crown Point Central, a school so small that seniors and pre-kindergartners eat lunch together in the cafeteria. The school has overcome a litany of rural obstacles so that 85% of its students now attend college, with an 80% on-time college diploma attainment rate. Recognized for its excellence throughout the region, Crown Point Central beat the odds and is now being studied by graduate students from Harvard and the University at Albany.

This chapter tells the story of how Crown Point Central fought for its students and succeeded in its mission to prepare them for college and beyond, despite its isolation and limited resources. Crown Point's story shows its success wasn't just about luck: It was about careful, intentional actions carried out daily by a wide range of stakeholders, from teachers to CFES (College For Every Student) staff members and community members. As Crown Point Central's teachers, administrators, and graduates can attest, the strategies leading to the school's success are replicable and can provide a practical blueprint for other rural schools seeking to motivate and prepare their students for higher education.

A Troubled Past

Crown Point Central wasn't always a model school—far from it.

Crown Point Central Superintendent Shari Brannock explains:

> In the late 90s, we were placed on the school need-of-improvement list. It had gotten to the point where something needed to change.
>
> We were missing consistency and continuity. [There was] no consistency with students. Part of that was people having to work in a system where leadership changed so often.
>
> New York State used to score you on 200 points, so if you were in the 150 range, you were doing okay. We had an 81 in math and a 115 in ELA [English language arts], so we weren't doing well.
>
> In my first ten years as a teacher, we worked with more than a dozen different superintendents and principals. It was bad. If I liked dinosaurs and taught first grade, and you liked dinosaurs and taught second grade, then no one ever learned about sharks because everyone was doing their own thing. We survived by shutting the door. We all worked in silos. We tried to stay in our element with the kids, but to avoid all the controversies and conflicts with leadership, we shut our doors. There was no leadership team. No one was working together.

Patricia Hall, retired elementary school teacher, recalls her time in the classroom:

> We worked as hard as we could, but we weren't seeing progress. And of course, the implied threat was that the school was going to close, and if there was one thing this community didn't want, it was to lose our school, because we are the center of everything. Without the school, the community wouldn't be the same, and that would be a tragedy for the community.

The First Step to Transformation: Coming Together

In 1999, CFES received a grant from the Charitable Venture Foundation to work with ten Adirondack schools. Crown Point Central was one of the schools invited to be part of the program, and they began working with CFES in 2000. That same year, the district took steps to begin working with

America's Choice, an organization that provides professional development and technical assistance that would change teaching and learning in the district. "We studied five different school models and selected America's Choice in 2001," said Brannock, who was School Treasurer then.

Helen Brannigan, who worked for the State Department of Education in Albany, happened to be driving by the school on her way to her seasonal house in the Adirondacks. Brannigan serendipitously dropped in and met with Brannock and this chance meeting led to state funding for America's Choice. "That involved three years of us getting support from people in Washington, where the National Center on Education and the Economy (NCEE) that ran the America's Choice model were based. America's Choice was the curriculum piece that guided us, the cog that started the wheel spinning," said Brannock.

To better understand what was happening at their own school, Crown Point Central educators "visited all kinds of schools from New York to California. We had great teachers, but we didn't work together," Brannock said. "After three years, we finished our partnership with America's Choice. We developed continuity in our teaching. We did things together and we created a totally different culture. In 2005, we were named a model school by America's Choice. Our scores shot up to 177 and 192. We were in the top three in our area, right there with Keene and Westport, the two wealthiest communities in our region."

A Second Ingredient to Success: An Unlikely but Symbiotic Partner

Separated by Lake Champlain and 15 miles, Middlebury College and Crown Point represent two different worlds. Middlebury, along with 18 or so other highly selective institutions in the United States, enrolls more students whose families are in the top 1% economically than those in the bottom 60% (Leonhardt, 2017). The difference in wealth between the two communities—Middlebury College and the town of Crown Point—is staggering. While the median household income in Crown Point is around $50,000 annually, that figure is tenfold greater for most Middlebury College students, symbolic of the gap between the haves and the have-nots across our country. While a Middlebury student might holiday in Europe or St.

Bart's, a Crown Point family is likely to vacation in a camper at Lincoln Pond, 10 miles northwest of town.

CFES has found that exposing rural children to college early and often is critical for promoting college readiness, so building mutually beneficial partnerships between rural schools and colleges has become a key part of CFES strategy. For Crown Point Central, a promising potential partner was hidden in plain sight, right across Lake Champlain.

"When we started working with CFES in 2000, they introduced us to Middlebury," said Brannock. Subsequently, Crown Point launched a partnership with Middlebury College that has had a huge impact for both institutions. Middlebury has given back to the region, while Crown Point's world has grown bigger. Despite their economic and cultural differences, Crown Point and Middlebury College have fostered a 20-year relationship that has benefited them both.

The first group of Middlebury College mentors were ten athletes from the men's and women's hockey teams who were part of a CFES-sponsored program led by then-hockey coach Bill Beaney, a native of the Adirondacks. Beaney recruited 200 college athletes from Middlebury, University of Vermont, SUNY Plattsburgh, Castleton University, and Saint Michael's College and sent them to 20 CFES schools in Vermont and New York State. While the colleges supplied the mentors, CFES trained them and supported the program on a daily basis.

That first year, and every year since, dozens of Crown Point students spend time on college campuses, breaking the barrier of isolation and exposure. "You can't be what you can't see," says Beaney.

Three Crown Point teachers also participated in a program with Middlebury College's faculty in the humanities, and Crown Point students did STEM-based service projects with Middlebury students, including cleanup projects on the shores of Lake Champlain.

Crown Point students were also expected to play an active role in their own advancement. As part of its emphasis on the Essential Skills™ (the key skills CFES has identified as defining college readiness, discussed in detail in Chapter 3), CFES program directors worked with Crown Point students on goal setting and leadership, and the students organized college- and career-readiness activities throughout the school. "CFES started Panther Partners. We called it that because both Middlebury and Crown Point share the same mascot, the panther. We also have a program called Senior Buddies," said Principal Tara Spaulding. "Senior Buddies meet with kindergartners once every two weeks and spend a period together, while the Panther Mentors support those in pre-K and beyond."

A Critical Step: Rethinking Instruction

Another key change was in the way Crown Point teachers viewed their instructional goals and each other. While well-intentioned, Crown Point's teaching culture had been one of individual silos, leading students to either repeat material from year to year or miss critical knowledge that no one thought to include in their teaching plans. The school recognized this was a problem and made a deliberate effort to change.

"We stopped teaching to the middle and began teaching to all ends, from the highest learners to the lowest learners. And now, if you go from a third grade classroom to a fourth and fifth, you'll see commonalities, so kids aren't having to learn routines and rituals all over again," Brannock said. "Looping and continuity and professional development were key. Every few weeks, we have data meetings and team-level meetings on assessments and teaching."

"We have a lot going on. It takes a lot of coordination, and we could not have done it without every single person buying in," Brannock said. "We had some challenges. We look at our data every few weeks. We had a teacher who came to me and said, 'I'm not doing this'. I said, 'Well, we're going to have to figure something out because we're all going to have to figure out how to do it'. She said, 'I give quizzes every week and tests every two weeks, and now you want me to use a rubric and a sourcebook—I can't grade these kinds of things'. She's an amazing English teacher, and so after a year of pulling teeth, she bought in. She saw results and she totally bought in."

Pedagogical Transformations

Crown Point's pedagogical transformation required not just a change in methods but radical shifts in culture and mindset. The changes fell into three basic categories: Strategy, values, and rigor. Shifts in all three areas happened gradually and were motivated by the school's cultural transformation.

Strategy

- Crown Point introduced two preparation periods for teachers. By the third year, teachers were writing their own genre studies. Feeling like they were navigators of their own destiny was critical for buy-in to curriculum and instruction changes. "If teachers are creating what they are teaching, they are feeling the power of ownership. This also allows them to go back to the drawing board when things don't go as planned instructionally and allows for reiteration of what needs to be taught, standards met, and yearlong plans to be developed," Spaulding said.
- Crown Point used surveys to assess what parents, staff, and students believed or perceived about their underperforming district. Personality tests were also administered to better understand how staff and students were wired. Figuring out who is like you and who is different personality-wise allowed staff to build on their strengths, understand their differences, and compensate for each other's weaknesses.
- Crown Point also looked closely and critically at district data to identify root causes of issues. Knowing where students were in terms of learning strategies allowed teachers to tailor student development and the organization of curriculum and resources. Crown Point also created a rotational schedule for Monday meeting times that allowed for whole group meeting time, team-level meetings, data meetings, and the development of a cross-curricular, cross-age unit each month.
- Establishing staff buy-in eliminated the cause of faults and nonconformance. If the educators were all working for the students, they collectively chose their desired outcome, and success across grade levels naturally followed. Crown Point faculty were also encouraged to continually question the what, why, who, when, and how of their work. They called this "Dig deep, root out."

Values

- Transform people through consistent, focused effort, always. "When staff is fed the same message for years, even decades, and when they know the people around them are all working toward the root cause together, even the toughest nut will crack and move toward being part of a TEAM (together everyone achieves more)," said Spaulding. "There is no wishy-washy, no back and forth," added Brannock, "No one wants to be on a losing team. No one wants to fail. Crown Point needed to transform using its biggest, yet unmanaged and un-unified, asset: Its people. To some degree, you find that out of 64 people, there are usually 52 opinions. When you find the commonality that reduces the differences and combines the similarities, you move them to a place where they can put students first!"

- Lead with your heart. Crown Point sees itself as a big family. "The kids know we have their backs," said Brannock. "We don't just know the student names, we know their parents', siblings', grandparents', aunts', uncles', and cousins' names. We know [if] they have pets, what their favorite color is, what street they live on. It's all in the details. And my mind is a steel trap when it comes to our students and how to make connections. When the students realize you are in the building for them—for the good, the bad, and the ugly—trust, respect, and relationships are built," said Spaulding.
- Celebrate small successes. "Small successes lead to big successes. We make it a point to recognize every success, big or small," said Brannock. "We have monthly assemblies for grades PK–6 that spotlight students who have exemplified a particular value, such as kindness, empathy, stewardship, enthusiasm. These values are also tied to a book of the month that ties into our reading program. We also recognize students quarterly for their reading goals. As for success in the classroom, there is constant communication with administration, families, and teachers about working toward and meeting instructional goals. Recognizing students, for small or large milestones, is crucial for their buy-in. We recognize quarterly honor roll in grades 4–12, yearly attendance goals, and birthdays throughout the year."

Rigor

- Recognize the task is difficult and the path is not smooth. "In the ever-changing world of education and state-driven educational policies/curriculum, you must go with the flow. The waters are choppy most of the time, even turbulent. There are no concrete answers, ever. And just when you think you have the standards mastered, they are modified. Stay in the boat, know there are many boats in the same water, and continue to paddle. We are all headed in the same direction," said Brannock.

- Maintain high expectations, and never grow complacent. Over the course of the initial five-year journey, Crown Point relied on high expectations to improve student performance from less than mediocre to topping the NYS (New York State) performance index. "With the ever-changing landscape of standards, assessments, and student achievement levels today," Brannock said, "one thing remains ... there is always room to improve, grow, and keep reaching for the sky! When you achieve success, push that much further. But know that success is student specific, not one size fits all. Know your students, know their ability levels, know their frustrations, and celebrate their successes."

A Kid-Centered Culture

The new Crown Point Central School that emerged was built on sound pedagogy, a culture of values, and college and career readiness (CCR) opportunities for all students. Superintendent Brannock's philosophy was to treat everyone in the school like family.

Sustained leadership was critical to achieving this. "Before it was like a revolving door of superintendents. We always had the potential, but without a leader, we weren't quite getting there," said Crown Point teacher Erica Peters, who graduated from the school in 1999. "We had all the care and the desire to get there but no leadership. Shari Brannock [who became Superintendent in 2003] pulled us all together to figure out how to get us to that next step where we're finally outperforming the people around us."

Even today, when Crown Point faculty talk about nurturing their students, two things stand out: Kindness and food. "Kindness works: A smile, a 'good morning', a hug, a 'how's your day'," Brannock says. "After a while, they are saying it to you before you can say it to them." Food is a metaphor for nurturing, and for how educators treat and respond to their students. They feed them, give them snacks, and fill the backpacks of poverty-stricken students with food on Friday afternoons. Social interventions involve food.

"If Patty loves chocolates, then she gets chocolates," Principal Spaulding said. Spaulding, like her colleagues, speaks to the culture of kindness. It's making sure students' basic needs are met and caring enough to know who likes chocolate and who likes licorice or peppermint. Further information on understanding poverty is contained in Box 2.1.

Box 2.1 Understanding Poverty

Crown Point's neighboring district, Ticonderoga Central School, was led by John McDonald for 20 years. Ticonderoga's poverty rate is so high that every student in the district now qualifies for free and reduced lunches, the most common metric for poverty. McDonald met with his faculty to talk about the most impoverished kids in the community, those who didn't have winter coats and never had money for lunch. At this meeting, McDonald asked his teachers, "How many of you know where those students live? How many of you have driven by their homes? What do you see when you drive by?" Some of the teachers noted that outside those homes there were satellite television dishes and snowmobiles. "How can they afford that stuff when they don't take care of their own children's basic needs?" one of the educators asked.

Poverty "is a miserable lifestyle," McDonald replied. "Families try to escape poverty with cable television, four-wheelers, snowmobiles, and worse—drugs, alcohol, and tobacco. Poverty affects everything in their world. Our kids need to know poverty isn't them; it happened to them." Here are ways to work with students who live in poverty:

- **Food**: Given the high correlation between poverty and food insecurity, we need to understand the link between food and health and academic achievement (Wight et al., 2014). A nurturing and caring environment can ensure that all students are fed. Every Friday, Crown Point students may pick up backpacks filled with food to take home.
- **Isolation**: Poverty is isolating, and schools need to find ways to break that isolation and expose students to new worlds through

assemblies and in-person and virtual college visits, and trips to cities and cultural sites.

- **Relationships**: Educators need to build human relationships with students and seek first to understand. "Educators should be the best bedside-manner people," says McDonald. "We aren't always."
- **Expectations**: "Poverty is not an excuse not to perform," McDonald said. With one of the poorest districts in the state, McDonald had more than half of his 12th graders taking rigorous Advanced Placement (AP) courses.
- **Apologize**: "Don't be afraid to apologize," McDonald said. "Too many of our kids come from harsh situations where parents and caregivers rarely say, 'I'm sorry'. These words from educators go a long way toward building human relationships."
- **Language**: Low-income families are less adept with language than middle class families. "I learned that I had to use 7th grade language for anything I sent home to families. Otherwise they couldn't understand what I'd written," said McDonald. "It's not intelligence. It's language facility."

In conversations with students, faculty, parents, and community members, there's consistency in how they describe their value-centered school:

- There is mutual trust, respect, and empathy.
- Everyone matters at Crown Point, and no one falls through the cracks.
- Staff believe, understand, and change.
- You can't be an educator unless you have contact with kids.

Exposure to the Bigger World

It's difficult for isolated, low-income kids to picture themselves thriving in the outside world, so CFES and Crown Point made an effort to bring the larger world and its possibilities to them. "Every week we have an assembly with speakers, college visits, [or] something going on that is outside their norm, which research has shown is way more beneficial than kids sitting in the classroom," Spaulding said. In the assemblies, K–6 students meet together, while older students meet and focus on college visits, financial aid information, or even student council votes.

"When we partner with CFES, we are giving kids a boost in what we are doing in their everyday lives so they are getting a more quality education, and they are realizing, 'Hey, I kind of like this'," Spaulding said. "You have CFES as a partner that's taking them on college visits, bringing kids up from New York City to shadow, sending our kids to New York City to shadow, so you are giving them more opportunity. There is not one week in this school year where our kids don't have an opportunity to do or see something different. Our junior class went to see *Hamilton* on Broadway and met all the actors, had a question and answer session, and had a tour of the city. Those are the kinds of things we've created along with CFES support, and it's really taken off."

CFES Brilliant Pathway Activities at Crown Point

As part of these initiatives, CFES hosts ten regular activities at Crown Point to promote CCR. These have been successfully adapted for the needs of other schools as well.

1. **College rally**: Over the last ten years, Crown Point has hosted a school-wide rally to promote its culture of CCR. Each year, the school-based CFES team (and CFES Scholars, students who actively participate in CFES programs) recruits dozens of college representatives and business and community partners to come to the school and talk to the Scholars about college and career pathways. Before the event, Scholars prepare questions for the visitors; each time Scholars ask good questions, they receive a stamp from that booth. Once they have five stamps, their name is entered into an ongoing raffle where they can choose college apparel, CFES swag, and other fun college- and career-related prizes. One year, Scholars were also given a chance to throw balls at a dunking tank that sank the principal and teachers. At the end of the event, all Scholars

sign a college and career pledge—a commitment to postsecondary pathway plans—that hangs in the building for the year.

2. **College visits**: All students in grades 7–12 visit at least one college every year. For example, every 8th grade class goes to Middlebury College for a tour of the campus and has a lunch discussion afterward with four Middlebury students about college pathways, classes, campus living, and sports.
3. **College and career fair**: This activity involves students in grades 4–12 and is planned and hosted by CFES Scholars. At the last fair, over 35 colleges and businesses were represented. As part of building school and college readiness, representatives come from different postsecondary pathways: Two-year, four-year, public, private, and vocational/technical schools. Each year more businesses attend, sharing information about careers in the region and the pathways to enter those careers. Other nearby schools in attendance include Ticonderoga, Westport, Moriah, and Minerva-Newcomb.
4. **Creation of a student leadership team**: This activity is a critical part of the Crown Point CFES program and its operation. Recognizing that 1) the small number of CFES staff at Crown Point was already stretched thin, and 2) there weren't enough true leadership opportunities, the CFES team created a student leadership team. Participating students must be in 9th grade and nominated by a teacher to join the team. Their roles range from event planning to mentoring and service activities. Team members gain schoolwide recognition, and leadership team members develop strong decision-making skills.
5. **Alumni panels**: In early January, alumni return to Crown Point for a panel discussion with students and families about college. Everyone loves the panel because the alumni are people the students know and can identify with—some recently graduated from Crown Point, others are familiar faces from a few years back.
6. **Service projects**: Crown Point students participate in numerous service projects throughout the year that are organized by the student leadership team:
   - Every month, the leadership team visits a nursing home in Ticonderoga. Students build friendships with residents and network with the on-site professionals. During the holiday

season, the school sends a group of students to several nursing homes in the area to sing Christmas carols to the residents.

- As part of community beautification, students build window flower boxes for the local post office, located next door to the school.
- In the spring, high schoolers participate in a Green Up Day, picking up trash, planting flowers, and reflecting on why this work is important.

One student leader collected over 100 prom dresses from the community and donated them to girls who wouldn't otherwise attend the prom because they couldn't afford a dress.

7. **Essential Skills workshops**: CFES professionals visit Crown Point regularly to implement their program there, including activities to help students develop the CFES Essential Skills. These activities include exercises that help students develop agility by urging them to think outside the box and consider new perspectives. They can include brainteasers and optical illusions to demonstrate how things aren't always what they seem to be and how we often need to adapt our way of thinking.
8. **Essential Skills activities**: **goal setting, teamwork, and leadership.** The monthly Panther Partners mentorship program provides another venue for Essential Skills development. Topics include team building, making good choices and the consequences of not doing so, sharing and accepting others' values and traditions, and respect. These workshops have proven to be a great way to strengthen connections between students and teachers, as well as between peers.
9. **Senior project portfolios**: This activity is another annual tradition at Crown Point. Through their English class, 12th grade students choose a project, which they research, write about, and present orally to a panel of adults. The panel typically includes a current teacher, recent grad, CFES representative, and mentor. Projects have ranged from building a guitar, baking, training animals for therapy, writing a short screenplay, building a hunting stand, and much more.
10. **Early college awareness week**: This is a school-wide pursuit that includes activities such as the following:

- college-gear raffle,
- teacher door-decorating contest,
- college facts and trivia on announcements each morning,
- elementary essay contest, and
- senior recognition at rally and treats are left in students' lockers.

Gaining and Maintaining Excellence

Crown Point's efforts and support of CFES initiatives soon started paying off and are continuing to yield significant benefits for the community. In 2001, just 52% of Crown Point's graduating seniors attended college. Today, 95% graduate from high school, 85% attend college, and 80% of Crown Point students who go to college graduate on time. In the Common Core State Standards tests, Crown Point now ranks in the top third among schools in the region.

Other indicators of excellence include the school's high levels of community support and loyal professional staff. "Even though our teachers are among the lowest paid in the state, we have little to no turnover," said Brannock, who exemplifies this loyalty. She's worked at Crown Point for 30 years, 20 as superintendent. The School Board President has been in place for 25 years, and in the most recent vote, 98% of the voters/residents voted to approve the school's budget.

Building a School of Distinction: It Can Happen Anywhere

After Crown Point education leaders shared their story of transformation, I asked them if they could transform another rural school in another part of the country. Without blinking, they all said in unison, "Of course!"

Was their transformation immediate? No—it was a three-year process, starting with creating the right culture of trust, respect, and empathy. There were hiccups years later, but hard work and dedication spur buy-in. The Crown Point team emphasized that their approach can work for other communities too, regardless of culture, socioeconomic status, or existing barriers. Superintendent Brannock and Principal Spaulding credit the following values for their success:

- **Trust**: We are all on the same ship. If it goes down, we all go down together. Get on the ship or get off.
- **Respect**: We are not the same, and that's okay. Conflicts—personality clashes, teaching-style differences, and management-style differences—are a natural part of different personalities working together. The key is to understand everyone's differences as well as their similarities. Have staff shadow peers, work across ages, and work across curricula because seeing is believing. Sometimes we take for granted the human capital we already have. Sharing it with others makes a huge impact. You can't understand students and how to address difficulties or embrace strengths unless we invest in social capital.
- **Empathy**: Leading with your heart will never lead you in the wrong direction, though there may be some palpitations along the way. If kids and adults know you care, not just for them but about them, they will commit to your plan.

Leading by Example: Portraits of the Crown Point Community

While much of Crown Point's success has been due to smart policies, supportive partners, and a warm, cohesive culture, none of these could have been realized without a supportive community. Here are the stories of some of the school's many stakeholders, from board members to students, and how they channeled their pride in their community into the pursuit of educational excellence. Their stories show that ordinary people acting with consistency and intention can together transform their world.

Mitch St. Pierre: A Bovine Podiatrist by Day, School Board Head by Night

When Mitch St. Pierre isn't running school board meetings, he's trimming the hooves of cows in Vermont. "What we do for a living is we go to farms and we take the cows, and we trim their toes so that they're shaped back to normal," he says. "We heal cows. We go to different farms every day. We might do 100 cows whose feet need to be fixed."

The oldest of 16 children, St. Pierre was born in Vermont and moved to Crown Point when he was 5. He's led the Board of the school he attended for the last 25 years. St. Pierre speaks warmly of the school's culture, "It's all about the kids. Everyone cares. We've cultivated a climate of trust."

St. Pierre shares his thoughts on Crown Point Central, "There used to be a lot of conflict in the building, not anymore. The Board meets with teachers twice a year. Now, instead of complaining like they did when I first joined the Board, they talk about all the good things."

St. Pierre also talks proudly about the community's support for the school. "Every year the community votes on the school budget. Last year, 100 votes were cast, and every vote but two supported the budget. The school janitor recently retired, but he came back because he loves the school."

"Teachers come here. They make less, but they stay. They don't want to leave. Teachers meet kids when they arrive in the morning on the bus," he said. Teachers here don't just educate children. They warmly welcome them.

Superintendent Shari Brannock

Shari Brannock's story is about hard work and a caring disposition. She was raised by her mother, Marie, in Putnam, which is two towns south of Crown Point. There, Brannock worked at the Putnam House, her grandparents' restaurant. She began working there at age 10, to help support her mom and two sisters. That was until the restaurant burned down and they were forced to move into a trailer. "I had clothes, food, and love," says Brannock. "I didn't feel impoverished; I felt lucky." When Brannock's mom remarried, the family moved to Ticonderoga.

"My mom's my inspiration," says Brannock. After dropping out of high school and raising three daughters, Marie got her General Equivalency Diploma (GED) and then went on to complete her associate degree at North Country Community College.

That example motivated Brannock, who was at the top of her 6th grade class at Putnam School before moving on to Ticonderoga Central. After Ticonderoga, she headed off to Hartwick College and later transferred to Siena College. While in college, Brannock returned home every weekend to waitress at the Putnam House and work at the local credit union.

After Siena, Brannock returned to Ticonderoga and began to move up the ranks at the credit union. Six years later, she was the vice president for loan operations when she heard about an opening at Crown Point Central. "They were looking for a treasurer. I met with the Board, and we seemed to click. They offered me the job," says Brannock. Her new career began—with a $4,000 pay cut.

Along the way, with support from her husband, Terry, Brannock completed two master's degrees: One from Castleton, the other from SUNY Plattsburgh. Ten years later, in 2003, Brannock became Superintendent. "I worked for 13 different administrators along the way. I learned something from every one of them."

Ask Brannock about her experience as superintendent, and she'll tell you how much she cares about the Board, her faculty, and the students. When a student's having issues at home and acts out in class, Brannock takes that child for a walk. As she says, "Discipline is handled with care and compassion, not a referral and a handbook of rules. That makes a big difference." And when the cafeteria staff doesn't have time to clean the tables after lunch, she steps right up. "Anything I ask of others, I do first!"

When Crown Point Central faced a $100,000 deficit a few years back, it grew dangerously likely the school would be forced to cut staff. So Brannock went to the Board and asked that they not give her a raise that year. Every teacher followed her example, and no staff members were cut that year. Now *that's* leadership.

We Are Family: Three Generations of Crown Point Leaders

Lisa Harrington exemplifies Crown Point values: Hardworking, family-oriented, and dedicated to young people. She applied those attributes as a teacher at Crown Point Central School, where she and her ten siblings graduated and her seven grandchildren now attend.

Recently retired, Harrington was an integral part of taking her alma mater from the brink of a state takeover in the 1990s to its current status as a ten-time CFES School of Distinction.

"My dad passed when he was 42, so my mom pretty much raised us 11 kids alone," said Harrington, whose parents also graduated from Crown Point. "It was hard, but we supported each other, and school was like a family. The school is the focal point of this town; it's the heart. The people on staff are rock-solid and very caring, and our kids know it."

After graduating from high school, Harrington went away to college for three years before returning home to raise her daughter, who has Down syndrome, with her husband, whom she had dated at Crown Point. She eventually earned a bachelor's degree in elementary education and a master's in special education.

"With America's Choice, you got out of your room and had team meetings," she says. "It was hard because school was still moving along while you were trying to make changes. One of the teachers said it was like trying to change the tire while driving. You took parts and kept adding on. Now it's just part of Crown Point."

Another of Harrington's daughters, Erica Peters, is carrying on the tradition as a 1st grade teacher at Crown Point. As a student, she just missed the school's turnaround when it adopted the America's Choice and CFES models, but she remembers the same kind of family atmosphere with dedicated teachers setting the tone.

"I loved going to school here," says Peters, who has a bachelor's degree in psychology and master's in education. "The teachers are really invested in the well-being of the kids, and I really felt that as a student. I do wish we had the kind of success they are having now when I was in school, because Crown Point had a negative connotation associated with being rural, like we didn't know anything. But I worked really hard and got a great education."

Over the years, as the school's reputation began to improve along with its test scores, the perception of Crown Point began to change. "I have friends ask all the time if I know of any houses for sale, because they want their kids to go to school in Crown Point," said Peters. "I love to hear that. It shows how far we've come."

Emily: The Odds-Beating Ivy Leaguer

The first time Emily realized she had a fighting chance at getting into an Ivy League school was midway through her junior year.

Once committed to pursuing this dream, Emily immersed herself in the college admissions process, took SAT practice tests, worked on college essay writing, looked into scholarships, and pursued anything else she could find about what it takes to get into an elite college.

Emily also relied on what she learned about CCR from being involved in CFES Brilliant Pathways. "CFES is really good at teaching you the importance of identifying a goal and then creating a pathway to achieve it," says Emily. "The reason it works so well at Crown Point is because the teachers buy in and will help you down your chosen path to success."

Through her elementary and middle school years, Emily took CFES and school-sponsored college tours, which led her to think more seriously about college. "We do a ridiculous amount of college trips for a school our size located in the middle of nowhere," she says. "CFES as a whole is constantly at the forefront of your mind in terms of having you think about doing something related to education beyond high school."

By her sophomore year, Emily started looking into schools with aerospace engineering programs. She eventually convinced her dad to take her on a two-week whirlwind tour of schools up and down the East Coast. After deciding to focus on strong engineering programs, Emily narrowed her list to 15 schools, with a top five that included Princeton, Columbia, Cornell, Massachusetts Institute of Technology (MIT), and Johns Hopkins.

Emily continued to work hard on academics and on improving her SAT scores, which peaked at an Ivy League-worthy 1520, including a near-perfect math score of 780. She also participated in after-school clubs, volunteered in the local community, and took on a leadership role with CFES by presenting at its national conference, starting a mentor program to help sixth graders transition to high school, and leading an adopt-a-college program for younger students.

Despite her seemingly stellar college resume, Emily worried that she was lacking certain credentials like extracurricular engineering activities and AP classes. Most of the stress was self-imposed, however, so when it got too intense, she would seek the support of teachers who she also considered friends.

"[Crown Point] teachers and administrators go out of their way to create a customized high school experience to make sure you are successful," she says. "They didn't necessarily have tailor-made advice for applying to Ivy League schools because it's rare, but in terms of support, especially emotionally and mentally, it was as good as it gets. For whatever reason, they have cultivated an incredibly supportive environment that works hand-in-hand with CFES."

In retrospect, Emily says the foundation for attending college was laid the first day she arrived at Crown Point, when she was enrolled in a CFES program known as Kindergarten Buddies. "It was a big deal walking around with a senior at that age," she says. "They were like idols to us. We even went to our senior buddies' graduation. Our school and CFES are really good about peer mentoring so kids have role models at a young age."

Currently living out her dream at Cornell, Emily is already seeing the bar being raised at Crown Point by younger students, including her younger sister, who, along with some of her classmates, is talking about compiling some impressive college lists.

"There aren't a lot of kids at Cornell who are from places like Crown Point," says Emily. "You go from 20 kids at the most in a class to a lecture of 450 really smart people. It took a little while to adjust, but I love it here and am grateful to everyone who helped me get here."

Erick: A First-Generation Student with a 24–7 Work Ethic

Emily's story may be exemplary, but she's hardly alone in seeing hard work pay off. Consider Erick, who graduated alongside her. Back in Crown Point for the holidays, he reflected on what it was like growing up in a town of 2,000 people.

Erick's situation wasn't easy. His mother passed away when he was in third grade, and his father worked 70-hour work weeks as an outdoor plant foreman doing cable and telephone installations to support his three sons. Despite his circumstances, Erick thinks of his upbringing as a rich one.

"Given my background, I could be like, 'There was a lot of adversity', but one very valuable attribute that my dad passed down to me is work ethic," says Erick, now a senior at the University of Rochester. "He has a 24–7 blue collar work ethic. I value education as much as I do because it took a lot of blood, sweat, and tears to get me where I am."

Erick credits his teachers at Crown Point for their willingness to work overtime after school to help him navigate the college application process and handle other obstacles he faced as an aspiring first-generation college student.

"They read every word of my personal statement and made sure my application was as good as possible," says Erick. "They didn't have to do that on their own time. The reason I was able to overcome adversity and defy the odds is that I truly had a village to help me through."

Mentors he met with regularly through CFES Brilliant Pathways were also part of the village. Erick idolized them and wanted to follow their example by attending college. That fire was stoked on CFES and school-sponsored college trips, including one in 6th grade to Marist that spurred him to start looking into what it took to get into college.

"When you have kids who are truly interested in college at a young age, they start asking questions and saying, 'I want to be there,'" says Erick. "That's when CFES and teachers can play a key role by telling students about the tools they need to get there. It's so much easier when your teachers are approachable because you view them as leaders but also friends. There's not so much of a power dynamic at Crown Point. It is a very egalitarian school."

As Erick grew older and more serious about college, he visited schools and eventually narrowed his list down to University of Rochester, Siena College, and St. Lawrence University. "I would say it was assumed I would go to college somewhere," he says. "My family definitely had high expectations, but they didn't have that college background and couldn't walk me through it. They supported whatever decision I made."

In many ways, despite the struggle of getting into Rochester, the hardest part was yet to come. "Initially, it was hard," says Erick. "It took a while to adjust to being around people who didn't have to worry about money and who had all these resources in high school." But he believes being on the CFES leadership team and practicing CFES Essential Skills such as perseverance and leadership helped him succeed at Rochester. "I eventually realized that I was on their level. CFES taught me that as a leader you need to take the necessary steps to do what needs to be done. It has been so foundational and important to me that I truly want to give back any way that I can."

After graduating from Rochester, Erick plans to earn his master's degree in social work from Columbia University, where he has already been accepted. He marvels at the journey he's travelled so far.

Conclusion

Chapter 2 tells the story of a rural school that lifted itself up from the state's warning list to a school being studied by Harvard for its exemplary student outcomes on test scores, and graduation and college attendance rates. The transformation was made possible in part by sound pedagogy and leadership, but it is mostly by ordinary people doing extraordinary things to change life trajectories. Superintendent Shari Brannock, Principal Tara Spaulding, School Board Chair Mitch St. Pierre, and students including Emily and Erick all worked hard and achieved exceptional results.

References

Aisch, G., Buchanan, L., Cox, A. & Quealy, K. (2017). Some colleges have more students from the top 1 percent than the bottom 60. Find yours. The New York Times. www.nytimes.com/interactive/2017/01/18/upshot/some-colleges-have-more-students-from-the-top-1-percent-than-the-bottom-60.html

Wight,V., Kaushal, N., Waldfogel, J., & Garfinkel, I. (2014). Understanding the link between poverty and food insecurity among children: Does the definition of poverty matter? *Journal of Children & Poverty*, *20*(1), 1–20. https://doi.org/10.1080/10796126.2014.891973

The Essential Skills

Building Blocks of College and Career Readiness

Over its 30-year history, CFES (College for Every Student)' most successful Scholars—those who graduated from college on time and secured well-paying jobs that moved them and their families out of poverty—were not those with the highest test scores or the best grades, but those who possessed the CFES Essential Skills™: Goal setting, teamwork, leadership, networking, perseverance, and agility. This chapter shows why CFES has identified these skills as critical and how we work with schools and communities to help students cultivate them.

Not Soft, Essential

At CFES, we recognize the foundational importance of these competencies. While many call these skills "soft" or "noncognitive," we dislike those terms. Calling them "soft" or "noncognitive" diminishes their value and gives them second-class status at a time when these traits are becoming more valuable than ever before. In 2015, CFES formally named these competencies as the Essential Skills.

That year, the Essential Skills became our third practice, replacing Leadership through Service. Our own research helped us understand that our CFES Scholars needed more competencies than leadership and that service—making your school and community a better place—needed to be and could be imbued in peer mentoring, sharing college pathway knowledge and other activities.

Essential Skills: A Trademark for Our Vision

Because of the value we place on these specific skills and their unique prominence in our model, CFES trademarked the term "Essential Skills" shortly thereafter. The trademark signifies that the term is the intellectual property of CFES. More importantly, it makes a statement about the value we place on the Essential Skills.

In addition, a growing number of educators and business leaders are starting to share our views on these critical skills. For instance, a few years ago, Allen Morrison, professor at the Thunderbird School of Global Management at Arizona State University, delivered some startling information to a group of corporate and educational leaders. "As knowledge and information have become commodities," he said, "they've come to take a back seat in the job market to applicants' networking ability and agility in developing new skills."

Joseph Fuller, professor at the Harvard Business School and an authority on America's competitiveness, offered a similar message: More than anything else, he said, businesses want employees with workforce readiness skills, such as teamwork and perseverance.

Morrison from Thunderbird warned that the workforce of tomorrow won't be the one we want and need unless we take action now. Helping students master the Essential Skills is a critical component of building that workforce, and we all need to develop the tools to achieve that.

Our Corporate Partners Agree

In addition, several of our corporate partners, such as Southwest Airlines, tell us that they can teach new hires how to do a job, but those employees won't last or be successful in today's workplace without the Essential Skills.

The Essential Skills Beyond College and Career

The Essential Skills aren't just useful for jobs and education. You need to use them in every area of your life, throughout your whole life.

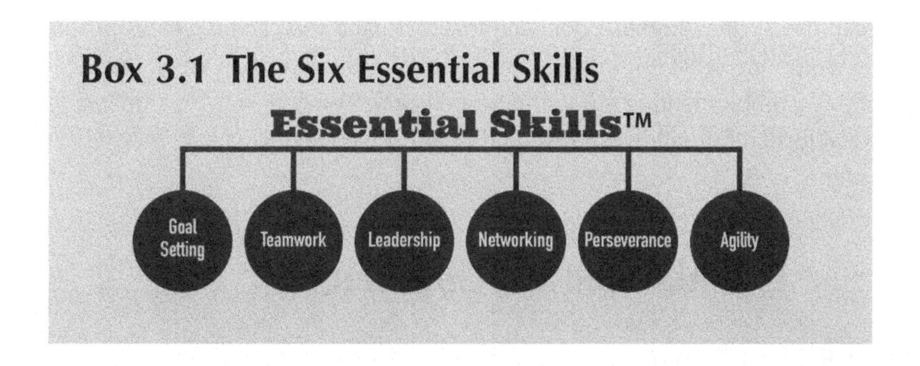

Organizations—corporations like Southwest Airlines and TransPerfect Technologies, as well as educational institutions including the University of Vermont and Harvard University—also use the Essential Skills. These competencies are foundational for high-performing organizations, not just individuals.

The Essential Skills are now one of CFES' three core practices, alongside Pathways to College and Career, and Mentoring. The Essential Skills evolved from the practice we call leadership through service, which helps young people identify and express their leadership potential by working to improve their school, neighborhood, and/or community. Leadership is now one of the six Essential Skills (see Box 3.1), and, as Brian Flores notes later in Chapter 4, service is inextricably linked to leadership.

Why Only Six Essential Skills?

The six Essential Skills promoted by CFES are not the only essential skills; Peru High School students (Box 3.5), for example, included communication as their seventh essential skill.

But our six happen to be the ones that CFES Scholars personally found most important for moving toward college and career readiness (CCR) and beyond. This was confirmed by a team of evaluators from the University of Michigan, who reported that "the Essential Skills promote social and educational uplift and ultimately help students become 21st-century workforce ready" (St. John et al., 2015).

In the sections that follow, we define each of the six Essential Skills and what each should mean to students, share an activity that adult leaders can use to help students cultivate that skill, and then share a short profile of someone who embodies that Essential Skill. We then offer practical tips for implementing student-centered programs that enable students to develop and practice the Essential Skills while serving as role models for others.

Essential Skill #1: Goal Setting

Definition: The process of determining a desired result that students envision *and* commit to achieving. Students have to know what they want so they can take steps to get there.

Why set goals? Setting a goal is like marking a destination on a life map: Students need to know where they're going to plan the best route. They can start where they are and go where they dream, but to get there, they'll have to set goals and identify the steps they will take to reach them. For instance, many career paths require a college degree, so one of the first important goals they can set is to go to college.

Goal-Setting Activity: Future Reunion

Introduction

In this game, students role-play to help them identify their long-term goals and aspirations and envision how they will attain those goals.

Materials

- printout and pen for each participant
- adhesive name tags (optional)

Instructions

- Explain to participants that they are about to attend a party 20 years in the future where they'll see all their classmates.

- Ask participants to spend 5–10 minutes writing down where they see themselves in 20 years.
- Give each participant a name tag to fill out (optional) to add to the reunion vibe. They could add their dream job and hometown if desired.
- Ask participants to mingle and "catch up" by discussing what they've been through in the past 20 years and what they are doing now. If your group needs more structure, pair participants for conversations, and have them rotate to a new partner every three minutes.

Discussion

- Was it difficult for you to imagine your life 20 years from now?
- Did this activity make you realize goals that you did not know you had?
- What are the steps you will need to take to move closer to your long-term goals?
- What steps can you take in the next few weeks to get you one step closer to reaching your long-term goals?
- Does the goal-setting process require you to have any other Essential Skills?

Reflecting and Connecting

- Be aware that it might be challenging for students to think about themselves 20 years from now. This activity not only challenges them to envision themselves in the future, but it is also intended to encourage them to think about what they can do now in order to move closer to accomplishing long-term goals. Although 20 years seems far away, what they do between now and then is what will make them who they will be.
- Remind students that time passes whether they are working toward their goals or not, so they need to be proactive to achieve goals that they have set. For example, a student might decide they will be an astronaut in 20 years, but that goal is unrealistic if they aren't laying the groundwork. Goals aren't achieved automatically.

Goal-Setting Personified: Angel

During his sophomore year at Seward Park High School in lower Manhattan, Angel found himself in detention because he had brought a knife to school—something he admitted was "stupid." He ruminated on his future. Would he drop out of high school like his older sister? Or was there something more for him? As he idled, Angel heard students in the hallway. They talked about visiting colleges and pursuing careers.

Seward Park's Principal saw something in Angel, so she approached him about joining the program, which met after school. "Sure, why not?" Angel said. He attended his first CFES meeting the next day.

That's when Angel began to set goals for himself. "I began to see myself as a college student, and it grew from there," he said. "I visited colleges. I met college students. They were role models and leaders."

Three years later, he entered the State University of New York (SUNY) Plattsburgh, where he became Student Body President in his senior year. A year later, he completed a master's degree at SUNY Plattsburgh. Recently, he completed the doctoral program at Teachers College, Columbia University. "If it hadn't been for goal setting, I wouldn't be where I am today," Angel said. See Box 3.2 for a list of phases in the goal setting process.

Box 3.2 Goal Setting Phases

- A short-term goal can be achieved over a day or a week. Angel's initial short-term goal was getting out of the detention room.
- A mid-term goal can be achieved in a few weeks or a month. Angel's mid-term goal was to join CFES.
- A long-term goal is attainable over many months or years.

  This goal is a step toward the student's dream goal, yet it is a significant accomplishment in its own right. Angel's long-term goal was to attain a bachelor's degree and ultimately a doctorate.
- A dream goal is the ultimate hoped-for achievement. It is when a student imagines the best job they could ever have or the best person they could ever be. Angel's dream goal is to become a college president. Don't bet against him!

Essential Skill #2: Teamwork

Definition: Collaborating with others to achieve set goals, since we can accomplish bigger and better things when we work together.

Why be part of a team? Technology makes it easier than ever to communicate and collaborate with each other, but if we all talk at once, it's impossible to get anything done. Like anything else, working well together takes practice. While being on a team can be challenging, it also allows students to maximize their strengths and bring out the best in each team member. Teamwork helps us achieve objectives in school, work, and life; service projects, group academic assignments, internships, friendships, and family relationships all depend on it.

Teamwork Activity: Blind Drawing

Introduction

In this activity, two-person teams must communicate well enough to draw an item sight unseen. While one person picks an item and describes it (without saying what it is), the other must sketch it based solely on that description. (The person describing the item can't see what the artist is drawing.) Partners switch roles after time expires.

Materials

- paper
- markers

- a small selection of everyday items (for example, a coin, a well-known company logo, a pencil, a bottle, a key, etc.) You could also use printed pictures instead of actual items.

Instructions

- Pair off students and ask each pair to sit with their backs to each other.
- One student in each pair should discreetly receive an object or picture, and the other should receive paper and markers.
- As one partner describes the object, the other draws it.
- At the end of the activity, all the drawings are revealed. The team whose drawing(s) is closest to the actual item or picture wins.

Rules

- Describers cannot tell artists what the item is; they can only give instructions.
- Describers cannot look at the artist's work during drawing time.
- Artists cannot ask any questions of their partners.
- Drawings must be completed within a three-minute time limit.

Discussion

- How well did the artist understand the instructions? How close did they come to replicating the actual item?
- What problems did each of you encounter during the challenge?
- Which one of you was a better communicator? Why?
- What was frustrating?
- Did your experience in the first round help you and your teammate draw a more accurate picture in round two? Why?
- What did you learn from the activity?
- What situations in real life do you think are like this exercise?

Reflecting and Connecting

- Although each partner had a completely different task, team members had to work together to accomplish their shared goal. On a team, different tasks may be delegated to different individuals, but every member should contribute.
- The two roles in this activity play to different strengths. For the describer, articulating ideas clearly and concisely is most important, whereas the artist requires good listening and interpretation skills.
- On a team, it is ideal for everyone to take on a task they are good at. However, you may need to take on tasks outside your comfort zone for the benefit of the team—like drawing even if you are a poor artist.
- Both partners benefit from thinking of their teammate's perspective when providing and interpreting information.

Teamwork Personified: Greg Muccio

Currently Director of Talent Acquisition at Southwest Airlines, Greg Muccio has worked at the airline for 19 years. "I go to bed every night excited about what someone on my team is going to accomplish the next day. It isn't about your agenda. It's about the team agenda," says Muccio.

Muccio has plenty of opportunity to get excited, since he hires 7,500 people at Southwest Airlines every year. "Ever since I was a little kid, I've put the other guys first," he says. "When I played sports, it was always about the team for me. I played defensive tackle in high school. If I could take out the blocker and let the other guy make the tackle, that was great by me because it was about the team. I wasn't very good, but I loved being part of a team." Muccio says that when you embrace your team, "you celebrate with others, never alone. A team is about humility and not taking yourself too seriously."

Muccio's colleague at Southwest Airlines, Luke Stone, Senior Manager of Talent Acquisition, says, "Greg excels at putting together teams of people to work on projects based on individual team members. He builds teams where individuals can learn from each other and further develop their skills and knowledge."

Essential Skill #3: Leadership

Definition: Leadership means that individuals are taking charge of their future. To do so, leaders must lift up their peers, help them, support them, and make their school and/or community a better place. Everyone can be a leader by helping those around them.

Why be a leader? When a student makes the effort to work toward their own goals, they're leading by example. Working hard and encouraging others to become college and career ready are important parts of the CFES experience. Whatever a Scholar's age, there are important ways to develop leadership skills. Being a leader will enhance their college and career opportunities. People with leadership skills are more likely to hold managerial positions as adults and earn higher incomes than those in non-leadership roles. To develop leadership attributes, students should challenge themselves, which will help pave the way for a bright career and future.

Leadership Activity: A-MAZE-ing Leadership

Introduction

Participants acting in a leadership role need to be able to inspire trust, communicate effectively, and care for their teammates to succeed at this challenge.

Materials

- tape, rope, or something to create a maze boundary
- items to serve as obstacles, such as chairs, cones, hats, or crumpled balls of paper
- a blindfold for each team of two

Instructions

- Mark off a square or rectangular area with tape, rope, or something similar to create a boundary.
- Place obstacles randomly on the ground inside the designated space.
- Divide the group into pairs.
- One partner will attempt to verbally guide their blindfolded partner from one end of the maze area so that the blindfolded partner does not touch any of the obstacles.
- After successfully navigating to the other side, partners should switch roles and try again.

Rules

- When one partner is inside the maze boundaries, the other must remain on the outside while providing instruction for getting to the end without touching any obstacles.
- The partner traveling through the maze must remain blindfolded and may not use any guidance or support other than the verbal instructions from their partner.
- Anyone who touches an obstacle or the maze perimeter must return to the starting area and try again.

Variations

- You may allow participants a couple of minutes of planning time to decide on their communication commands.

- The activity can be conducted one pair at a time or with all pairs at once.
- If, during the activity, participants find an "easy" pathway, you may rearrange the obstacles. If the group challenges this, remind them that this activity models real life (that is, conditions change, and you need to be ready to adjust your strategy/approach).

Discussion

- How did you feel while doing the activity?
- What did you enjoy about it?
- Was it difficult? Why?
- Did you trust your partner immediately when you started?
- How did your partner support you?
- Would you be able to go through the maze on your own without instruction?
- What factors are important for trusting and working with someone else?
- What communication strategies worked best?
- How can this activity be translated into developing positive leaders?

Reflecting and Connecting

- The obstacles represent problems the group faces either personally or as a team. They are everywhere in life. A good leader can help you become aware of potential pitfalls as you try to reach your goal.
- Communicating clearly, calmly, and concisely is an important leadership skill. In this game, leaders who are effective communicators will be the most successful in guiding their teammates to success.
- If you had multiple blindfolded participants navigating the maze at the same time, it is likely that conflicting directions were overheard from other leaders. This is similar to having too many leaders on one endeavor—it is difficult to know which directions to follow. Being an effective leader requires strong communication and a teammate who is dedicated to following your directions.

Leadership Personified: Brian Flores

Brian Flores spent 15 years as a scout and coach with the New England Patriots before becoming the Head Coach of the Miami Dolphins. During his time with the Patriots, he won four Super Bowl rings. He's been a 16-year friend of CFES, inspiring its Scholars and educators and hosting luncheons for the CFES Board with Patriot players. Recently, Coach Flores led a webinar for CFES college- and career-readiness advisors and CFES educators and Scholars.

During the webinar, Coach Flores shared what leadership looks like as he talked about helping CFES Scholars become college and career ready. "Leadership is about service," he said. "On a daily basis, I'm trying to figure out different ways to try and help people succeed—coaches, players, equipment guys, training staff, medical staff. How do I help them become the best version of themselves?"

Flores gave examples of mentor leaders from his youth growing up in Brooklyn, before he played linebacker at Boston College. Among these mentors were his 1st grade teacher, his parents, Patriots Coach Bill Belichick, and CFES board member Scott Pioli, who hired him as a scout for the Patriots in 2004.

"Education is very important to Scott, just as it has been to me and my parents, who came to this country from Honduras as immigrants," said Flores. "They always stressed that the way to make a better life for yourself was through education, so when Scott brought CFES to my attention 16 years ago, I was all in."

Flores suggested that college- and career-readiness advisors take the time to earn the trust and respect of their students before attempting to provide guidance, just as he does with his players. "It's about building a relationship and finding a way to connect," he said. "There are very different types of leaders. Some are loud and boisterous; some are quiet and reserved; some are rah-rah; some are just thinkers and say nothing, and when they speak, everyone listens. They come in all shapes and sizes, but at the end of the day, you can't lead unless people trust that you have their best interest in mind."

When asked what kind of leader he considers himself to be, Flores said it depends on whom he's trying to motivate. "Part of leadership is dealing with different types of people and pushing the right buttons for each individual," he said. "Some people need that motivational speech, while others need an arm around them."

"As mentors, teachers, and coaches, we need to instill confidence in our young adults and children. It goes a long way in building leadership."

Essential Skill #4: Agility

Definition: The capacity to be adaptable and responsive to challenging and uncertain circumstances. It can be hard when big things in life change, but when a person sees these challenges as opportunities or adventures, that's agility!

Why do I need to be agile? Agility helps people succeed in a changing world. It allows a person to embrace new opportunities and circumstances and ultimately be comfortable with uncertainty and change. We know, for example, that many of the jobs of tomorrow, especially the high-paying ones, do not exist today. Thus, students might need to change their own course, even if they've planned carefully. An agile person can adapt and adjust and overcome hurdles that arise. A student's success in college and career depends on knowing the questions to ask, working with the people who can help them find the answers they need, and becoming comfortable with being uncomfortable.

Agility Activity: But Then ...

Introduction

Participants will create a story line using random photos and transitional prompts that will help them think productively about changing circumstances and unexpected challenges.

Materials

- assorted interesting photos printed on cardstock

Instructions

- Divide students into small groups and distribute five photo cards at random to each group.
- Groups should spend 5–10 minutes coming up with a story of a hypothetical person's pathway through college and career, using the cards as illustrative tools (metaphorical interpretations welcome). Between each card, students should use the phrase "but then" or "and so" to indicate that something unexpected has happened to their imaginary character and say how they adjusted. (Example: "Ben grew up in a city, but then his family relocated to a rural area when he was 18, and so he became a farmer. But then there was a drought, and so he put up a windmill. But then lightning struck his windmill, and so he went back to college to study the climate.")
- Ask each group to choose one spokesperson to share their story with everyone.
- Pick out any notable examples of adaptability that come up during each story to highlight scenarios of agility.

Discussion

- Where do you see yourself in 10 years? 20 years? 30 years?
- What are some obstacles that could get in your way?
- How might you overcome those challenges or change your initial plan?
- Will your pathway take unexpected twists and turns? How will you deal with those challenges?
- Are you comfortable with change?

Reflecting and Connecting

- How can you connect this activity to real-life instances in which you might need to adjust, adapt, or redefine the path you take to reach your goals?

- This exercise pushes students to think metaphorically, which may be easy for some and difficult for others. Be encouraging and positive as groups work through this activity.
- Creativity is key. Remind students to be thoughtful in the story lines they create and to maintain a positive outlook.
- Connect this process to the concept of agility by identifying parts of the story that can be linked to either challenges or changing circumstances in college, career, life, and so on.
- Discuss how the group had to assess options, embrace challenges, and deal with consequences.
- If a group is struggling to come up with a story, remind them to take another look and change their approach. This too demonstrates agility!

Agility Personified: Brett McClelland and Mallory Carpenter

When Brett McClelland and Mallory Carpenter arrived at Beekmantown Central School in northern New York as new CFES Gaining Early Awareness and Readiness for Undergraduate Programs (GEAR UP) Fellows, they walked into a school in major transition. The elementary, middle, and high schools all had first-time principals who were unsure how to utilize their services.

Rather than pushing initiatives too soon, McClelland and Carpenter sought input on how best to help students, coupled with a willingness to try anything. It wasn't long before they earned the trust and respect of teachers, allowing them to implement their own CFES-based activities on their way to building one of the most successful GEAR UP programs in the region. In many ways, McClelland and Carpenter define agility. They taught students how to use agility in their own lives, but they also practiced it themselves by pivoting to the needs of the school.

Not surprisingly, when the COVID-19 crisis swept across the country, the fellows once again relied on agility to find new ways of reaching students. Like many schools across America, Beekmantown faced an unprecedented need for online student support for daily homework assignments, CCR, and mentoring. McClelland and Carpenter created videos on Essential Skills for students, as well as more subject-based content, such as a science video titled "Improve Our Earth and Improve Ourselves."

They also worked with principals on ways to provide virtual mentoring and tutoring to students who were struggling during the crisis and needed extra support. Providing links to virtual campus tours, online college fairs, and financial aid webinars helped ease the stress of the college search process. McClelland and Carpenter also shared CFES-produced resources, including live webinars, that reinforced Essential Skills.

The foundations of Essential Skills that the Fellows laid prior to COVID-19 paid off during the pandemic. CFES schools that emphasized Essential Skills, including perseverance, agility, and leadership, experienced strong student engagement during the COVID-19 crisis, with Beekmantown leading the way with a 97% online attendance rate.

"There's no question that teaching students the Essential Skills throughout the year helped them during the shutdown when they needed to utilize the skills more than ever," said McClelland. "The relationships we built with teachers and staff prior to COVID-19 really helped when we needed to come together quickly to find ways to help our students not only survive but to thrive through this unprecedented situation."

Beekmantown also benefited from resources provided by CFES' college and corporate partners in the form of online programming, weekly virtual science cafes, and live chats with leading scientists and other experts in a broad range of fields. CFES webinars featured college diversity officers talking about retention, and financial literacy experts, corporate leaders, and college admissions professionals.

Essential Skill #5: Perseverance

Definition: The ability to overcome challenges to achieve a person's goals. When something sets a person back, the person must decide to keep trying.

Why is perseverance important? Failures and mistakes are part of life. Perseverance allows a person to overcome those challenges and turn them into something productive. Having perseverance is more likely than almost any other quality to lead to success; when a student has perseverance, they can use failure as a motivating tool, which will help them move forward throughout college, career, and life.

Perseverance Activity: Mission: It's Possible

What is an Essential Skills Mission?

Missions are a great way to get real-life experience while testing your skills. The world is your laboratory, your training ground, and your obstacle course—get out there and put your skills to use!

Your Perseverance Mission is to:

1. Identify a skill you are interested in mastering through practice.
2. List any materials you need to get for your skill practice.
3. Set a schedule for your practice.
4. Identify a supportive person with whom you can check in on your progress.
5. Make your practice a habit until you master that skill!

Remember these Perseverance Tips:

- Sticking to your practice schedule is the most important part of mastering your skill. It's best if you can work on it every day.
- Get creative with reminders to practice: Colorful calendars, notes on the mirror, phone alerts—anything that will remind you it's time to work on honing your new skill.
- Accept that failure will be part of the process. Remember that every failure is an opportunity to become better on your next attempt.
- Use the power of positive thinking—believe that you can do it!
- Apply your attitude of perseverance to everything you do in life.

Need Some Help Picking a Skill?

Not all of the following suggestions are "serious" skills—some are just fun. The important thing is to pick something you are interested in learning and sticking with it through practice.

Try learning how to:

- Say "hello" in 10 different languages,
- type without looking at the keyboard,
- tie a bowtie,
- master the tango,
- cook a family recipe,
- juggle,
- memorize a poem,
- spin a basketball on your finger,
- tie six different kinds of knots,
- create origami,
- learn sign language,
- whistle with your fingers,
- build a website,
- write, direct, and produce a YouTube video, or
- do a cartwheel.

Perseverance Personified: Kristin Thorpe

Fifteen years ago, a CFES mentor from Middlebury College met with Kristin Thorpe, then a high school junior at Crown Point Central School, and asked her, "Why can't you do it? Why shouldn't you attend a college like Middlebury?"

"I remember vividly when I told her that I wanted to be a high school teacher," said Thorpe. "Middlebury's one of the most selective and expensive colleges in the country. It's like a small Ivy League college. It took me by surprise, but I decided to apply, and I got in. I thought I couldn't afford it. Turns out it cost me only $1,000 more to attend Middlebury than SUNY

Geneseo, a state school that had been my top choice. It's crazy because Middlebury costs three times as much as Geneseo, but they gave me lots of financial aid," said Thorpe.

"So I went to Middlebury, and while I was there, I paid it forward. I was heavily involved in CFES. I was the Head CFES Mentor at Crown Point. I came back every week to mentor Crown Point students. I helped kids with goal setting."

Not only did Thorpe mentor students, but as the Head Mentor, she had to recruit and organize ten of her Middlebury College mentor peers.

"Middlebury was really difficult for me. I was always studying. I'd never struggled before. I was a math major, and I failed the abstract algebra class that was taught by my advisor. I then retook that class with a different professor and got one of the highest grades on the final."

"My professor from the first class told me that he thought I wasn't cut out to be a math major. I don't like being told that I can't do something. That's when my perseverance really kicked in. I also stepped back and set goals to succeed in that class," said Thorpe.

Thorpe's advice to other rural students: Talk to people—reach out. Persevere. Don't be afraid of things that are difficult. Develop a strong work ethic.

Fifteen years ago, Thorpe said she had "a huge passion for equity in education." Now living with her husband and three kids in Nevada, teaching middle school math, she's fulfilling her own prophecy and continuing to build dreams for others. "I tell my students today, to never let anyone make them feel incompetent. Sometimes we don't know things because we've never been given the chance. That doesn't mean we can't understand it if given the chance," said Thorpe.

Kristin Thorpe's story is about lots of Essential Skills: Leadership, goal setting, and networking. She encompasses all six of the Essential Skills, but it's perseverance especially, that allowed her to succeed in college and other phases of life.

Essential Skill #6: Networking

Definition: Turning an acquaintance into a supporter. A person's network can include mentors, teachers, family, friends, and people you meet through extracurricular activities. In fact, anyone can become part of a network. As

Shari Brannock of Crown Point says, "We need to do it together. Working alone doesn't work."

Why should I network? Even the most talented people need help from others to achieve their goals. Networking is an essential skill that can help a person develop supportive relationships that connect them to academic and career opportunities now and in the future. The expression, "Who you know is more important than what you know," sums up why having a network is important. A network is comprised of what a person knows, and those relationships can play an important role in a person's success.

Networking Activity: Social Media Scavenger Hunt

Introduction

Social media is a good way to expand your network, keep in touch with your contacts, and make sure everyone in your network is aware of what you have going on. To use social media as an effective networking tool, you'll want to make sure your profiles are presentable and give an accurate idea of what you're all about. This scavenger hunt will help you see what you might need to change in your social media.

Instructions

Log in to your favorite social media platform and see if you can find the following things in your profile or in the profiles of others:

- an embarrassing photo that is visible only to some people,
- an embarrassing photo that is shared publicly,
- a post in which someone was rude or disrespectful,
- five people in your network that you spent time with during the past week,
- someone in your network that you haven't ever met in person,
- a post that shared too much personal information,
- information about a person's hobby that is new to you,
- sensitive personal information, such as a home address,
- a photo that you wouldn't want posted in the hallway of your school,
- someone in your network that could help you edit a college application essay,
- someone in your network who has been supportive of your goals,
- the account of a college you might want to attend, and
- the account of a corporation or business in a career that interests you.

Reflecting and Connecting

Did you find anything that surprised you? Social media can be a great networking tool, but it can also give people the wrong first impression of who you are. Seventy percent of employers use social media to screen candidates; 57% are less likely to interview a candidate they can't find online, and 54% have decided not to hire a candidate based on their social media profiles (Camarneiro, 2018). Here are some ways you can make sure your social media profiles are helping you network and not hurting your future:

- Follow the college account and business account you found in the scavenger hunt. Seeing their posts will inspire you to follow through on your goals and get you familiar with what is going on at that campus or in that industry.
- Use social media to reach out to organizations that might help you achieve your college and career pathway goals. For example, if you are a female interested in computer science, get involved with @GirlsWhoCode.

- Interact more with the people you identified as supportive of your goals and spend time with them in person as well. Social media can help you network, but make sure it's not the only way you interact with your supporters.
- Keep everything you share on social media appropriate.

Networking Personified: Don Outing

Growing up in a single-parent home in 1970s Baltimore, Don Outing never gave much thought to networking. He was more concerned about rising out of poverty by any means necessary, which he did through hard work in the classroom and on the field as a four-sport star.

Outing is now the Vice President for Equity and Community and the Diversity and Inclusion Officer at Lehigh University. When he looks back, he realizes his early success was due in large part to his network of supporters, which included his mother, sisters, teammates, coaches, and teachers.

It's why Outing chose to spend his life helping young people change their life trajectories through careers in STEM. As Founding Director of the Center for Leadership and Diversity in STEM at West Point from 2009 to 2014, Outing and his network of partners, including CFES, impacted the lives of more than 10,000 students.

"I wanted students to know that failure was acceptable, but that not doing something to rectify the failure was unacceptable," says Outing. "I asked them, 'Do you know how many great mathematicians struggled and repeatedly failed over and over again on their way to solving complex mathematics problems? You don't think they relied on a network of supporters to help them achieve the success that they did?' "

Outing speaks from experience. He remembers the move into public housing in Baltimore actually "feeling like an upgrade." Despite the odds, he continued to excel in football and in school, taking thermodynamics and differential equations, prompting recruiting battles between the likes of Bear Bryant at the University of Alabama, the University of Maryland, and Boston College, and a late push by the military academies.

The Naval Academy won out. Outing arrived in Annapolis in the fall of 1979 as one of only 200 African Americans on campus. Though he didn't think of it as networking at the time, Outing built strong bonds with his classmates. "We called ourselves the 7th Battalion [only six officially existed] and met for fellowship and mentorship," says Outing. "I came from Baltimore, so for the first time in my life, I found out what it meant to be a minority."

Outing's growing network at the Naval Academy included Capt. Charlie Robinson, whom he credits with helping him remain in college. "I had a 1.11 grade point average in my first semester and was going to be asked to leave if I didn't turn things around," said Outing. "Captain Robinson was the first African American marine officer I'd ever met. That relationship had a huge impact on my life and helped define the relationships I've tried to form with my mentees. I didn't want to disappoint him."

Outing made the Dean's list the next three semesters, an achievement that served as a catalyst for what would become a career in academia. He earned his master's degree from Rensselaer Polytechnic Institute (RPI) and was hired to teach mathematics at West Point. The senior faculty recommended that Outing get his PhD so he could return as an assistant professor.

Unsure if he could handle doctorate-level work, Outing again relied on a member of his network for guidance. Gary Krahn, Head of the Department of Mathematics at West Point, showed Outing an article about three African American women who had just graduated with PhDs in mathematics from the University of Maryland.

"I said, 'Yeah, so?'," recalls Outing. "Then he explained that this had never been done before, and that only nine African Americans in the entire US attained PhDs in mathematics that year. Gary knew how to touch a nerve in me because now I saw it as my duty and obligation to get my PhD."

After graduating with honors from RPI, Outing returned to West Point driven to enlighten underrepresented minorities about the opportunities in mathematics. "I had this passion and vigor, and I wanted to share it with as many people as possible. It was like I was sitting on a huge secret, and I needed to get it out there."

Outing launched the West Point Robotics Workshop, which inspired thousands of students to consider careers in STEM, including CFES Scholars across the country. "My core principles and values were in line with CFES," said Outing. "But what I really like is the passion I feel when I interact with CFES and their staff. It's never about them. Empowering children is always their goal."

Outing continues to inspire young mathematicians like Dr. Samuel Ivy, who succeeded him as Director of the Center for Leadership and Diversity in STEM at West Point. "Don invited me to give a talk at West Point when I was a senior at Morehouse, and it just blew me away," says Ivy. "He kept in touch with me and has worked very hard to increase the representation of mathematicians of color within the department."

Outing continues to pay it forward in his new role at Lehigh. "I had inspiration along the way from other African American mathematicians who exposed me to the work they were doing, and now it's my turn to build the network," he said.

How the Rubric Works

The Essential Skills Rubric was developed as a self-reflective tool. It can be conducted in the classroom, as it allows scholars and school communities to assess results in 30 minutes or less.

1. Scholars can start by completing the Essential Skills Rubric Online Assessment hosted on the brilliantpathways.org website, which enables us to identify who they are, their grade level, and the school they attend.
2. Next, they consider the series of statements in Box 3.3. These statements align their attitudes and skills related to how they demonstrate proficiency in each of the Essential Skills.
3. Finally, scholars will receive their results in the form of a spider chart (Box 3.4). Once it's clear where they excel and where they need practice, we can provide scholars and educators with content to further develop their skills.

This tool is helpful not only to scholars for the purposes of self-evaluation but also helpful to school communities, as they provide intelligible feedback. We will work with scholars and campus leaders to help scholars achieve the highest level of mastery with our activities and workshops.

The spider chart depicts all six components of the Essential Skills. When complete, scholars can see which skills stand out, and which skills need more development. By plotting multiple students on the same chart,

Box 3.3 Rubric for Essential Skills

Essential Skill™	1 Acquiring	2 Developing	3 Adapting	4 Advancing
Goal setting	I just go day-by-day and get things done as I need to.	I follow the goals my teachers set in class.	I use a planner to set and track my school goals, and I am working on doing the same with my personal life.	I have clearly defined short-, mid-, and long-term goals and a list of specific steps to achieve my goals.
Teamwork	I don't like to contribute or do the tasks I am assigned in groups.	Occasionally I make compromises to accomplish a common goal.	I have a positive attitude about the task(s) and the work of others.	I perform all duties of assigned roles, and I contribute knowledge and opinions to the group.
Leadership	I don't consider myself a leader and do not seek out leadership opportunities.	I tend to let others make the decisions but occasionally contribute.	I understand myself enough to be able to contribute in times of need while allowing others to do the same.	I use my skills to help other people succeed or become engaged.
Agility	I don't like change and don't adapt to new circumstances.	I know what I need to do, but I don't take the steps to adapt.	Change is stressful for me, but I manage to take the steps needed to adapt.	I remain calm and productive during changing times and act on opportunities even when I don't have all the information.
Perseverance	I often give up on the first try.	I am willing to try out other ways.	I seek and refine suggestions on how to move forward.	I don't let setbacks deter me from achieving my goal.

Essential Skill™	1 Acquiring	2 Developing	3 Adapting	4 Advancing
Networking	I rely on myself for everything I do.	I rarely ask for help from acquaintances but recognize when I need help.	I reach out to others in an effort to broaden my network.	I regularly seek to broaden my network and utilize those within it to support my goals.

Box 3.4 Spider Chart with Essential Skills™ Rubric Results

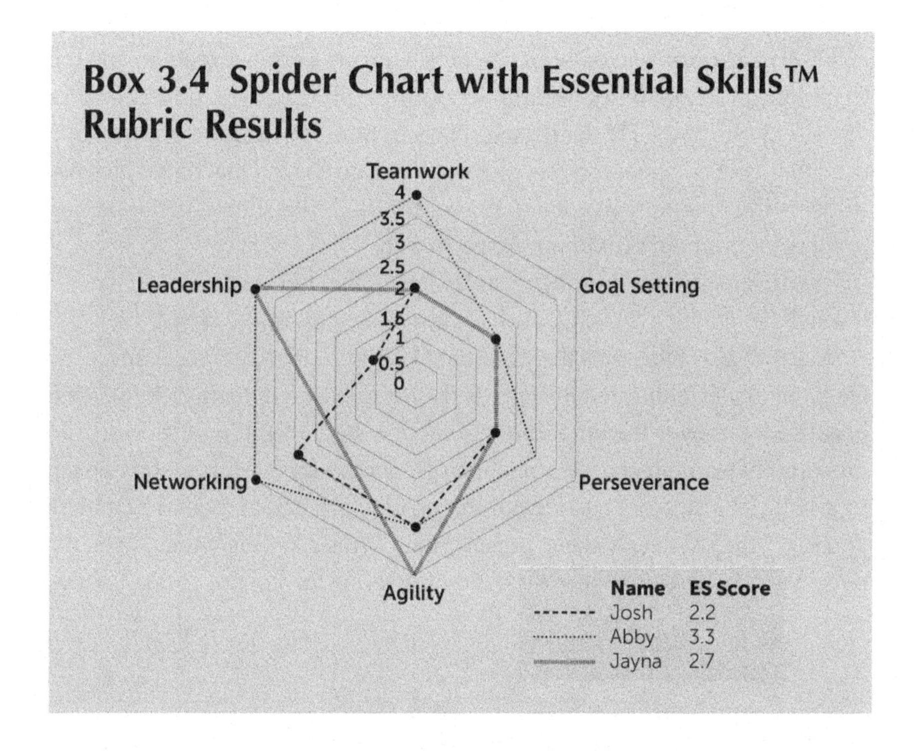

educators and program facilitators can get visual confirmation of which areas need support.

In this example, we've compiled results from three 8th grade students who took the assessment earlier this year. Abby scored the highest, averaging 3.3 points for each of the six Essential Skills. Goal setting, though, is an area she needs to work on. In fact, each of the three students in this example scored lowest on goal setting—perhaps this will be the next area to focus on.

Bringing the Essential Skills into a Florida Classroom

CFES Scholars develop the Essential Skills in many ways. CFES engages students in interactive exercises that allow them to define, practice, and then discuss the skills and how they can be applied to real-life situations. Game play is a great opportunity to connect abstract content to actual behavior changes. Postgame reflection and discussion enable participants to draw connections and build the Essential Skills. CFES uses digital tools such as MAP APP (Resource 3.1), and some CFES educators teach the Essential Skills in classroom settings.

Kelly Larrow is one of those teachers. Larrow, a science teacher and the CFES liaison at Mulberry Middle School in Polk County, Florida, teaches three sections of a CFES leadership class to 6th, 7th, and 8th graders. She used to try the "one-shot approach," but because she felt that didn't give her students the time they needed to master the skill, she shifted her approach to focus on a single skill for an entire month.

Larrow uses a three-pronged approach to help her students: 1) Discover the skill, 2) practice the skill, and 3) ultimately, master the skill.

Larrow also integrates the Essential Skills into her science classes. "The Essential Skills help students in their overall development and success because it removes the emotion. Instead of a student getting frustrated and thinking they are incapable or feeling discouraged, I put this in the context of a skill. So instead of a student thinking they are bad at math, I reframe it and say, 'You just need to keep persevering.'." This takes the emphasis off the person and places it on the skill. "It's empowering for students," says Larrow.

Resource 3.1 MAP APP

MAP APP is CFES' web-based game in which players use the Essential Skills to become college and career ready. Players can role-play based on situations they are likely to experience on their own brilliant pathway toward CCR.

Bringing the Essential Skills Together: The Power of Peers

A common thread in the success stories shared above is that the individuals involved didn't only commit to improving their own lives but to uplifting others around them. A powerful characteristic of the Essential Skills is that they don't merely cultivate a mindset for survival but for service.

CFES has found that peer mentoring is a practical and engaging way for students to put the Essential Skills to work. Peer mentoring embodies all the Essential Skills and is a good way to build CCR. Here are some of its many benefits:

- **Peer mentoring supports students academically.**

  Peer mentoring keeps students involved in school and in their education. This is important for students who are transitioning to a new school or new grade level. When students become peer mentors, grades almost always improve. Peer mentoring is a school-based relationship that benefits everyone—from potential dropouts to aspiring valedictorians.
- **Peer mentoring can help students become college ready.**

  Peer mentoring helps students prepare for college and succeed once they get there. This is particularly important for first-gen students who need someone outside their household to help them plan for this next big step. In addition to creating a supportive, college-bound community where students can have productive, ongoing discussions about college with a peer, peer mentoring helps students develop time management and teamwork skills, improve study habits, and build leadership qualities.
- **Peer mentoring helps students become leaders.**

  When acting as peer mentors, students don't sit back and listen to someone else's instructions. Mentors are front and center, making it happen. Mentors are role models who show younger peers what it takes to succeed. Mentors take charge of shaping the overall mentoring program and planning activities that encourage others to get involved.

Mentors play a vital role in the success of their mentees' achievements, from getting better grades to earning college scholarships.

- **Peer mentoring can help students become career ready.**

  The benefits of peer mentoring last a long time, providing leadership and networking skills that support students in future jobs. Ben, who was part of the Leadership Lunch program at Peru High School, decided he wanted to become a teacher because of peer mentoring. Some peer mentoring programs use the Brilliant Career Lab, CFES' interactive website that enables students to investigate STEM careers as an activity. This allows mentees to explore careers with their mentors. Other peer mentoring programs bring in professionals to share career paths with both mentors and mentees.

Leadership Lunches: Peru's Peer Empowerment Program

Chris Mazzella, Principal of Peru High School, had 40 high school students do a four-hour summer training that centered on Essential Skills. The students were trained in the six Essential Skills, to which they added a seventh: Communication. To deliver mentoring and teach the Essential Skills, the high school students then created a year-long program in which they supported 7th graders during lunch twice a month.

The high school students also participated in their own lunch workshop facilitated by Mazzella twice a month at which they developed their own leadership skills. In the spring, these same high school students organized a program called Positive Action Week. Each morning, students made a public service announcement to share the theme for the day. They developed lunchtime activities where students wrote positive notes to a peer or teacher, put stickers on lockers with positive messages, and ended the week with a day focused on eliminating intolerance and embracing kindness.

Peer Empowerment Mentoring Program

Four years later, Mazzella's students, all now in college, reflected on the impact of Leadership Lunches.

- Hunter: "It was mutually beneficial. Many older kids showed growth and opened up and developed leadership skills. It definitely changed behaviors. This experience motivated me to continue to mentor in my career and as a college student."
- Samantha: "It helped me be more confident and let me learn teamwork. All the presentations were collaborative. It allowed me to find strengths and weaknesses and my voice when working on a team. The biggest thing was leadership put it into practice. We learned to communicate effectively. Having to present to younger kids was a huge growth experience for me. I was forced to get out of my comfort zone and learned how to plan a clear and effective presentation. The Leadership Lunches connected our community that supported younger students."
- Ben: "Definitely made me a better communicator. It also impacted my career choice to be a teacher. The leadership programs in the school created a positive atmosphere. You had to work hard at making the commitment to make the connection with the younger students for them to trust the mentors. Developing a community within the school is essential for students to have a sense of belonging."

Building a Peer Mentoring Program

A well-designed peer mentoring program benefits both mentors and mentees, as well as the entire school community. Here are suggestions for building a school-based peer mentoring program, based on strategies developed by CFES Brilliant Pathways.

Step 1: Build Your Leadership Team

The core leadership team is a group of student and adult leaders who are responsible for the mentoring program's setup and administration. The team will work best if its student members are from different social groups, ranging beyond the obvious leaders. For instance, students who had to repeat a year of school can relate to academically struggling mentees. Students from all social groups can be excellent mentors. In fact, the wider this range of students, the more likely it is that the program will be successful. The only rule to follow is to be sure that everyone is committed to the program and committed to working together.

Step 2: Define Goals for Your Mentoring Program

A peer mentoring program can achieve many things, but it's most likely to be effective if you set realistic goals. Write a statement of your program's goals and vision. This should be a sentence or two that you can use to focus your core leadership team and communicate your mission quickly to any audience. It should answer these questions: "What are you doing?" and "What is the purpose of your program?"

Step 3: Secure Approval and Support from School Administrators

Since peer mentoring is going to be a part of your school culture, it needs to be officially recognized and approved. Highlighting how mentors can devise creative solutions to longstanding problems can make this an easy sell. At one New Hampshire school, for instance, it was very easy to convince the Principal to sign off on a peer mentoring program because she had wanted to do more for unmotivated 9th graders. These were the exact students the older students had targeted as potential mentees. Family support also helps, so communicate with parents and caregivers. Although peer mentoring programs are student-led, let students know that adults are always available to offer help.

Step 4: Develop Your Mentoring Calendar

The earlier you do this, the more organized your program will be! If your program involves multiple schools, be sure to involve a student and administrator from each school in the planning because each will have a different understanding of how the program can work within their schedule. Follow these steps to build a calendar together:

- Include your program's **start and end dates**. Allow planning time at the beginning of the year to kick things off and time for wrap-up discussions at the year's end.
- Fill in **all mentoring events** that will take place throughout the year, including training, kickoff activities, mentor check-in meetings, group events, and special field trips.
- Mark the weeks when the mentoring program has **time off** because of vacation, testing, class trips, and other prescheduled events.
- Plan **celebrations** and be sure to mark them on the calendar.
- **Give everyone a copy of the calendar**—mentors, mentees, administrators, other teachers. If everyone has your schedule before they set theirs, they can plan around the mentoring group activities.

Step 5: Select Your Target Mentee Group

The way you select mentors and mentees should be based on the resources and needs of your school. If your program is about helping with transitions, for example, then your mentees might be 9th graders who might be having difficulty adjusting to high school. If you're trying to engage young males through sports, athletes with academic difficulties would be a good group to identify as mentees.

Step 6: Design Your Mentor Application

At some schools, mentors are handpicked by faculty members, while other schools ask students interested in mentoring to fill out applications. Design your mentoring application to be a resource for pairing mentors and mentees with similar experience and interests. In addition to asking for basic information (name, age, gender, schedule availability, reason for interest in the program), make sure the application asks questions that relate to your program goals and description.

Step 7: Train Mentors

Since the mentor–mentee relationship is the program's foundation, mentors must be comfortable in their role. Training is vital and should happen early. Mentors should learn about the commitment they're making and their role. Once they finish their initial training, they can pass along training tips to the next group of peer mentors.

Step 8: Plan Activities

Peer mentoring is often centered on academics but be sure to plan social activities as well. Since peer mentoring is for everyone, be sure activities are varied enough to attract a range of students. Some kids like to play soccer; others prefer a poetry slam. Free food is always important, so, where possible, plan an activity that engages participants as they snack. Make sure you plan some activities for the first few mentoring sessions. Mentors and mentees will probably be a little nervous, and structured interactions can help relieve the pressure as they get to know each other.

As your core team plans each activity, make sure both mentors and mentees understand what to do and what is expected of them. Receiving written information about what will happen before an event gives mentors structure and support, along with time to clarify any sources of confusion. At this planning stage, adults need to be on hand to provide the necessary structure, but students will want to gradually take on more and more responsibility as the program moves forward.

Step 9: Plan a Kickoff

The kickoff will mark the program's official start. Core mentors who help plan this event will feel invested in the success of the program. If mentors are dedicated to the peer mentoring program, mentees will see their commitment and match their enthusiasm in weekly meetings.

To start the year off, plan a group activity—something that can be photographed and reported on for the school newspaper or posted on social media platforms. Don't worry if mentors and mentees haven't been paired or even selected yet—you never know how many kids you'll draw in with a great kickoff. Make it memorable.

Step 10: Mentor–Mentee Sessions

Mentors and mentees should have regular, scheduled meetings, but the frequency and setting of the meetings is up to you. For instance, high school students in Olathe, Colorado, meet their mentees in the middle school cafeteria. Other programs alternate meeting on the athletic field and in a classroom.

The first few mentoring sessions ought to be held in rapid succession to allow mentors and mentees to get to know one another quickly. For instance, if you're planning to have mentors meet every other week for the rest of the year, hold weekly meetings for the first two or three weeks.

Mentors and mentees will explore interests and aspirations together during structured events, such as college visits, weekly meetings, leadership workshops, and so forth, but you should also connect during informal gatherings. There are many ways for mentors to stay in touch with mentees, including social media, text messages, or just stopping by a mentee's lunch table to say hello.

Tips for Adult Leaders: Take the Back Seat

Adults involved in peer mentoring programs need to understand their roles are different from their typical responsibilities as teachers and administrators. Rather than leading the group, they must sit back and let students take the lead. It's important that both students and teachers understand the adult coordinator's role and responsibilities. With a strong line of communication and a shared commitment to success, students and adults can help one another define and refine the adult role. Here are guidelines that adults should follow:

- **Rule #1: Listen**

Interactions between the adult coordinator and students need to be conversations, not lectures. Teachers, who are used to setting the agenda, need to adjust to this new role, while counselors and coaches, who are used to a more collaborative approach, might have an easier time. Once the lines of communication are open, and mentors and mentees see that adult coordinators are truly receptive to their suggestions, they will feel comfortable and able to explain what they want and need from the program. This two-way communication, combined with the trust that is built throughout the course of a peer mentoring program, is crucial to maintaining momentum and ensuring long-term success.

- **Rule #2: Be There, Be Approachable, and Be Supportive**

Even though peer mentoring is a student-driven program, adult coordinators play a crucial role. They may work on the administrative requirements of the program, such as distributing and collecting mentoring applications, but they may also support the program by hurling a dodge ball in the gym with mentors and mentees. Regardless of the adult role on any given day, their presence and support are fundamental to keeping the program running.

- **Rule #3: Think of Us as a Team**

Student leadership is crucial to the creation and management of a successful mentoring program. However, shared leadership between adults and students is a matter of finding the right balance. This requires teamwork and agility.

A slightly informal, mutually respectful atmosphere between mentors and adult leaders makes it easier for students to ask for help when they need it and for adults to find their place without stepping on anyone's toes.

Adult coordinators also benefit from the support of their peer mentoring team. Rather than having to run every detail of the program, they can delegate some of the responsibility to their students. In other words, everyone is contributing something to the program, but no one person has the burden of doing all the work.

The teamwork aspect of peer mentoring—the sharing of responsibilities between students and adults—is especially important for adults. Students will come and go. Some will enter the program as timid, uncertain mentees and become confident, self-assured mentors before they move on to college. While students on the leadership team will be involved in program planning for the following year, it is the adults who provide continuity. Adults can lean on their peer mentors when they need help in managing the program.

- **Rule #4: Have Patience, Believe in Student Leadership**

As bright and skilled as they may be, mentors and mentees are still relatively inexperienced when it comes to building an effective and sustainable program for the school and community. It will take time (and trial and error) for them to build their own pathways to success. Adults need to be generous with time and exercise patience as students learn to take ownership of the mentoring program. By waiting for students to work out details for themselves, adult coordinators show students that they have confidence in them.

Peer mentoring is a creative approach to addressing challenges in schools. For a program to remain effective and sustainable, students need to create solutions that work for them. Mistakes may happen, but these can be valuable learning experiences that will help strengthen and sustain the program.

Student leadership summits are a leadership development opportunity that builds agility, networking, teamwork, goal setting, and, of course, leadership. During these workshops, which are planned and facilitated by CFES Scholars, participants address leadership topics and skill areas, share their leadership experiences, and brainstorm activities designed to make their schools and communities better places. Topics focus on early college awareness, goal setting, leadership development, peer mentoring, healthy habits, and social responsibility. The summit traditionally features a welcome and/or keynote speaker, breakout sessions to encourage discussion, and a closing session to share group findings and next steps. See Box 3.5 for an example of an agenda for a CFES student leadership summit.

Conclusion

Since trademarking the Essential Skills in 2015, CFES has seen interest in these competencies grow exponentially. Business leaders at Southwest Airlines and educators at Harvard Business School realize that the Essential

Box 3.5 CFES Student Leadership Summits

SAMPLE AGENDA

9:30 a.m.	**Welcome, introductions, and event overview**
9:50–10:50 a.m.	**Group discussions. Sample topics:** *Leading with Accountability and Responsibility* *Community Building and Empowerment 101* *The Leader's Identity: Who Are You? Communication Etiquette*
11:00–12 noon	**Group discussions. Sample topics:** *Leadership beyond the Position* *Communicating Effectively*

Skills are critical for growth and success. Chapter 3 shares how CFES became aware of their importance and how CFES is helping its scholars and educators develop the Essential Skills. For each of the six skills, the chapter provides a definition, an activity to develop the skill, and a profile of a person who embodies that skill.

Because studies have found that rural youth are more susceptible to doubts about their intelligence and ability to compete in college even when they have the same level of high school preparation and achievement as their peers (Engle, 2007), the Essential Skills are especially important for them. Although we dissect each skill individually, CFES knows that people do not develop these skills one at a time. We know that those with an exemplary skill have multiple competencies. Brian Flores personifies leadership, but his success as a coach also depends on networking, goal setting, agility, and perseverance competencies. Kristin Thorpe succeeded at Middlebury as much because of goal setting, leadership, agility, and networking as perseverance.

References

Camarneiro, A. (2018). Should employers look at social media when hiring? LawDepot blog. www.lawdepot.com/blog/should-employers-look-at-social-media-when-hiring/

Engle, J. (2007). Postsecondary access and success for first-generation college students. *American Academic, 3*(1), 25–48.

St. John, E., Milazzo-Bigelow, V., & Stillman, P. K. (2015). *College for every student: Middle school survey* [Unpublished evaluation]. University of Michigan School of Education.

College- and Career-Readiness Advisors

Navigators to a New World

The Power of College- and Career-Readiness Advising

Growing up in Mulberry, Florida, near the citrus groves, Maria never thought she'd become the first in her family to attend college. That changed in 10th grade when her math teacher, Mr. Lambert, took Maria and three classmates to visit nearby Polk State College. "It opened up a new world for me," said Maria.

But in 11th grade, the complexity of the college admissions process threatened to derail Maria's dream. That's when Mr. Lambert stepped in and showed her how to sign up for tests, fill out financial aid forms, and move through the admissions maze. "Mr. L. badgered me about deadlines and supported me at every turn. I never could have done this alone," said Maria, who has now graduated from the University of Central Florida.

At schools across the United States, millions of students, most from low-income households with limited college and career knowledge, sit on the bubble. They're qualified for college, but they don't get the kind of college- and career-readiness (CCR) support that Maria received from Mr. Lambert. In fact, that's part of his job: Mr. L. is a CCR advisor. We need thousands more like him.

This chapter highlights the critical role qualified CCR advisors can play in supporting rural students on their journey toward higher education.

It also outlines the overwhelming obstacles—cultural, financial, and logistical—that discourage the pursuit of higher education in rural communities. All too often, promising rural students are actively discouraged from considering college, despite the obvious benefits it brings to their future income, quality of life, and potentially, the future vitality of their communities. As discussed in the previous chapters, rural students are no less intelligent or capable of college work than their urban and suburban counterparts, but to overcome their obstacles, they need consistent, knowledgeable, and personalized guidance and mentoring, which is often more than their overworked school counselors can offer.

This is where CCR advisors—specially trained and certified educators, college students, community volunteers, and others—can make a difference. This chapter shows how CFES (College for Every Student) recruits and trains CCR advisors and shares practical examples of how they motivate, educate, and empower students.

The Rural Trap

CCR advising is critical for rural students. Consider Jon and Sinead: Both grew up and attended school in the northeast corner of Vermont, a heavily forested area known as the Northeast Kingdom. They didn't know many people in their communities who had attended college so they didn't have trusted individuals to turn to for the college and career readiness (CCR) advice they needed.

Jon: Too Late, Too Overwhelming

Jon never thought about going to college until his senior year, when a coach from Castleton University, about two hours south of his hometown, contacted him about playing soccer there. "I visited, and I loved the Castleton campus," he said. "I didn't even know about Castleton until the beginning of my senior year. When their coach said I could start for them, I was over the moon."

A few months later, Castleton accepted Jon. But he didn't enroll. Instead, he stayed home to work in a restaurant to support his younger siblings.

"There were some family setbacks, and the money part scared me, so I decided I couldn't go. People needed my help. My grandmother needed my help. My family is falling apart right now, and they definitely need a stable person. Family has always been a big thing for me."

Jon wished he'd had someone to advise him earlier in high school so he would have been more prepared. "My high school could do a lot more to help kids understand what college is all about and what type of scholarships are available," he said. "Had I known that there were scholarships available when I was a freshman, I would have tried harder. My mother didn't care. She told me I'd be better off financially by getting a job and not paying a lot of money and borrowing a lot more."

Sinead: No One to Help

Jon's classmate Sinead described herself as "one of those kids who thought I would go to college from the time I was in kindergarten until I was in 10th grade." That changed during her junior year when Sinead started thinking about other options based on conversations with family and friends. She did not want to burden her parents with college debt.

She worried that her father, who is a crane operator at a granite shed, might "roll over and die because he works so hard." The idea of adding to the financial stress of her father and mother, who runs a housecleaning business, was not something she wanted to do because they "already struggled with making payments."

She described the need she felt to help her family: "I've seen the things that they've gone through, and I just want to step up and help. They've had a tough life. I want to work and be able to help my dad with payments and things because he struggles. At first, my dad wanted my sister to go to college, but that changed and he told her, and later me, that we didn't need a college degree to get a job. He didn't tell me not to go, but he didn't push me to go to college."

In the end, Sinead landed a job as a bank teller in Harwood, 15 miles from where she grew up. "Life is hard, and you need money to survive. No one pushed me, and no one has shown me how to move down that path to a better life," she said.

Obstacles to Advancement in Rural America

Jon and Sinead's stories exemplify the obstacles promising rural students face when pursuing higher education. In both their stories, we see a number of common issues at play:

- **A lack of social capital:** Rural communities such as Jon and Sinead's in Vermont's Northeast Kingdom often lack the networks needed to inform families about the benefits of college. Rural parents who did not attend college have limited knowledge about colleges and college admissions, which negatively impacts their children's postsecondary educational pursuits (Howley, 2006). A shortage of knowledge about college options in rural communities inadvertently results in parents discouraging their children from attending college.
- **Inaccurate and misleading information:** Students make decisions about going to college based on information that is often inaccurate and misleading. Jon's mother told him that he'd be better off not going to college, even though he would have ended up in a far better place financially with a degree from Castleton than just a high school diploma.
- **Trusted individuals might not be the right advisors:** Students make decisions about their postsecondary future based on advice from parents or other trusted individuals. Unfortunately, those individuals do not always have accurate knowledge or even the best interest of the student in mind. For instance, the push to attend college from one parent and the pull to stay close to home from another can cause confusion rather than create clarity, often resulting in hasty, pressure-induced decisions (Reidel, 2018).
- **School counselors are not enough:** Students from rural schools, especially those like Jon and Sinead who would have been first-generation college students, need support from outside the home to successfully move down the pathway to college and a career. Rural schools have counselors, but evidence suggests that they have neither the time nor the skills to adequately provide CCR support, especially for low-income students like Jon and Sinead (Belasco, 2013). While some counselors have attempted to assume this role, too many of them

> struggle to handle the hierarchy of needs they face, from abuse in student homes to course scheduling. It's unsurprising that they often have little bandwidth to help students on their college and career journey. A recent survey of 5,300 middle and high school counselors reported that they wanted to help students graduate high school and attend college but lacked necessary resources and time, much of which is spent on nonstudent administrative work. Thus, most bubble students never find anyone to encourage and help them understand college terminology, test taking, and how to apply to and pay for college. More often than not, formal education for these students ends with a high school diploma (if that), and they end up staying in their home communities, making minimum wage.

These obstacles not only impose limits on the lives of individuals but they impose limits on their communities and the overall economy as well. More than ever, state policymakers see postsecondary credentials as not just beneficial but essential for the economic and social well-being of both individuals and society (Perna & Finney, 2014).

In rural states like Vermont, as noted in Chapter 1, there are expected to be thousands of job openings in the next decade that will require education and training beyond high school. However, postsecondary enrollment in Vermont is below the national average of 68.4%, with only 60.2% of Vermont high school graduates choosing to attend a two- or four-year postsecondary institution (Vermont Student Assistance Corporation, 2016). Vermont consistently ranks in the bottom 10 states for the percentage of grads it sends to college (NCHEMS Information Center for Higher Education Policymaking and Analysis, 2016).

CFES' Strategy: College- and Career-Readiness Advisors

The lack of social capital in Jon and Sinead's Northeast Kingdom community meant that it had few people with a postsecondary education and a well-paying job to serve as role models.

CCR advisors are especially critical for the postsecondary aspirations of students from low socioeconomic backgrounds and first-generation

Box 4.1 Who Are Today's CCR Advisors?

Ask first-generation students who helped them on their pathway to college, and they will rarely tell you it was a college counselor. A recent CFES study of rural students found that 85% of first-gen students had more than one CCR advisor. The people who supported first-gen students down their pathway were 58% teachers (not including counselors), 34% school staff and administrators, 32% community members (including pastors and priests), 18% corporate/business leaders, and 14% coaches (Dalton, 2019).

students, such as Jon and Sinead (Box 4.1). In 2012, just over half of 18 to 24-year-olds from the lowest family income quintile who had earned a high school diploma or GED in the past year enrolled in college, compared to 81% of students from the highest family income quintile (Snyder & Dillow, 2015).

CFES has developed an innovative solution to support students like Jon and Sinead by training and credentialing college- and career-readiness advisors who help students develop the knowledge and skills they need to move down the pathway to college and career. Over the last two years, CFES has trained (and with the University of Vermont) credentialed 5,000 CCR advisors. Thus, instead of one fragmented, overworked counselor in a rural school, there can be a dozen or more CCR advisors in that school and community to help students deal with admission and financial aid deadlines, understand how to pay for college, complete applications, find internships, and meet other CCR challenges. A CCR advisor could have helped Jon and Sinead navigate the influx of questionable information they received and likely guided them toward a realistic postsecondary decision that would have put them in a better long-term financial position.

An Unlikely College- and Career-Readiness Advisor

Ask Paul Luna how he ended up in college, and he'll tell you it was his father. But there's nothing traditional about Paul's pathway.

Paul is now President and CEO of the Helios Education Foundation, a philanthropic organization that has invested a quarter of a billion dollars to help first-generation, low-income, and traditionally underrepresented students pursue postsecondary degrees. He grew up 80 miles east of Phoenix in a rural community of less than 2,000 people called Miami. It's in the heart of the Copper Corridor of Arizona, which consists of communities built on mining operations. Copper mining has been, and continues to be, the major industry in Miami, employing more than 700 people.

Paul's father was a first-generation Arizonan and a copper miner for 46 years. Attending college was not an option for him, but his goal in life was to make sure that college would be an option for his children. The elder Luna prioritized education for his family and created a college-going culture in their home.

Paul was an excellent student and talented baseball player. In fact, he was a good enough infielder to catch the attention of Stanford's Assistant Coach, who sent Paul an admission application and encouraged him to apply.

Paul, however, had other ideas. He wanted to follow his sister and his friends from Miami to a more familiar place, Arizona State University (ASU), and he didn't plan to fill out the Stanford application.

But Luna's father said, "It would be disrespectful not to complete and return the application." So, Paul followed his father's advice.

A few months later, when an acceptance letter that included an academic scholarship arrived from Stanford, Paul was resolute. He still planned to attend ASU. That's when his father sought the advice of engineers at the copper mine. The engineers told him that Stanford was a once-in-a-lifetime opportunity and that his son needed to attend Stanford. So at his father's insistence, that's what Paul did.

Navigating a college system that he knew nothing about proved challenging for Paul. Not only was the academic experience different than anything he had tried before, but he also had to manage living away from home in an urban community where he was one of very few Mexican-Americans. The social and cultural differences were immense. However, through focus and perseverance, he ultimately graduated with a degree in civil engineering. He pulled through and overcame the barriers that stand in the way of many first-generation college students.

When Paul is asked who served as his CCR advisor, he'll credit his dad. Who would have thought that his father's wisdom and dreams would benefit not just his son and daughter but thousands of other first-generation, highly deserving youth served by the Helios Education Foundation today? That's the sort of impact a CCR advisor can have.

Study Confirms the Value of College- and Career-Readiness Advisors

A recent University of Vermont study of rural high schools showed the huge impact CCR advisors could have on increasing readiness of students for college and career nationwide. The study included prior research showing how the support of an advisor can have a major impact on whether a student chooses to apply to college. When they're available, school counselors can play a critical role in helping students traverse the challenges of high school and providing insight into the many options available to them following graduation (Hurwitz & Howell, 2013). The problem is that very few low-income students, especially from rural America, have access to high-quality counseling.

The University of Vermont study found that if just five more students from each of the state's 76 high schools enrolled in college, Vermont would rise from the bottom ten to the top 20 for college attendance rates. If students had a CCR advisor, those increases would be achievable. See Box 4.2 for an explanation of why CCR advisors are so important from Scott Thomas, Dean and Professor, College of Education and Social Services, University of Vermont.

Advising the Advisors: Training CCR Advisors

The college admissions and financial aid landscape is complex and changes quickly, so it's essential that those charged with guiding students toward college have accurate, up-to-date knowledge as well as a way to stay up-to-date as higher education evolves. To ensure the effectiveness of CCR advisors, CFES has designed a certification program to equip advisors with the knowledge, skills, and resources they need to succeed. See Box 4.3 for information on the CCR advisor certificate.

Box 4.2 Why CCR Advisors are so Important

By Scott Thomas, Dean and Professor, College of Education and Social Services, University of Vermont

For many students at selective college campuses like the University of Vermont, most days growing up were a CCR day. When one is surrounded by college-educated family members and attends well-resourced schools from kindergarten through high school, it reinforces the assumption that college is a rite of passage rather than a privilege. But for many other K–12 students—in fact, perhaps most of them—far less guidance (or conflicting guidance) comes from home and the support from knowledgeable CCR advisors becomes especially important.

Many years ago, my colleagues and I traveled around the country comparing the college-going resources for students attending schools in low-, mid-, and high-income communities. The results of that years-long examination revealed that students who do not proactively seek contact with counselors and/or attend a high school where college enrollment is not the norm are less likely to receive sufficient college counseling. In other words, students with the greatest need for college counseling likely face the greatest structural barriers to receiving that counseling. We also concluded that a one-size-fits-all approach to improving college counseling is likely to be ineffective.

Years later, CFES Brilliant Pathways is training and credentialing CCR advisors and providing a model that adapts these valuable advising resources to the school and community contexts that they serve. Our partnership with CFES Brilliant Pathways is designed to help address the structural inequities to information and resources that lead to durable findings from across the country. Our commitment to this partnership is based on evidence that CCR advisors make a difference in college going for students lacking the built-in advantages known to best ensure college access and success. Being a first-generation college student who experienced the quiet power of a CCR advisor that forever changed my life, I know firsthand how this can transform individual life trajectories, families, and communities.

Box 4.3 CCR Advisor Certificate

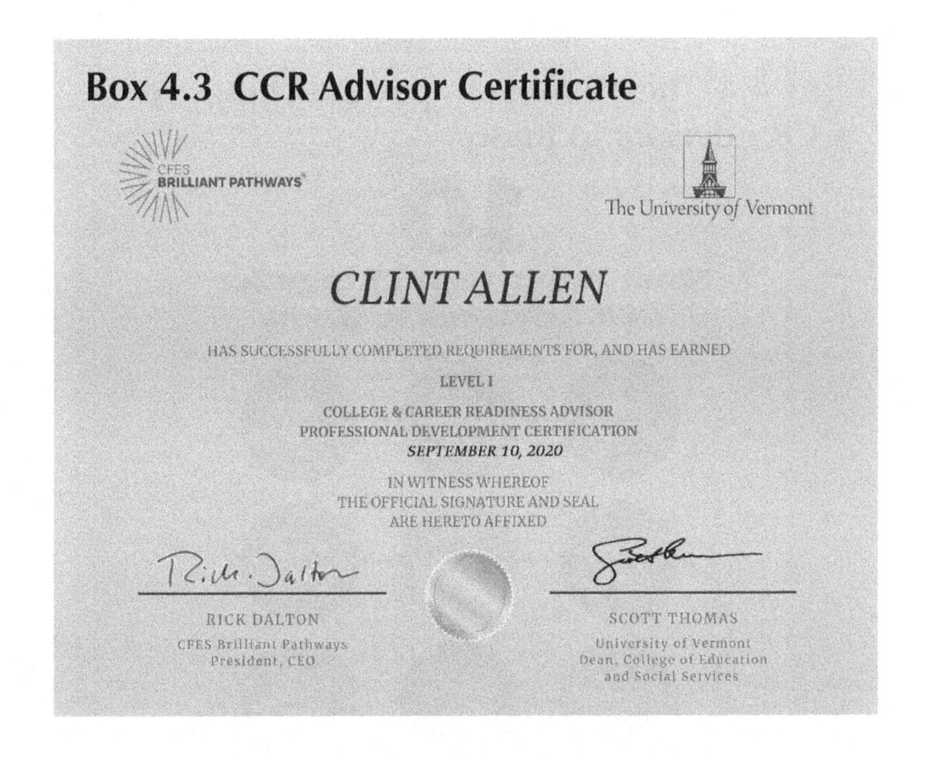

The core of CCR advisor training is an inspiring and informative six-hour online (or in-person) workshop introducing new advisors to educational experts, theoretical background, best practices, and practical exercises. The workshop also offers participants the opportunity to meet and network with like-minded changemakers. Following the workshop, CCR advisors participate in ongoing professional development (monthly webinars and virtual discussions about CCR), tap into CFES resources (digital and other), earn a credential that is certified by the University of Vermont, and even receive college credit.

CFES surveyed our staff, college officials, corporate and business leaders, and K–12 educators to find out what knowledge and skills students most needed to be college and career ready. The ten elements in Box 4.4 reflect those responses. Note that every one of these elements changes fast and frequently, so advisors must stay mindful of both the changing college landscape and the changing needs of their students.

- **Paying for college:** Advisors help students understand how to afford college (grants, scholarship, loans, etc.) and navigate the financial

Box 4.4 The 10 Most Important Things For CCR Advisors To Know

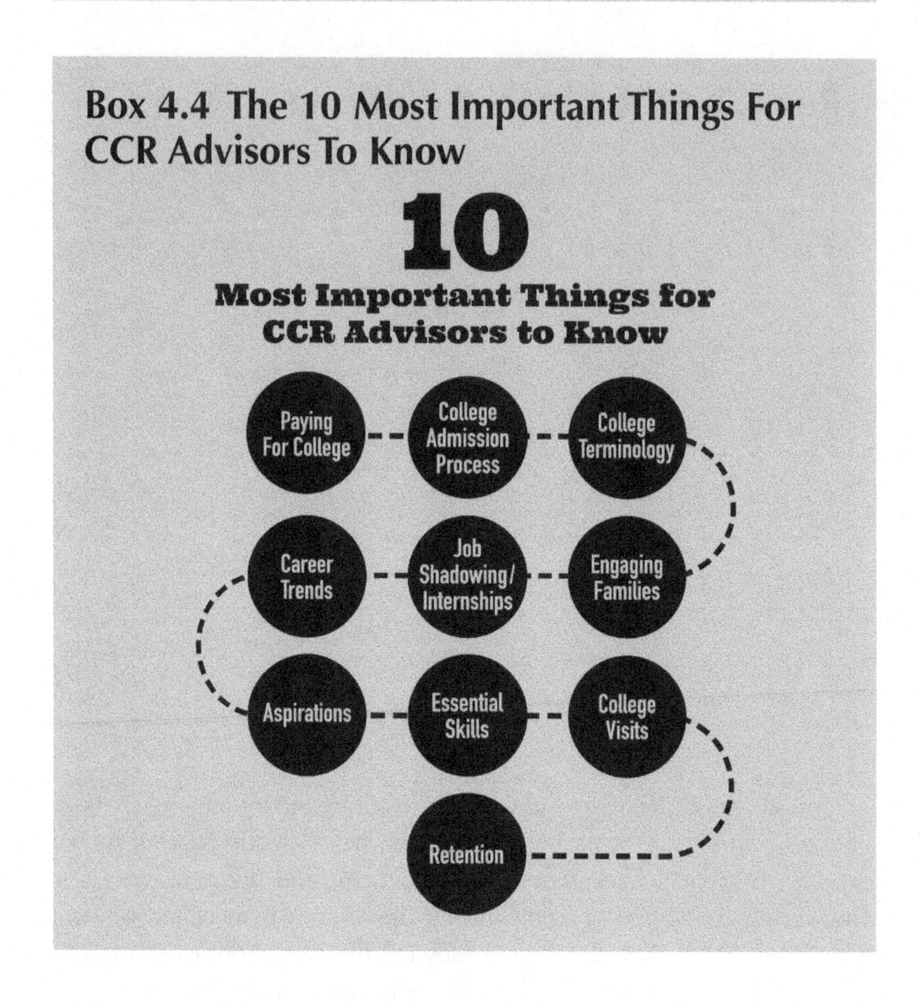

aid process (e.g. Free Application for Federal Student Aid (FAFSA) completion).

- **College admissions process:** Advisors make sure students are aware of the timeline for applying to college and steps required for admission. This includes researching colleges; being aware of deadlines for applications, financial aid, and scholarships; and planning for college.
- **College terminology:** Students are exposed to college vocabulary to build their knowledge about college pathways. This terminology includes words like major, minor, loan, merit scholarship, and athletic scholarship.

- **Career trends:** Advisors help students track the direction of fast-growing, in-demand jobs and understand the skills required for success within those particular fields.
- **Job shadowing and internships:** Students can't be what they don't see. Job shadowing and internship opportunities expose students to the workplace. Advisors assist students in finding these opportunities.
- **Engaging families:** Advisors invite families to be part of the process by building relationships and providing information to prepare a student for success together.
- **College visits:** Visiting college campuses in person or virtually allows students to see themselves as college bound, while also exposing them to experiences that will enable them to make an informed decision about where to apply/attend. Advisors help students connect with colleges and universities that might be a good fit for them and their interests.
- **Aspirations:** Advisors focus on nurturing and celebrating a student's interest and ambition of achieving their future goals.
- **Essential Skills**: These are six critical skills students need to develop and practice in order to be successful in college, career, and beyond. Advisors help students develop these skills.
- **Retention:** Advisors ensure that students stay in college and attain a degree on time.

The Impact of College- and Career-Readiness Advisors on Schools: Principals' Perspectives

At a CCR advisor training session in Florida, we asked three participating principals to talk about why they wanted to attend, why it was important for their staff to attend, and how CFES supports their CCR goals. This is what they said:

> **Michael Young (Mulberry High School):** We were looking for a framework that would provide students with direction, a way to tie things together. We were trying to reframe our belief that high school is the final step and help

them see their high school teachers as their biggest influence. When I ask my students who the most powerful person is, it's their middle school teacher. How do I change that so my students are talking about their high school teachers?

We are here today not to create another thing; it's something to inform how we work. Our job is to help them find purpose and hope. If we can give them that little bit, even if it doesn't come out until years later, we've made an impact. As teachers, we aren't good listeners; we're good tellers. We have to remember the relationship piece. We can help students get so much further if we remember that.

I'm a first-generation student. I knew I needed something beyond high school. My middle school English teacher ended up being my senior English teacher and told me I was a good writer. It made me think I could be a writer, so I majored in English. She was my CCR advisor!

I find my purpose now in helping other people find their purpose, even more with adults than with students—helping them be their best person.

Cynthia Cangelose (Mulberry Middle School): We're larger than ever before, so I'm looking for places for my children to belong. CFES is a place for kids to find belonging. We have groups for kids who are at risk in the traditional sense, but CFES allows us to look at the "risk" of not going on. [We make] connections by having high school kids come back before they graduate to show middle school kids what comes next.

I was the first in my family to go to college. I had six siblings, and none of them went to college. I'm inspired every day to give students the direction I didn't have.

LaShawn Frost (Booker Middle School): [What's] imperative for me [is] to give our students an opportunity to excel in whatever they choose. Our motto is "to inspire tomorrow's leaders," and CFES gives us a framework to do that. We have a college- and career-readiness day every Wednesday. We talk about it so our students are encouraged to think about careers.

The research shows how students feel lost during middle school, but relationships and inspiration make a difference. It has an impact. It is critical that we cultivate hope and inspiration in our students, and this is a way to do that. We look at the whole child.

One notable question: "We are preparing students for a world we can't foresee and a future we don't understand. How do we do that?" My answer: "Think back to the conversations we had earlier about mentors in our own lives. Our teachers didn't understand the world we would be entering either, but here we all are, able to utilize technology we could never have

> believed would exist, and we recognize the skills our teachers/mentors instilled in us well beyond academics."

Every month, CFES hosts a webinar at which an individual shares expertise on a topic that directly relates to what a college and career advisor needs to know. Past speakers include Brian Flores, Head Coach of the Miami Dolphins, who talked about leadership; Don Outing, Vice President for Equity and Community and the Diversity and Inclusion Officer at Lehigh University, who spoke about how we can help students succeed in college before they arrive on campus; and George Pataki, former Governor of New York, who spoke about leadership and preparing for jobs of the future.

College- and Career-Readiness Advising Success Stories

The CCR advising program has proven to be both practical and effective, and CCR advisors have successfully shepherded thousands of rural students through college into fulfilling careers. An example of one of the case studies used in the CCR advisor trainings is given in Box 4.5. A few of the students' stories are listed below.

Drew Malone: From Rural Kid to TV Producer

Drew Malone, CFES Scholar, graduate of Crown Point 2014, and 2017 graduate of SUNY Plattsburgh, shared his story of the impact of college and career advising on his professional life. Aubrey Bresett, who was one of Drew's CCR advisors, not only inspired him to pursue television production, she helped guide him during his time at SUNY Plattsburgh.

> In the fall of 2012, I traveled with a group of Crown Point Central School peers and teachers to the CFES National Conference in Albany, New York. Our school was being recognized as a School of Distinction, and we were there to accept the award. During the first day, Aubrey Bresett, Communications Director at CFES, pulled me aside and asked if I'd do an interview for a

local television station. As she was setting up, Aubrey asked me about what I wanted to do for a career and where I wanted to go to college. I wasn't sure what I wanted to do, and I didn't know where to go. I'd been procrastinating far too long.

Aubrey told me it's okay to not have it all figured out. Then she shared her own personal journey: how she attended SUNY Plattsburgh for TV/video production and later worked at Mountain Lake PBS in Plattsburgh. She told me all about the program, the contacts she made, and what she learned. I was so engaged with what she told me, I immediately wanted in.

From then on, I was set on Plattsburgh. I was accepted into their TV/video production program a few months later.

I ended up graduating from Plattsburgh in three years because I'd completed 30 credits in high school. After I got my bachelor's, I started looking for a job. I had a cousin who was working at Time Warner Cable News (now Spectrum News), and she suggested that I apply for a position as a news producer. Two weeks later, I got a call for an interview, and I got the job. I became a morning news producer right out of college. I worked in the control rooms with a producer, director, and an audio operator. It was a producer's job to keep things running smoothly in the room. I had that job for roughly two years and over a year of that time was servicing our markets in Buffalo and Rochester.

Natan Arrazate: A Journey of Resilience and Growth

Natan grew up in Van Horn, Texas, and shared his story of blazing his trail to college as a child of immigrants with the help of his CCR advisor:

> As a first-generation college student, navigating the journey of a postsecondary education was like learning a different language. Both of my parents are Mexican immigrants with only a high school education. I grew up watching them struggle to keep good-paying jobs, and I felt an immense pressure to do well in school, with dreams of getting ahead in life. My parents constantly reminded me about the importance of a college education and how it was important to my future.
>
> When it came time for me to start applying to college, my parents lacked knowledge about the process and were not able to assist me as much as they wished to. I later came to understand that this was very common for [those] who were first-generation college-bound students. This lack of knowledge was

especially true when I had to go through the financial aid process. My parents knew that I could apply for financial aid, but they didn't know where or how to begin.

Applying for the Free Application for Federal Student Aid (FAFSA) was a lengthy process. It required me to submit not only my own personal and financial information but also [that of] my parents. For a student who was the first in the family to apply for federal student aid, I was completely overwhelmed by the application and all of the information that was required. Nobody in my immediate family was familiar with the application, so I had to turn to other resources. When I was a senior in high school, I found a collegiate mentor at my high school. The mentor was a college student from El Paso Community College who was volunteering his time to help students complete the FAFSA. He was able to explain the application process and assist me with collecting the required documents.

His role expanded beyond helping me. It included talking to my parents and ensuring them that the information they were giving us would be secure and used appropriately. It wasn't easy. My parents were hesitant to give me access to sensitive information, such as Social Security numbers and income tax returns. It wasn't until we continued to educate them and they knew how this information would be used that they felt comfortable and allowed me fill out the application.

After completing the FAFSA, I quickly learned that this was the least of my struggles, given the support I received from the collegiate mentor. My lack of knowledge came to light when I started my postsecondary education at a community college. I chose to go down that path because of the promise of less-expensive classes. That is something I was hearing while applying to colleges. I quickly found this to be true, and my first semester came with a big financial aid stipend to cover other college expenses like books and such. I grew up with limited financial resources, but I realized later that I had very little financial literacy. Managing my own money was never something that I was tasked with, let alone something that I was good at.

I was not well educated on the responsibilities I needed to meet as a student in order to continue receiving my financial aid package, such as maintaining a certain GPA. During my first year in college, I became ineligible for financial aid because I had poor grades. I was faced with the dilemma of either dropping out of school or finding a way to pay for a full semester out of pocket. If I found a way to pay for it out of pocket, I would also have to pass with straight A's. I knew I couldn't disappoint my parents and family members. I had to pick up a part-time job to help my family with these added expenses.

As with many low-income, first-generation college students, my transition to college was difficult, and the added stress of working and going to school made it more difficult. I had to navigate a whole new system with little support from my family and friends. My first year of college was a turning point for me. Things didn't go well, but that's when I realized that I had to become self-sufficient if I wanted to avoid that setback again.

Becoming self-sufficient meant that I had to seek out resources on my own. However, I found that I wasn't the only person going through this struggle. I built a community of students who were in similar situations, and together we were able to find a network of resources that were available at the college to better assist us. One of our main focuses was to find ways to navigate the financial aid process. I found community workshops that explained the process in detail and attended financial literacy classes that taught me how to better manage my money. These resources were extremely helpful not only to me but to my family as well. My financial aid journey was one of many lessons learned from careless mistakes, but with the proper guidance from my mentors, I was able to bounce back from my setbacks.

With this new attitude, I was able to continue my studies at the community college and later transfer to the University of Texas at El Paso to pursue my four-year degree. I continued to expand my network of support, asking my professors to become mentors who could help me stay motivated and on course. Those initial mistakes led me to be more assertive, persevere, and follow my passion. You can imagine how it felt during commencement—such an immense pride to become the first in my family to graduate with a bachelor's degree.

Workshop for College- and Career-Readiness Advisor Training: A Sample Schedule for Virtual Training

Session 1: Opening (Live)

The opening session provides the foundation for the five pre-recorded sessions. This live session features a keynote speaker and other experts who share the latest research and best practices for how to help young people realize their postsecondary dreams. They explain the necessary building blocks for advisors seeking to reach students from diverse backgrounds and provide the tools to carry it out. **Format: Live video meeting (one hour).**

Content

- Welcome and Introductions
- Defining CCR
- Advisor's Role in Helping Students Become College and Career Ready
- Exploring Trends and Changes in the CCR Space
- Skills Needed to be a CCR Advisor
- Fostering a CCR Culture

Resources

- Building Blocks of CCR
- What Every CCR Advisor Should Know
- College Readiness Timeline

Session 2: The Value of Mentoring

A mentor can significantly improve a young person's quality of life by supporting their pathway to college and career, thus helping them realize their full potential. For example, mentors can inspire personal gains in academic performance and attainment of goals. This session emphasizes the value of mentoring and provides participants with an understanding of mentoring tools and strategies central to the role of a CCR advisor. **Format: On-demand webinar (45 minutes).**

Content

- The Importance of Mentoring and Utilizing Mentors
- Developing Partnerships
- Mentoring to Support Pathway Exploration

Resources

- Mentoring Tips: How to Get Started
- CFES Mentoring Handbook
- Getting to Know You Activity
- Scholar Map Activity

Session 3: Essential Skills™

While there are different paths to college and career, certain skills are vital for all of them. CFES calls these the Essential Skills: Goal setting, teamwork, leadership, agility, perseverance, and networking. Essential Skills are interconnected, overlapping, and indispensable when preparing students for success in college and career. In this session, participants learn about these critical competencies, how to integrate the Essential Skills into the classroom, and ways students can apply these skills in a college and career setting. The pre-recorded session will address how the six skills should be introduced and nurtured by CCR advisors, while providing sample activities and practical application strategies. **Format: On-demand webinar (45 minutes).**

Content

- Defining the Essential Skills and Their CCR Role
- Integration of Essential Skills in the Classroom
- Sampling of Activities
- Practical Application of Essential Skills

Resources

- Definitions of Essential Skills
- Social Media Scavenger Hunt Activity
- Mission: It's Possible Activity
- Future Reunion Activity
- Evaluation Tool: Rubric for Essential Skills

Session 4: College Readiness and Paying for College

Cost is the number one reason why students from low-income households choose not to attend college and also the top reason they drop out of college. We need to help students see college as an investment and an opportunity to climb out of poverty, rather than a place to accrue debt. This means helping students understand how to meet deadlines and become paying-for-college experts who are informed and able to make smart financial decisions. This session focuses on helping students build a support system of friends and mentors to find answers and resources, tap into federal aid and scholarship opportunities, get to know people at the financial aid office, and learn the paying-for-college lexicon. When students own the paying-for-college process, they truly become college ready. **Format: On-demand webinar (45 minutes).**

Content

- Your College Journey
- Building a Knowledge Pathway
- Building a Network of Support in College
- Paying for College

Resources

- Creating a College-Going Culture
- Evaluation Tool: College-Readiness Rubric
- Engaging Families
- Financial Aid Primer
- Available Scholarships

Session 5: Career Readiness

The United States job market is evolving at its fastest pace in history. Emerging technologies are creating new career opportunities that only a few years ago seemed unimaginable. One thing hasn't changed, however: the need

Box 4.5 Case Study

Here is one of the case studies used in the CCR advisor trainings. CCR advisor candidates read this case study and then work together to answer the questions at the end of the study.

Westminster Consolidated Case Study

Westminster Consolidated, a K–12 school in the rural Chenango Valley of central New York, is located in a town of 3,200 residents. The school is the largest employer in the community, followed by a convenience store chain and a half dozen stores and businesses.

Here are some pertinent facts about the school:

- There are 410 students currently enrolled.
- Ten years ago, enrollment peaked at 786 students.
- The class of 2019 had 31 students. Four enrolled in SUNY schools and eight in community colleges; four planned to enter the service; and the remainder are pursuing jobs, almost all of which pay minimum wage.
- A decade ago, 62% of Westminster's students enrolled in two- or four-year colleges.

In May 2019, a team from BettaTech, a digital design and manufacturing corporation with plants and offices in 320 sites around the world, visited Westminster to explore the possibility of setting up a small plant there. Sharon Ruether, the Head of the BettaTech search team, graduated from college 40 miles from Westminster and thought the bucolic Chenango Valley would provide an ideal lifestyle for future BettaTech employees. "I saw the location as a perfect place for one of our plants. It offered wonderful recreation opportunities. It supported heartland values," said Ruether.

But six weeks after the team visited Westminster, in June, Ruether met with State Senator Robert Lambert, who represents the Central New York district in Albany, to explain BettaTech's decision to establish a plant elsewhere. "It was a tough choice. I wanted BettaTech to create jobs in the Chenango Valley, but we were concerned about meeting workforce goals. Where would we find future employees? Frankly, we looked at Westminster Consolidated postsecondary placement trends, and we didn't see a viable future for the corporation."

In September, Senator Lambert appointed a commission of two individuals to visit Westminster Consolidated to explore workforce development concerns. Over two days, the commission conducted focus groups and one-on-one interviews with students, parents, teachers, and administrators. Here are some of their findings:

- Principal Kay McDonald believes that it's better to have fewer graduates going to college: "In the past, our grads who went off to college, especially four-year places, never came back once they left Westminster. More of our kids are now staying and settling in town. College is for families who are better off."
- Only three 12th grade students knew what the FAFSA was, and only two 11th graders had ever been on a college campus.
- Westminster has one part-time counselor, Grant Judge, who works with all students. "I deal with a crisis or two every day," he said. "I don't have time to talk with every one of our kids about postsecondary opportunities." Following the commission's visit, Grant Judge took an early retirement.

You are hired as Westminster's first full-time CCR advisor. What's your short-term (three months) and longer-term (18 months) plan?

for a college education to land a high-paying job in STEM and other growth industries. A person with a high school diploma makes an average salary of $35,580, while associate degree holders earn $58,240 and bachelor's degree recipients make $68,190.

A CCR advisor plays a critical role in helping students shape their future by exposing them to a broad range of career possibilities. In this session, participants learn how to help students identify strengths and weaknesses that will play a key role in narrowing their job focus to lead them down a successful career path. Participants acquire necessary tools to help students identify, pursue, and secure jobs using CFES resources, partners, an alumni network, National Advisory Board members, and other supports. **Format: On-demand webinar (45 Minutes).**

Content

- The Difference CCR Advisors Make
- Helping Students Identify Potential Career Paths
- CFES Tools
- Current and Future Jobs and the Credentials They Require
- Activity: Helping Students Find Jobs

Resources

- Career Exploration Video
- STEM Readiness
- Brilliant Career Lab
- Heads Up Activity
- Tips for Landing a Job

Session 6: Topics of Today

The amount of change that has occurred since March 2020 is unprecedented in United States modern history. The COVID-19 pandemic disrupted traditional education models, forcing K–12 and higher education leaders to rethink every aspect of educational delivery and engagement. The call to end racial injustice in America is another defining moment that is motivating individuals and organizations to rethink priorities to ensure that Black lives truly matter.

The purpose of this session is to explore these and other current topics with a focus on how education can help level a socioeconomic playing field that remains far from equitable. Other areas of discussion include how best to support students as a CCR advisor in the post-pandemic world, how to engage students virtually, and ways that students from rural areas can revitalize their communities by moving back home to launch startups or work remotely for major employers. **Format: On-demand webinar (45 minutes).**

Content

- COVID-19: Engaging Students Virtually
- Black Lives Matter: Systemic Racism
- Local Community Issues and Perspectives
- Rural: You Can Go Home Again

Resources

- Best Practices for Virtual Learning
- Video: Education Levels the Socioeconomic Playing Field
- Video: Technology and Rural Communities

Session 7: Closing (Live)

The live one-hour opening session and five pre-recorded sessions are designed to equip participants with the tools to support students in the areas of mentoring, CCR, Essential Skills, understanding how to pay for college, and current topics of the day. The live closing session brings all of these topics together by showing participants how to integrate them into a cohesive plan. Participants will hear from an expert speaker, engage in collaborative breakout discussions for case study strategies, and learn next steps to take as a newly-minted CCR Advisor. **Format: Live video meeting (one hour).**

Content

- Bringing the Elements of the Training Together
- Breakout Session: Case Study Strategies
- Sharing Breakout Recommendations
- Next Steps and Closing Remarks

Resources

- Case Study
- CCR Toolkit
- Planning Tool
- Access to Member Section

Conclusion

As the United States economy moves away from small-scale agriculture, mining, and other traditional industries, rural areas need to explore new areas of economic expansion—and in today's digital economy, this requires cultivating a college-educated workforce. But deeply entrenched cultural, financial, and logistical obstacles to higher education remain in rural America, meaning young people from rural areas need guidance and support if they are to successfully pursue higher education. This chapter outlined CFES' practical and proven strategy for supporting college-bound rural students: Train and certify teams of CCR advisors to raise aspirations and to serve as mentors and information resources for students. CCR advisors support students by sharing knowledge, introducing them to opportunities, keeping them accountable to their goals, and helping them cultivate the Essential Skills so they can succeed on their own.

References

Belasco, A. S. (2013). Creating college opportunity: School counselors and their influence on postsecondary enrollment. *Research in Higher Education, 54*, 781–804. https://doi.org/10.1007/s11162-013-9297-4

Dalton, R. (2019). *Focus group study of CFES Scholars: Moving down the pathway to college and career* [Unpublished manuscript]. CFES Brilliant Pathways.

Howley, C. W. (2006). Remote possibilities: Rural children's educational aspirations. *Peabody Journal of Education, 81*(2), 62–80.

Hurwitz, M., & Howell, J. (2013). *Measuring the impact of high school counselors on college enrollment. Research brief.* College Board

Advocacy and Policy Center. http://secure-media.collegeboard.org/digitalServices/pdf/advocacy/policycenter/research-brief-measuring-impact-high-school-counselors-college-enrollment.pdf

NCHEMS Information Center for Higher Education Policymaking and Analysis. (2016). *College-going rates of high school graduates – directly from high school*. The National Center for Higher Education Management Systems. www.higheredinfo.org/dbrowser/index.php?submeasure=63&year=2016&level=nation&mode=map&state=0

Perna, L. W., & Finney, J. E. (2014). State of attainment: Three ways that states can help more students access higher levels of education. CURRENTS. https://repository.upenn.edu/gse_pubs/297

Reidel, J. C. (2018). *An examination of the college decision-making process of high school students in rural Vermont: A cross-case analysis* [Doctoral dissertation, University of Vermont]. Graduate College Dissertations and Theses. https://scholarworks.uvm.edu/graddis/908/

Snyder, T. D., & Dillow, S. A. (2015). *Digest of Education Statistics 2013*. National Center for Education Statistics, Institute of Education Sciences, U.S. Department of Education. https://nces.ed.gov/pubs2015/2015011.pdf

Vermont Student Assistance Corporation. (2015). *Vermont's class of 2012: Highlights and challenges for pursuing a postsecondary education*. https://assets.documentcloud.org/documents/2500749/2015-special-report-class-of-2012-highlights-and.pdf

Business Collaboration and Job Readiness

How to Find, Launch, and Retain Partnerships

Fried catfish, shrimp gumbo, hush puppies, cherry cheesecake—the table groans with food. "Raised 'em ourselves. We've got over 10,000 acres of catfish ponds," explains Gene Raffield, Chief Executive Officer of Raffield Fisheries and community task force member who was part of the Gulf County Project we set up, which that is described in Chapter 1.

It's 1988, and I'm sitting with Raffield, one of the Florida business leaders who helped launch the project in Gulf County, Florida. That project transformed academic performance and college readiness in Port St. Joe and Wewahitchka, Florida, and sparked what would later become CFES (College for Every Student) Brilliant Pathways. Raffield Fisheries hosted dozens of task force meetings and exposed Gulf County youth to employment opportunities in the region. Since 1991, rural CFES schools have partnered with more than 800 businesses like Raffield Fisheries that have offered financial, in-kind, and mentorship opportunities (Dalton & Erdmann, 1990).

As the familiar adage goes, "it takes a village to raise a child"—and nowhere is this more true than in rural education. Rural families and schools, which have limited time, resources, and money, often find it difficult to provide students with the knowledge and opportunities they need to succeed in the world of the future. This is where CFES' intentional collaboration with caring citizens such as Gene Raffield, along with local businesses, nonprofits, and other allies, can fill crucial gaps.

This chapter explores these partnerships and outlines the critical roles they play in not just providing financial support for schools but in helping schools prepare students for the professional world. It shares some of the many creative ways educational partners have supported schools and their students, as well as presents practical advice on how to identify and recruit potential partners and how to retain existing ones. The chapter also shares stories that illustrate the impact partners have had: Sometimes, it only takes the right mentoring or the right exposure to outside opportunities to change a student's life for the better.

Building a Community of Supporters: Examples of Rural School–Business Partnerships

School partnerships can take a number of forms, depending on the size and needs of the community. The Gulf County Partnership, for instance, involves two school districts and several businesses, including Raffield Fisheries, the paper mill, a local dentist, and the Gulf Coast Chamber of Commerce. Some partnerships have included one school and one business, while others involved one business and multiple schools. About half of our business partnerships last for 12 months; some fizzle out because one or both partners are not responsive, while others are designed for the short-term. The rest are sustained from year to year, affecting hundreds of students and educators.

The six partnership examples that follow show the varied forms partners can take, from consortia to nonprofits, from emerging to one-year collaborations, as well as some of the ways that partners are supporting local schools and students.

- Through a partnership with DentaQuest—a company that provides dental insurance and other oral health care services, CFES recruited four dentists and seven dental hygienists in northern New York to help 750 rural students in 12 schools understand both the value of oral hygiene and possible career paths in the oral health care professions.
- In Western Texas, a partnership with Blue Origin—an aerospace manufacturer and suborbital spaceflight service company—brought tutors to Van Horn High to prepare students for the math and science portions of the ACT and SAT. The same tutors later returned to explain

how students could apply to and attend the University of Texas at El Paso, the nearest public college, then return to their hometown and earn a six-figure salary working for Blue Origin.

- A partnership with Champlain National Bank in northern New York is providing financial literacy education to students and families in a dozen schools.
- International Paper's Ticonderoga mill partnered with eight Vermont and New York schools to clean up trash on the southern end of Lake Champlain while helping students learn about the balance between the environment and industry.
- Watershed Alliance—a Lake Champlain-based environmental education program—hosts science fairs at the CFES Center and at CFES schools to build STEM competency and careers in ecology for students in both New York and Vermont.
- Huiana is a nonprofit that helps Hawaiian Island youth develop workplace skills through internships. Dozens of students from two rural CFES high schools, Konawaena and Kohala, participate in Huiana career readiness activities each year.

Where Are the Partners?

Rural communities have fewer prospective business partners to choose from than their urban counterparts and even fewer that are in the industry sectors projected to flourish over the next decades. Despite these obstacles, CFES has helped create and/or nurture partnerships with 800 businesses for its rural schools, promoting CCR through mentoring, internships, speakers, apprenticeships, and job shadowing opportunities. Here are some steps you can take to identify promising partners to support your school community.

Finding Business—and Other—Partners

In rural communities, potential partners are often hidden in plain sight. Here are some places you can start looking for rural partners:

- **Community banks** are committed to being good neighbors; their charters require them to serve their communities. They can introduce you to other partners or become partners themselves. For instance, they have supported rural CFES schools by helping students build financial literacy. Champlain National Bank provides financial literacy to Adirondack schools, and Kona Credit Union offers an event called Reality Fair in rural Hawaii schools to help students with financial planning.
- **Chambers of commerce** are organizations that provide services to businesses and commerce. Gilbertsville Mount. Upton Central School tapped into its regional Chamber of Commerce in nearby Cooperstown, New York, to recruit businesses to participate in its first career fair.
- **Community foundations** exist to make communities better places to live, and therefore make excellent partners. The Adirondack Community Foundation provided a grant to CFES to promote family engagement in area schools. With an $800 stipend, AuSable Valley Central School was able to provide gas cards, dinner, and childcare for families. Eighty families attended the school gathering, up from nine families the previous year.
- **Families**, including grandparents, aunts, and uncles of teachers, students, and board members, may have connections to prospective business partners. When Gilbertsville Mount Upton Central School needed businesses to participate in their career fair, it tapped into every one of the families that were part of the school community.
- **Government agencies** at the state and federal level can be a good source of volunteers who can partner with schools and provide programming in rural communities. There are dozens of government agencies, and each represents a different career path: Volunteers can bring knowledge of agriculture, justice, energy, and fish and wildlife services, to name a few. For instance, Peter Emerson of the Vermont Fish and Wildlife Department works with students to help them understand and appreciate the natural environment of northern Vermont; recent activities he organized focused on habitat restoration of Atlantic salmon.

- **Health care** partnerships in rural communities can be fostered through hospitals and urgent care facilities. In northern New York and Vermont, CFES schools organize health care fairs and health care activities with the University of Vermont Medical Center and its satellite facilities. Additionally, SIM*VIVO, a business in Willsboro, New York, that produces medical training modules and surgical simulators, partners with a dozen rural schools to introduce students to health care professions through medical simulations.
- **Nonprofits** seek to provide services regionally, and they need you as much as you need them. In Hawaii, for example, Konawaena and Kohala High Schools partner with Huiana, which provides internships to prepare Hawaiian Island youth for the labor force of the future. Huiana also helps Hawaiian youth develop workplace skills through applied internships related to students' career pathway interests. Participating students engage in school-based learning, hone in on career interests, gain job readiness and workplace skills, and reflect on and develop their work ethic. Nearly 5,000 miles to the east, the ECHO, Leahy Center for Lake Champlain partners with 15 CFES schools in northern New York and Vermont to enhance STEM learning in the Lake Champlain Basin and Adirondack region. Activities focus on community-based science learning opportunities, including STEM festivals. ECHO and CFES cohost festivals that include an ECHO truck filled with engaging activities for all ages, such as a 12-foot wind wall, a 15-foot "soil tunnel" showing the science of healthy soils, coding robots, giant blue building blocks, a 30-foot Lego racetrack, and more.
- **Retirees** often settle in rural communities, and they can serve as mentors or contacts with businesses where they may have been previously employed.
- **Service organizations** such as Rotary International or Kiwanis International are committed to serving others and improving the world. Their members are business and community leaders who can be good leads to business partnerships.
- **United Way Worldwide**'s mission is to advance the common good in communities. Although United Way Worldwide is known more for raising funds and distributing them in communities, it can also help you identify potential business partners.

Showing Rural Students the World: How Partners Can Help

Businesses, nonprofits, and volunteer mentors can introduce rural students to information and opportunities that would otherwise be unavailable to them. The following sections showcase some of the creative ways that CFES partners have shared their talents and expertise with students. These innovative programs and activities tend to fall into two general categories: college-readiness training and career education.

College Consortia: Envisioning College Life

One of the most successful CFES outreach activities involving partner participation is an annual event in which 400 grade 10 students from the Leatherstocking cluster in central New York gather on a college campus for a day. They meet educators and representatives from higher education and industry while learning about CCR. Typically, as many as 50 business leaders attend, leading small groups in discussions and activities focused on workplace trends, skills, and training.

Bringing Urban Initiatives to Rural Communities

CFES has partnered with a range of major corporations to support programs in urban America. These partners include Ernst & Young (EY), Colgate Palmolive, General Electric (GE), Southwest Airlines, LPL Financial, TransPerfect, MetLife, Jopwell, the Atlanta Hawks, the Boston Celtics, and several New York City law firms, including Schulte Roth & Zabel LLP, and Cadwalader Wickersham & Taft LLP.

These partnerships can also offer value to rural America, and some urban corporations are even willing to reach out to rural schools. Corporations are increasingly recognizing the value of rural investment—rural communities can be sources of customers and their future workforce. Businesses like EY, GE, and Southwest Airlines have worked with CFES to partner with rural schools across the United States.

An Urban Partnership Sparks a Rural Mentoring Program

Ten years ago, CFES Brilliant Pathways developed a signature volunteer program for EY that morphed into College MAP (Mentoring for Access and Persistence). Now operating in 37 cities, College MAP is recognized as one of the most innovative and high-impact corporate volunteer mentoring programs in the United States. CFES provided the curriculum and a network of college partners.

EY originally provided mentors for 11th and 12th grade students in urban schools to help them become college and career ready. EY volunteers work in small groups with these students to demystify and assist in the process of applying to and paying for college. According to EY, 90% of College MAP Scholars go on to college, and employees who are College MAP mentors have longer tenure and receive higher performance ratings than their peers.

When the principal of a rural school in northern New York learned about College MAP at a CFES meeting, he asked, "Why can't we do that?" In response, CFES professionals helped the school recruit and train 20 mentors to use the College MAP model to support 40 rural students in grades 11 and 12. The lesson here is that while rural and urban students face different sets of challenges, many of the strategies originally designed for urban communities can be successfully used in rural communities as well.

The Impact of the Rural Mentoring Program

John was one of the rural students who benefited from the College MAP hybrid. He was a mediocre student who hadn't considered higher education, until a community mentor encouraged him to buckle down academically and think about college. The mentor urged John every day to study, offered weekly reminders to sign up for the ACT, and provided hands-on help in finding financial aid.

Today, John is a college junior with a 3.62 GPA. He's proud of what he has accomplished, but he also gives credit to the mentor and program that helped him. "There's no way I could have done this without lots of help from other people," he says. "My mentor pushed and pushed me to do better—to stop settling for average and raise my own standards."

A few months into his college journey, John reached out to two longtime friends who had dropped out of college and convinced them to give it another try. His "if I can do it, you can too" attitude paid big dividends: Today they room together at SUNY Canton. They all have GPAs above 3.6. They're all on track to graduate and enter the 21st-century workforce. Together they offer a great example of what can happen when aspirations are instilled and fulfilled (Dalton & St. John, 2017).

College MAP Modules: An Example of a Program that Works

CFES developed 24 months of college-readiness modules that were adapted for northern New York mentors who, in turn, supported rural students in 11th and 12th grade. We include this information to provide an example of the types of information and skills college-bound rural students need to acquire, as well as to spark inspiration for other programs that can enhance rural education and motivate students.

Junior Year

September: Orientation

Mentors get to know scholars and encourage them to start thinking about college as an option after high school. Mentors outline the steps needed to prepare for college at this time.

October: Success Starts with Each Student

With help from mentors, scholars assess their current status: What do I value? What mission should I be working toward accomplishing? What needs to change so I can reach my full academic and personal potential? Scholars identify their goals and come up with strategies for attaining them.

November: College Knowledge

Mentors help scholars understand different college options, including general characteristics of colleges, and what majors, minors, and other areas of interest are offered on a college campus. Scholars take inventory of their strengths, interests, and long-term plans to determine possible majors/minors and their personal pathway to college and career.

December: Major Match

Now that scholars know the basics of college, mentors help them think about potential future majors. Scholars also assess college preferences (big vs. small, far vs. near) and develop a list of features that are important to them.

January: College Match

After identifying personal values and potential areas of academic interest, scholars identify a preliminary list of colleges that align with their needs and interests. Mentors emphasize that the list may change (and that's okay!) as scholars continue to research colleges and learn more about their own preferences.

February: Financial Awareness

Mentors help scholars address how to pay for college. Scholars are introduced to the concept of financial literacy, with a focus on money management. Mentors talk with scholars about how their decisions today will affect their finances in the future.

March: Making It Real

Scholars look to mentors for insight about the pros and cons of each college and adjust their list. Mentors help scholars understand how majors/minors relate to career options. Scholars continue researching information about scholarship opportunities, including grants.

April: University Campus Visit

Scholars and mentors visit a university campus together and then reflect on the experience.

May: Senior Summer Game Plan

Mentors encourage scholars to get involved in clubs, volunteer opportunities, and internships during the summer to build their existing student profile and show colleges that they are hardworking and interested in their future.

June, July, August: Preparing for Senior Year

Mentors keep in touch with scholars through email, phone calls, text messages, and/or online resources. Mentors remind scholars of timelines and the importance of getting ahead and keep the lines of communication open to continue fostering a stronger mentoring relationship.

Senior Year

September: Back in the Game

Mentors review scholars' summer activities, especially their involvement in projects such as internships, volunteer organizations, and scholarship research that will enhance their student profile, placing a strong emphasis on the need to focus early.

October: Small Liberal Arts/Community College Campus Visit

Scholars and mentors visit a small college campus and make comparisons in preparation for the college application process.

November: Application Workshop

Mentors help scholars with their final applications, including essays, transcripts, and other requirements. Mentors offer access to their workplace, a quiet space with access to copy machines, laptops, and telephones, to help scholars assemble their applications.

December: Checkpoint

Mentors check in with scholars to make sure they are on track with college application details and deadlines, offering encouraging words and opportunities to understand the bigger picture through community service, holiday giving efforts, and other activities.

January: Financial Aid Workshop

Mentors ensure that scholars and their families have all the information they need to consider their options and help them understand that college is an investment.

February: Leadership Career Panel

Scholars interact with business leaders and others who have recently graduated from college and can provide valuable insight. Scholars are encouraged to engage in conversations that emphasize the importance of college in creating a career path.

March: College Knowledge—The Real Deal

Mentors educate scholars on proper college acceptance protocol and encourage them to ask questions about what to expect once they are college students. Topics may include time management, social life, healthy behavior, and other areas that won't be found in a college profile book.

April: The Final Decision

Mentors help scholars understand their financial aid package (Chapter 10) and remind scholars to weigh all their options when making final decisions and to discuss options with their family, counselors, mentors, and other trusted individuals.

May: Culmination

Mentors and scholars celebrate the culmination of the program and the beginning of the next chapter in the scholars' lives. Mentors encourage ongoing communication after graduation through phone calls, texts, social media, and emails.

Opening Up the World of Work: Another Benefit of School–Business Partnerships

Students are reluctant to study for jobs they don't see around them, so a rural student who has never met a software designer, a surgeon, or an attorney is unlikely to become one. This is another reason why school/business partnerships can be so valuable: Businesses can provide students job shadowing and internship opportunities, help them see pathway connections, and provide in-kind and direct support to both schools and students.

But the benefits of school/business partnerships go both ways: Schools can provide businesses access to their future workforce and help businesses build goodwill in the community, while improved schools can help businesses with hiring new and maintaining current employees.

The forms of career education that businesses provide are as varied as the businesses themselves. Here are some examples of successful initiatives.

Aviation Day with Southwest Airlines

Southwest Airlines offers programs to expose students to the airline industry in urban sites throughout the country. When I contacted Greg Muccio, Director of Talent Acquisition at Southwest, Airlines to see if they would do a program for rural schools and students, Muccio said, "Why not? We're always looking to build the pipeline for future employees."

CFES Brilliant Pathways and Southwest Airlines teamed up for Aviation Day to educate students across the Adirondacks about the growing number of good-paying jobs in the airline industry and how to access them.

The Campus Reach Program at Southwest Airlines identifies and engages future Southwest employees at an early age to inspire an interest in aviation careers. Teams from Southwest facilitated aviation lessons and classroom activities with students at ten Adirondack rural schools.

"Aviation Day was an opportunity for us to share with students what companies like Southwest look for in employees so they can start honing those skills now," said Muccio. "The Essential Skills™ that CFES teaches, like agility, leadership, and teamwork, are exactly what we want when we hire."

Jobs within the airline industry are diverse and call for a wide range of skills. Some of the most popular jobs include customer service representative, airline administrative support, flight attendant, pilot, operations agent, security officer, air traffic controller, maintenance technician, aircraft mechanic, sales representative, facilities technician, reservations clerk, and inspector.

During the CFES Aviation Day, Southwest organized activities tailored to different grade levels. These included aviation charades and leadership lessons based on the experiences of a woman named Bessie Coleman, who overcame obstacles to gain her pilot's license and became the first African American woman to fly solo in the United States; a paper airplane making contest and a teamwork-based session; a personal branding lesson, in which students created a personal brand statement; and information sessions about all the opportunities in the airline industry.

It's also worth noting that aviation careers are relevant for students in the Adirondacks looking to build their professional lives close to home. Nearby Plattsburgh, Albany, and Burlington airports employ upward of 2,000 people. Albany International Airport employs over 1,000 people, with salaries ranging from minimum wage in food services to more than $100,000 for aircraft mechanics.

DentaQuest: Promoting Dental Health and Dental Careers

DentaQuest provides services for dentists and dental programs around the country. In 2016–17, they established a program with CFES to improve oral health and expose students to the oral health profession in 12 Adirondack schools, impacting 750 students. The partnership focused on children from low-income rural families, who are particularly vulnerable to tooth decay because of their limited knowledge about proper oral health care and the importance of dental health, as well as their challenges in accessing preventative dental care, including a lack of transportation to dental offices.

CFES enlisted four dentists and seven dental hygienists to visit schools, and CFES trained students as peer mentors in the schools. These professionals and mentors communicated to students the importance of proper oral health and demonstrated how to practice it.

The dentists and dental hygienists also provided knowledge about career options in oral health care. Schools in the program had students complete career interest surveys to identify participants for the initiative. The New York State Dental Association donated toothbrushes, dental gloves, and floss to support the initiative.

In addition, elementary school students received dental screenings and fluoride treatments from the dental hygienists and dentists working with their schools. After screenings, dental professionals generated reports on each student. School nurses then passed screening results from the reports, as well as dentists' contact information to parents so that students and their families could establish a dental home.

Logan, a former CFES Scholar, volunteered her time to kick off an oral health care mentoring effort. At the time, she was studying in a dental program at the SUNY Canton, and Logan returned to Crown Point Central to train 75 high school students in best practices and enlighten them about career options in oral health care.

A health care career fair hosted by CFES and Champlain Valley Physicians Hospital in Plattsburgh, New York, featured careers in oral health care. Representatives from the hospital worked with students, engaging them in activities related to health care, while four regional colleges offered students information about career pathways in health care.

Career Fairs: Bringing Businesses and Students Together

Several CFES schools host career fairs each year, bringing a range of businesses to their gymnasium to talk with local students and those from neighboring schools about the workplace. Konawaena High, in the hills above Kona on the big island of Hawaii, and Alexandria Area High School, surrounded by Minnesota lakes, are examples of schools that host annual career fairs. Career fairs are a good way to audition prospective business partners. Businesses get to know the school, and educators and students have an opportunity to get to know them.

In 2019, Gilbertsville Mount Upton (GMU) educators decided they wanted to host a career fair, their first ever. What's unusual is that GMU is located in a town of just 900 residents and few local businesses, but that didn't deter Principal Heather Wilcox and her colleagues.

"It starts with relationships," said Wilcox. "We asked every student, every faculty member, and every family to tap into their networks—'Who do you know?' And when they said they knew someone from a bank or an airline or the Baseball Hall of Fame, we said, 'Invite them!' One of our staff members joined the Chamber of Commerce in Cooperstown just so he could recruit people to the career fair."

Lisa Ruland, a GMU counselor, noted an overlay of strategies that she and her colleagues employed: "I spoke with pre-K–6 students several times before the fair about career exploration to get an idea of their interests and aspirations." Ruland strategically used social media to recruit businesses. She also guided students in preparing for the event by tying questions to the

Essential Skills. She oversaw every detail that makes an event successful, from encouraging businesses to bring visual aids to providing name tags and a light lunch.

GMU ended up with 33 different businesses represented at its first career day, from local loggers to startup high-tech companies. Heather Wilcox said it was a "huge success. Every one of the 340 students in the pre-K–12 school attended. Students were so engaged that we had to ask them to leave the fair to catch their buses to go home at the end of the day."

Previously, GMU tried fireside chats where business leaders answered students' questions in the auditorium. That didn't work. But the career fair, said Wilcox, "exceeded our wildest dreams." Part of the success, according to Wilcox, "was that the job fair was hands-on, and our students could meet and talk with business leaders. Additionally, the fair drew a direct link to career readiness."

An activity to test students' knowledge of careers is contained in Box 5.1.

Box 5.1 Resource: Career Heads-up

Introduction

This game is a fun way for students to test their knowledge of common careers, help them connect their interests to career pathways, and learn about some careers they might not have previously considered.

Materials

- A Career Heads-Up card deck for each group. The printable cards, created by CFES Brilliant Pathways, are formatted for 3" x 4" cardstock name badge inserts and should be printed using two-sided print settings.
- If players don't have printing capabilities, simply write career words from the word bank below on slips of paper or notecards.

Instructions

- Give each group of two or more players a set of Career Heads-Up cards. The pile of cards should be placed face down in the middle of the group.
- The first player takes the top card from the deck and, without looking at the career name written on it, holds the card to their forehead for the other players to see.
- The rest of the group gives the player clues to help them guess the name of the career. They can describe things people with that career do, say, wear, and so on. They can also give examples of people who have that career. They cannot use any words that appear in the title of the career as part of their clues.
- The player holding the card has three guesses to get the right answer.
- If the player guesses correctly, they keep the card and earn a point. If they are unable to guess the correct career, the card goes in the discard pile, and it is the next player's turn to guess.
- If no one in the group is able to describe a player's card, the group can pass, and the person who is guessing chooses another card.
- Play continues until all cards are used. The player with the most points at the end of the game wins.

Variations and Reflections

- If you have more time, players can sort the cards by career clusters, levels of education/training required, or other categories.
- Ask students which careers they could picture themselves having in the future and connect their current interests to possible careers.
- Review or research the careers that students were unfamiliar with or unable to guess.
- Allow this activity to be the start of many conversations around career goals, postsecondary pathways, and skill development,

which will help students build knowledge and become college and career ready.

Zookeeper	**Chef**	**Teacher**
Sports Announcer	**Bank Teller**	**Hotel Manager**
Dentist	**Video Game Developer**	**Judge**
Park Ranger	**Construction Worker**	**Nurse**
College Professor	**Artist**	**Scientist**
Mechanic	**YouTuber**	**Dog Trainer**
Astronaut	**Waiter**	**Dancer**
Television Producer	**Reporter**	**Computer Programmer**
Paramedic	**School Counselor**	**Politician**
Engineer	**Architect**	**Coach**
Plumber	**Police Officer**	**Real Estate Agent**
Author	**Veterinarian**	**Welder**
Firefighter	**Farmer**	**Pilot**
Librarian	**Musician**	**Baker**

School-Embedded Career Activities

Volunteers from local businesses and other organizations can also introduce students to new career opportunities and how to prepare for them through school-based programs. For instance, 9th graders at Peru Central School in northern New York completed a career interest survey and then researched jobs that fit their interests, and then later shared what they learned with peers.

At Keene Central, in the Adirondack region of New York, high school students do mock interviews with local business leaders, developing skills that they can later use when applying for internships, summer jobs, and college.

And four times annually, the Career Café at New York's Cherry Valley-Springfield Central School provides students the opportunity to meet and chat with local business leaders over lunch. Lunches are scheduled around specific career clusters—agriculture, business, education, engineering, fine arts, health, information, technology, public service, and trades.

Partners Everywhere: The Power of Online Partnerships

Even isolated rural communities can take advantage of the world's talent by seeking out online partners. Online partnerships can transcend the limitations of geography and allow students to connect with business leaders in a variety of sectors anywhere in the world. The coronavirus shutdown has forced all schools to become more adept at online learning, and this new knowledge can and should be applied to cultivating business and educational partners. For instance, Jopwell, a diversity hiring startup that helps companies recruit underrepresented ethnic candidates for jobs and industries, recently led an online session on financial literacy that was attended by rural educators and students.

An example of a successful long-term virtual program is the ECHO Collaborative. This is a collaborative between CFES and the ECHO Leahy Center for Lake Champlain—an innovative science and nature museum located on the waterfront in Burlington, Vermont—which engages CFES Scholars, families and their communities in interactive scientific discovery, nature and the care of Lake Champlain. Home to more than 70 species of fish, amphibians, invertebrates, and reptiles, and major traveling exhibitions, ECHO exposes CFES Scholars to STEM-related concepts. The collaborative incorporates the following virtual activities:

Engineer It!: Students and families can try engineering design challenges at home with materials they might already have around the house.

Science and Stories Online: These online science-driven stories, directed by an ECHO youth programs manager, use songs, books, and a hands-on component around different seasonal topics.

Citizen Science Challenge: Different plants or animals are highlighted, challenging students to get outside, make observations, and discover wildlife.

Science Spotlights: Anyone can do these quick science experiments at home.

Animal Ambassadors Cam: This gives students a virtual visit to the animal habitats at the ECHO Center, such as a baby turtle tank. An invasive species can also let students peek into ECHO's invasive species tank and exhibit.

Science Hacks: Local television station WCAX shows science projects that families can do at home that are focused on gravity, magnetic fields, chemistry, and other STEM topics.

How to Grow Partnerships: Starting, Maintaining, Sustaining, Retaining and Strengthening

Strong, lasting partnerships are like any other healthy relationships: They must be built on respect, communication, and consideration of the needs of all parties. Here are suggestions to build and strengthen partnerships over time:

Starting

- **Identify school needs.** Schools should first identify their needs before approaching a prospective business partner. Examples of needs include exposing students to STEM careers and building interest in STEM; providing CCR advisor support for students (Chapter 4) or helping students understand how to interview (as was done at Keene Central School, described above).
- **Identify potential partners.** The first part of this chapter provides a list of where to find prospective partners—places like the United Way Worldwide or Rotary International—and resources in your community, such as retirees.
- **Ask.** The most important step is to simply ask a business if they would like to partner, giving them specific details on what they can provide. Be sure to list ways the partnership will impact students, help the business, and provide value to the region. Invite leaders of the business to visit your school, and when they visit, make sure they meet students and ensure their time is respected with a tight schedule. *Do not ask for financial support at this time!*
- **Build a shared vision.** Successful partnerships require a vision that is shared by both the business and school. It's critical to not become an "adopt a school" initiative! When a school is not on an equal footing

with a business partner, it doesn't take long for resentment to grow. At CFES, we've seen this destroy dozens of partnerships.

- **Top leaders need to buy in.** The superintendent needs to believe in and support the partnership, as do key business leaders. If the decision makers don't buy in, the partnership is doomed. Top leaders do not need to be part of the everyday components of the partnership, but they do need to receive regular communication about what's happening.

Maintaining and Sustaining

- **Commit to student success.** The core of a school–business partnership needs to be student success. That might translate into career readiness and/or better oral health, as in the DentaQuest partnership.
- **Partnerships need champions.** "I wasn't shy," said Lisa Ruland, one of the champions of the GMU career fair. "I utilized my connections when talking with faculty and staff about their students' interests and the connections they had. It created real buy-in and made this a unified effort."
- **Partnerships must meet the needs of both the school and business.** Whenever you meet, review goals and discuss whether the partnership is letting both the school and the business achieve its objectives. There is always a need to make adjustments, and these should be addressed quickly.
- **Partnerships need clear goals and agreed timelines.** The northern New York mentoring partnership was modeled after EY's College MAP, and its goals centered on college readiness. Goals were clear, and there was a monthly timeline to meet them.

Retaining and Strengthening

- **Develop a team.** Partnerships that are led and implemented by one person don't survive. Individuals get burned out. Individuals leave. A successful partnership requires significant resources to succeed, the most important of which is personnel time. The Sophomore Summit in central New York builds CCR for 400 students in 10th grade. The summit has been successful for more than a decade in large part because a team from the schools and regional businesses and colleges plans and guides the event each year.

- **Communicate.** Champions communicate well with their counterpart at the business. They return phone calls and emails within 24 hours. The partnership graveyard is littered with poor communicators.
- **Promote success.** Use news and social media to trumpet partnership highlights. Display partnership pictures and pennants in lobbies and offices and have an end-of-year ceremony where partners are recognized.

Conclusion

In 2015, the CFES mission statement evolved to include career readiness alongside college readiness. Several forces drove CFES to incorporate career readiness into our mission. Without enough skilled and trained workers coming through the pipeline, our country was (and still is) facing the challenge of filling millions of jobs. More than half of the new and high-paying jobs are in STEM, yet too many young people are unaware of workplace options and what is required to secure these jobs.

Collaborations with businesses can go a long way toward narrowing this skills gap. This chapter shares where and how a school can find a business partner; the anatomy of business partnerships with rural schools; ways to adapt an urban partnership to fit a rural setting; steps to start, sustain, and strengthen partnerships; and examples of high-impact partnerships and how they changed students' lives.

References

Dalton, R. & Erdmann, D. (1990). *The chance to dream: A community success story*. Plan for Social Excellence, Inc.

Dalton, R., & St. John, E. (2017). *College for every student: A practitioner's guide to building college and career readiness*. Routledge, Taylor & Francis Group.

Building Readiness for College

CFES (College for Every Student) Brilliant Pathways defines college readiness as "the level of preparation a student needs to succeed in college." So what are the skills, knowledge and behaviors a student needs to achieve that level of preparation and readiness?

In previous chapters, a set of personal competencies—the Essential Skills™—were identified as a vital component of college readiness, degree attainment, and success in the workplace and beyond. In addition to the Essential Skills, college-going students need a supplemental suite of skills and knowledge, from self-awareness about their own possible career interests to financial literacy, to practical knowledge and expectations about life as a college student.

This chapter explores what it means to be college ready and how to build that readiness in rural youth. Some of the strategies CFES has successfully leveraged to promote college readiness are discussed. Among these are diagnostic tools that show the skills and knowledge college-bound students need and provide a useful assessment tool for teachers, mentors, and students alike. College partnerships are another effective tool: Over the last four decades, we've seen school–college partnerships strengthen student performance, build college knowledge, raise aspirations, change learning in the K–12 classroom, and transform the culture of both schools and colleges.

This chapter will then share some ways partnerships build college readiness by showing examples of high-impact partnerships, tips to help students take advantage of partnership opportunities, and advice for becoming college ready.

College Readiness Starts Early

College preparation isn't just for high school seniors. Students need to start cultivating the habits, skills, and mindset for academic and professional success as early as middle school. For this reason, CFES has developed a number of resources to introduce younger students to the idea of college and to the steps they will need to take to get there. Box 6.1 shows the CFES Scholar Map, a visual schematic of the college-readiness journey that students complete with the guidance of their mentors and Box 6.2 shows the key that accompanies the Map. Box 6.3 shows the CFES College-Readiness Rubric, a diagnostic tool that helps students better understand where they are on their educational journey. CFES has also developed a list of practical, age-appropriate steps that mentors can help students take to start forging their own college pathways.

Box 6.1 CFES Scholar Map

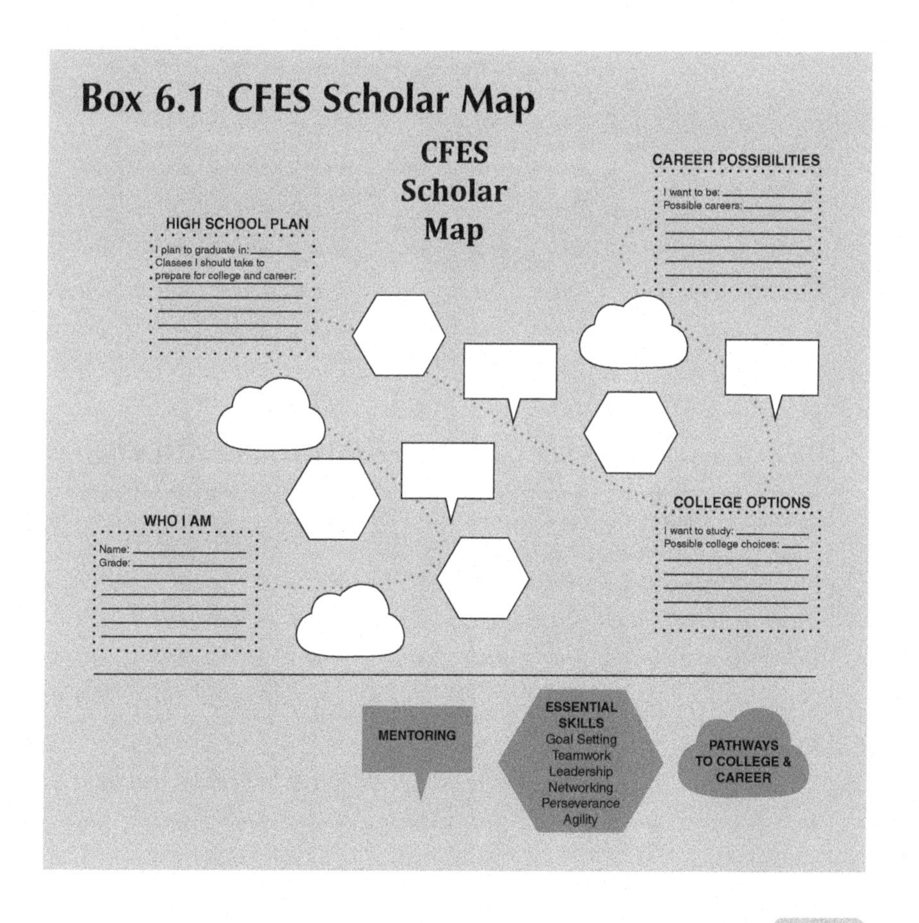

Box 6.2 CFES Scholar Map Key

Plan, Options, Possibilities: The circles are pivotal moments on a Scholar's college and career journey. Scholars can begin mapping their Brilliant Pathway by starting with "Who I Am" or with "Career Possibilities" or at any other point on the map.

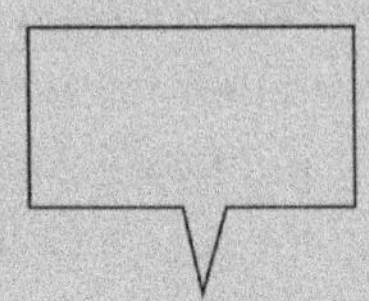

Mentoring: Use the rectangles to help students identify ways in which their mentor can support them in moving down their college and career pathway.

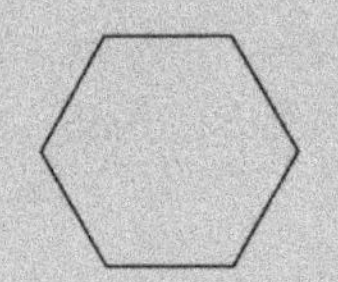

Essential Skills: Use the hexagons to initiate discussions, participate in activities, and make ongoing improvements in developing the six Essential Skills (Goal Setting, Teamwork, Leadership, Agility, Perseverance, and Networking).

Pathways To College and Career: Use the clouds to help Scholars identify how college and career pathway knowledge can help them move down their Brilliant Pathway. These steps can include college research or campus visits, job shadowing or internships and many other activities.

Box 6.3 The CFES College-Readiness Rubric

Acquiring	Demonstrates self-awareness of personal preferences	Aware of basic options after high school	Beginning to show interest in learning about careers	Confronts learning opportunities with fear
Developing	Identifies own strengths, needs, and preferences	Open to learning about college options when presented	Shows ability to utilize tools to research options	Open to new learning opportunities with as little effort required

Adapting	Can express personal strengths, needs, and preferences specific to certain situations	Plans to fulfill requirements for postsecondary success; makes changes based on feedback	Understands requirements needed for success; takes action based on needs	Invites the unknown, even if extra effort is required; learning appears to be very important
Advancing	Advocates for self in education, employment, and within the community	Invested in own education with an understanding of the importance of a postsecondary degree or credential of value	On track with exceeding credentials for set path	Seizes every opportunity as a valuable learning experience; always striving for improvement

It's important to note, however, that none of these tools are intended as road maps for students to navigate on their own. Rather, they collectively represent a long-term project with many interconnected components in which teachers, volunteers, and school partners must provide critical information and support. Above all, they must impress upon their students that it's never too soon to start working towards their dreams!

The Mental Journey Toward College Readiness

As the previous chapters have shown, many of the steps toward college readiness involve cultivation of a college-going mindset. CFES has identified the qualities of a college-ready mindset and the stages students pass through on the way to attaining it. Below are two conceptual tools used by CFES that incorporate our benchmarks for college readiness to evaluate students' personal and intellectual growth as they advance toward college and future careers.

The CFES Scholar Map

The Scholar Map is a tool designed to move students down the pathway to college and career. It helps students visualize where they are headed and understand how the CFES program and/or practices can ready them for postsecondary opportunities.

There are many ways to complete the Scholar Map, and each scholar's Brilliant Pathway to college and career will be unique. However, each student's trajectory will have some common themes, represented by the shapes on the Scholar Map. These represent the CFES core practices (Mentoring, Essential Skills, and Pathways to College and Career) that will help scholars move along their own Brilliant Pathways.

Box 6.2 shows the CFES Scholar Map itself. As you can see, the map illustrates that the path to college is long and one must start the journey early. To succeed in college, one must first have a plan to succeed in high school and, as noted earlier, this is not a path for a student to navigate alone—the guidance of a mentor is essential to help the student develop self-knowledge and master the Essential Skills needed for academic and professional success.

Here are some of the ways CFES mentors help students get the most meaning and value from their Scholar Maps:

- **Keep mentors, schools, and CFES program directors in the loop.** We ask that all CFES Scholars complete the Scholar Map annually, but this is an activity that program directors can facilitate and support. School teams, mentors, educators, and others who work with scholars on postsecondary planning should be comfortable using the map with scholars as well.
- **Connect the dots.** This tool incorporates every element of the CFES program. Mentors should look at what scholars are already doing and tie their progress on the map to activities and/or CFES experiences that they have had or will have. For example, you might ask scholars to share a reflection about visiting a college campus, exploring careers on the Brilliant Career Lab website, meeting with their mentor, or participating in an Essential Skills workshop.
- **Start at the end.** When thinking about the future, it's sometimes easier for students to work backwards. Help them identify potential career

interests and professional goals and then move backwards through the mapping tool. This exercise can be conducted using the Brilliant Career Lab website (www.brilliantcareerlab.org), which guides students though a 60-question interest assessment to help them identify potential career fields, while also providing additional information about job outlook, courses to take, job description, etc.

- **Keep it simple.** This tool is meant to help students become aware of their options and visualize the steps they need to take to pursue college and career possibilities. Building knowledge about college and career pathways, developing the Essential Skills, and interacting with positive role models will make it easier for students to map their futures.

In summary, the CFES Scholar Map is intended to help students see themselves as college ready and empower them to take the steps needed to advance toward their goals.

The CFES College-Readiness Rubric

Conceptually related to the CFES Scholar Map, the CFES Brilliant Pathways College-Readiness Rubric (Box 6.3) outlines the attitudes and academic and study skills necessary for entering college. It can be a powerful tool for assessing where scholars are in their roadmap and the steps they still need to take to move through their postsecondary journey.

Combined with college and career readiness (CCR) guidance described in Chapter 4, the rubric can increase the number of students who attain college degrees and thus contribute to the building of a more skilled and well-rounded society. In addition, the College-Readiness Rubric is helpful not only for students' own self-evaluation, but also for school communities, as they can use the rubric to assess the actual efficacy of their own CCR practices and allocate resources more effectively.

The College-Readiness Rubric is a holistic assessment focused on four areas, three of which are highlighted in the Scholar Map: the Essential Skills, Pathways to College, Pathways to Careers, and Academic Skills.

The online assessment hosted on the Brilliant Pathways website (www.brilliantpathways.org) takes 30 minutes for students to complete and includes a series of statements that span the four disciplines. CFES asks students to focus less on what they think is the right answer and more on what they would do in a given situation. Their answers reflect their current developmental state in each of these areas.

For students, understanding where they stand in their college and career pathway involves a critical reflection process. CFES is intentional in helping scholars move through their journey, which starts with an understanding of their past and current situation to help shift their mindset from feelings of inadequacy to the confidence and motivation needed to take positive steps toward a successful postsecondary journey.

The College-Readiness Rubric in Action

Over the years, CFES has found the College-Readiness Rubric to be an accurate reflection of students' readiness not just for college-level academic work, but for navigating the complex world of college admissions and advancing toward a degree. Here are some examples of students who've reached different points on the college-readiness journey.

In Chapter 2, we heard from Erick from Crown Point Central, who overcame the obstacles of growing up in a low-income, single-parent family to become a student at the University of Rochester. Erick is an example of the benefits of mastering the four areas of the College-Readiness Rubric. From a young age, Erick knew he wanted to go to college, and while he didn't know the steps to get there, his desire was a powerful motivator. However, as we know, motivation alone isn't enough. Without the Essential Skills, it would have been easy for Erick to give up on his dreams, but because he knew how to apply the Essential Skills—among them, goal setting, leadership, and building a network of supporters—he was able to gain admission to the University of Rochester and persevere when faced with yet more obstacles. He was further motivated to succeed by the sight of his father working 70-hour weeks to support his family. "You need to take the necessary steps to do what needs to be done," Erick said.

In Chapter 4, we learned about Sinead, who had been invested in the idea of going to college from the time she was in kindergarten but gave up on her dream and instead opted for a job as a bank teller. In terms of the College-Readiness Rubric, she had reached the Adapting stage in Pathways to College and the Advancing stage in Academic Skills. However, her Essential Skills remained at the Acquiring stage. Because she lacked the Essential Skills, when obstacles arose and fear about paying for college increased, instead of thinking of ways to persist in her college-going plan, Sinead decided to discard it. She was still at the Developing stage in Pathways to Career, which led her to give up her dream and instead become a bank teller.

What could have changed things for Sinead and kept her on the path to college? She needed support earlier in her journey to push her to pursue her goal. Access to the College-Readiness Rubric might have made a difference by identifying the areas in which she needed further growth—such as developing perseverance, networking, and goal setting skills—so she could receive the support and direction she needed.

Julie, whose story is looked at in more detail below, faced many obstacles early on in life, but supportive guardians helped her move from Adapting to Advancing in the Essential Skills. Because of this, she understood her strengths and knew how to advocate for herself to achieve more in life. During her high school years, she showed a keen interest in academics, showing she had reached the Advancing stage in Academic Skills. This prepared her to pursue multiple college tracks. Unlike many of her rural peers, Julie also took the initiative to learn about college options, showing she had reached the Advancing stage in College Pathways as well. This allowed her to avoid a pitfall common to many students from rural America: ending up at a college that was a poor fit.

Julie's Journey: Kentucky to Harvard

Julie, now a senior at Harvard, grew up in a low-income household in rural Kentucky. Her father left before she was born, and her mother passed away when Julie was just a toddler. When her grandmother died from breast cancer, Julie's great-grandmother stepped up to raise her.

CFES arranged the visit that introduced Julie and 18 other Kentucky youth to Harvard. Students from First Generation Initiative led the campus tour and then conducted a Q&A session on college awareness, life at Harvard, and paying for college.

Julie is an outlier. Even students who do everything right—take the right classes, master important skills, and find their way to college—may not necessarily find the *right* college. Many well-qualified rural students are not able to attend the quality colleges for which they are prepared, and this number is on the rise. Estimates vary for the number of students who fall prey to this phenomenon known as "undermatching," though the number in the United States is considerable. One estimate is that 28% of college students are undermatched and were qualified to attend more rigorous institutions (McDermott, 2013).

Unlike Julie, most low-income youth who enroll in college attend poorly-resourced local institutions, which often saddle students with elevated loan debt and have higher dropout rates. Students who attend top-tier colleges are more likely to graduate and go on to earn roughly 25% more over their lifetimes than those who attend less selective colleges.

Julie is attending Harvard at no cost to her. There are other Julies who would also do well at top-tier colleges.

How to Help Students Become College Ready: A Practical To-Do List

The CFES College-Readiness Rubric and Scholar Map are effective tools to help students cultivate a college-ready mindset. But college readiness means more than just academic and emotional readiness. Along with solid academic and personal skills, students need financial literacy and a familiarity with the constantly changing college admissions landscape. Moreover, preparing for and applying to college requires students to jump through a number of logistical hoops—hoops that rural students and their parents may not even know exist. The following list shows the many practical steps mentors, teachers, and other allies can take to help students from middle school onward navigate the road to college:

- Help students develop the Essential Skills.
- Help students develop good study habits.
- Encourage students to set academic (and personal) goals by evaluating their strengths, interests, and skills.
- Engage students in service projects, leadership opportunities, clubs, sports, and other extracurricular activities.
- Match students with mentors—someone to look up to who is a positive role model—or serve as a mentor yourself.

- Teach students how to research colleges using the Internet and books, and by asking people who have attended college.
- Familiarize students with the standardized tests that are required for college entrance—like the SAT and ACT.
- Encourage students to talk with friends and family about college.
- Familiarize students with financial aid, college financing, and resources to help pay for college.
- Help students choose the right high school courses to meet college admissions requirements and prepare them for their future careers.

Tips for Grades 6–8

- Help students develop good habits, such as completing assignments on time, being proactive, and participating in class.
- Encourage students to ask teachers and family members lots of questions about colleges and careers.

Tips for Grade 9

- Introduce students to their CCR advisors to begin talking about and exploring colleges and careers.
- Encourage students to tell their teachers they're planning to go to college and to talk to their families about planning for college.
- Ensure students have a Social Security number (and memorize it).
- Encourage students to study seriously—grades earned in 9th grade will be included in their final high school grade point average (GPA).
- Get students involved in extracurricular activities, both in and out of school.
- Take students to college fairs, college campuses, and virtual (web-based) college tours.
- Help students research opportunities to job shadow or volunteer in a career field of interest.

Tips for Grade 10

- CCR advisors should talk to students about postsecondary enrollment options and appropriate courses.
- Encourage students to take the Preliminary SAT/National Merit Scholarship Qualifying Test (PSAT/NMSQT) for practice. Instruct them to check the box on the test sheet that releases their name to colleges so they can start receiving information from them.
- CCR advisors should discuss students' PSAT scores with them to identify areas of strength and areas that need work.
- By now, students should become familiar with college admissions requirements (SAT/ACT scores, GPA, etc.)—make sure they've mastered this information.
- Encourage students to take SAT II Subject Tests in recently taken courses while the material is fresh in their minds.

Tips for Grade 11

- CCR advisors should meet with students to review their transcripts and talk about college options.
- Encourage students who haven't yet taken the PSAT to sign up for and take it in the fall.
- Have students make lists of colleges that meet their most important criteria (such as size, location, areas of study, living options, and cost).
- Encourage students to request information and applications from colleges of interest by mail or the Internet.
- Have students discuss colleges of interest with their CCR advisor and family.
- Ensure students stay involved in extracurricular activities.
- Have students think about who they will ask to write their recommendations.
- Encourage students to apply for on-campus summer college programs for high school students (although scholarships are generally available, most charge a fee).

- Have students practice completing college applications.
- Ask students to compose rough drafts of their college essays and ask teachers and other trusted supporters to review them.
- Familiarize students with the Free Application for Federal Student Aid (FAFSA).
- Assist students in developing a financial aid application plan, including a list of the sources of aid, requirements for each application, and a timetable for meeting the filing deadlines.
- Help students select courses that will position them to meet admissions requirements while they apply to colleges in the fall of senior year.

Tips for Grade 12

- Encourage students to enroll in Advanced Placement (AP)/advanced level courses, if available.
- Encourage students to re-take the SAT/ACT if needed.
- Help students finalize their college lists.
- Visit college campuses with your student(s).
- Ensure students complete their college applications and keep track of deadlines.
- Have students request letters of recommendation, if required.
- Encourage students to write their college entrance essay(s).
- Help students apply for scholarships.
- CCR advisors should meet with their students to review their application checklists.
- Assist students with filing the FAFSA and other necessary financial aid documents once they've decided on a college.
- Help students weigh their college options once financial aid awards and college acceptance letters are received.
- Be sure students accept the college offer of their choice and start their college careers.

College Partnerships: A Critical Support for Rural Students

The previous sections showed the importance of regular mentoring and guidance in cultivating college readiness among rural students. However, such mentoring is typically beyond what already busy teachers and school counselors can provide. And as we saw in Chapter 5, students cannot be what they cannot see—to pursue a career, students need to be able to picture themselves in that career, which means they need to be exposed to it. Just as meeting and talking to professionals from a range of industries opens career pathways for rural students, meeting college students and instructors and experiencing campus life can make higher education feel more attractive and less intimidating for them as well—provided students can actually make these contacts.

This is why college partnerships are such a critical part of CFES' college-readiness strategy. Colleges provide role models, mentors, and knowledge and activities for schools and students, and schools provide service and training opportunities for college students, as well as a pipeline of potential future students. In short, well-planned college partnerships can be a win-win arrangement for both schools and colleges.

Six Ways Colleges Can Partner with Students

College partnerships, like business partnerships, can take a number of different forms, depending on the schools and communities involved and the needs and strengths of each. Colleges can help students and their schools by providing support, resources, and knowledge that schools alone cannot.

What Colleges Can Teach Students About College Readiness

- **Paying for college**: How to afford college (grants, scholarship, loans, etc.) and navigate the financial aid process (FAFSA completion, etc.)

- **College admissions process**: Timelines for applying to college and steps required for admissions, such as college research, application deadlines, financial aid and scholarship applications, planning for college, required courses, and test scores.
- **College terminology**: Essential college vocabulary for understanding college pathways, e.g., major, minor, loan, merit scholarship, athletic scholarship, etc.
- **Engaging families**: Inviting families to be part of the process by building relationships and providing information to prepare the student for success.
- **Aspirations**: Nurturing and celebrating a student's interest and ambition of achieving their future goals. For instance, every year, kindergartners in Keeseville, New York, dress up in caps and gowns and march to Pomp and Circumstance. Pictures are taken of the kindergartners and they serve as motivation as these students move toward college.
- **Retention**: Steps to ensure students succeed in college, meaning they stay and attain a degree on time, can begin long before students start college.

Here are examples of the different ways that colleges partner with schools and help students become college ready:

Mentoring Partnerships

College students are ideal mentors because they relate well with K–12 students and can demystify college in ways older adults can't. In Chapter 3, we saw Kristin Thorpe return to her high school as a Middlebury College mentor; at CFES, we often hear our scholars talk about the impact of "kids who look like me, who faced many of the same challenges."

One of the reasons why Middlebury has been such a good mentoring partner, as noted in Chapter 2, is legendary coach Bill Beaney, a champion for mentoring at the college who recruits athletes to serve as mentors from his hockey team and other teams throughout the college. Over the past 30 years, Beaney has recruited 5,000 college student mentors.

Mentoring programs and initiatives can take a number of forms. Here are some examples:

- Through a program called Mentor Madness, hundreds of college students, most from Middlebury, the University of Vermont (UVM), and SUNY Potsdam, mentor 3,000 K–12 students in 20 northern New York and Vermont schools during a day in January each year. In addition to exposing high school and college students to the mentoring experience, it creates buzz about mentoring. We have found that schools become more committed to mentoring programs and that college students and community and business leaders step up to become full-time mentors.
- Thirty-five students from SUNY Potsdam are mentoring 90 grade 8 students from Malone Middle School. The college students will follow the cohort through high school, with new college students stepping in as others graduate. Every year, the Potsdam and Malone students meet four times, twice in Malone and twice on the Potsdam campus, which is about an hour away. Students have opportunities to engage in real time Q&A sessions with college students, as well as focus on the Essential Skills needed for a college setting. The meetings also offer opportunities to learn about postsecondary opportunities in education, STEM, and civic engagement.
- College 101 is a virtual mentoring program for rural Kentucky students sponsored by Berea College. It began with 75 grade 11 students who were mentored by CFES professionals. Because the components of the college application process, such as college essays, standardized tests, and applications, can be overwhelming, CFES professionals break the process down into phases to make goals manageable. These advisors help alleviate stress for students and their parents by providing information, assisting in the financial aid process, and helping find the best fit colleges for each student. The Kentucky students work with their mentors to create a timeline, narrow their college selection, and apply for financial aid and scholarship opportunities. College 101 then follows students into their freshman year of college.

College Visits and Meetings

To become college ready, rural students need frequent exposure to college—the earlier the better. Visiting college campuses, either in person, as Julie did at Harvard, or virtually, allows students to see themselves as college-bound while also exposing them to experiences that will enable them to make informed decisions about where to apply and ultimately enroll. Here are some of the many ways CFES schools have brought the college experience to their students.

- Each year, 20,000 CFES students spend time on college campuses where they take tours, engage with college students, and meet with financial aid, admissions administrators, and teaching faculty. An example of exposing large numbers of students to college is the Sophomore Summit, an annual event in which 400 grade 10 students from the Leatherstocking cluster in central New York gather on a college campus for a day. Thirty higher education leaders meet with students in small groups and in college-readiness sessions that focus on understanding the ABCs of college.
- Another strategy is to hold an alumni day, in which recent high school grads are invited to return to their old schools to share insights about college life. These events are often held in early January when college students are still home for the holidays.
- CFES schools throughout the country celebrate college readiness for an entire week. The week involves college rallies, college trivia contests, college poster contests, and college students and faculty visiting schools to talk with students about college life, how to pay for college, and the admissions process.
- Every March, seniors from Kohala High School take part in the "Next Steps" meeting with admissions and academic advisors from University of Hawaii at Hilo to engage in discussions about the transition from high school to the first year of college.

Summer Partnerships

Summer breaks are a great time for high school students to get a taste of college life, since they're not constrained by their usual class schedules, and college campuses typically have more free space for them to explore and time to show them the ropes.

- College Explore, a three-day residential program, gives rising juniors and seniors a chance to experience life on a college campus and receive guidance on going to college. CFES Scholars submit an online application that includes a personal statement and references. Accepted students have attended a dozen different colleges, including Skidmore College, Roger Williams University, and Paul Smith's College.

- In late May, West Point offers a four-day, on-campus residential experience for middle school students at which they fly drones, build robots, learn how to make sound waves, and have other hands-on STEM experiences while being mentored by cadets.
- Health-Start, a residential, week-long program sponsored by the UVM, exposes rising high school juniors and seniors to the world of modern medicine through active learning labs, lectures, panel discussions, demonstrations, and hospital visits. Students learn from clinical and scientific faculty at the College of Medicine and College of Nursing and Health Sciences at UVM.

Academic Partnerships

In academic partnerships, colleges give high school students a boost by letting them experience college-level coursework—either through formal for-credit courses or informal learning experiences. Below are a few examples of successful academic partnership models:

- Dual-enrollment programs let academically able high school students take introductory college-level courses through a participating college while still enrolled in high school. This both speeds up their trajectory toward college graduation and saves on college tuition, an important concern for rural students. For instance, Crown Point graduate Drew Malone, who we profiled in Chapter 4, took English, American history, algebra, calculus, and other courses at his high school and paid $500 to receive transferable credits from North Country Community College. This let him arrive at SUNY Plattsburgh with 30 college credits, allowing him to complete his bachelor's degree in three years. Syracuse University Project Advance, an example of this approach, serves several CFES schools in rural New York (TBS Staff, 2020).
- West Point has worked with CFES to expose thousands of CFES Scholars to STEM through mobile robotics workshops where students assemble

and program robots with the help of West Point professors and cadets. More than half of those students are from rural communities.

- Elisa New, Professor of American Literature at Harvard, offers an online poetry course to 11th and 12th graders. In fall 2019, 350 students from 25 schools in low-income communities across the country took the 12-week Poetry in America course that offers four credits (Gibson, 2020).

Comprehensive Partnerships

Multi-faceted, comprehensive partnerships connecting high schools, colleges, and businesses have not only provided college readiness for students, mostly of high school age, but they have changed the culture of both schools and colleges. An example of such a partnership is the seven-state, nine-partner program, Partners for Educational Excellence, introduced in Chapter 1. Another comprehensive partnership that grew out of that program is the Gulf County Project, also described in Chapter 1 (Gentry, 2019). For the last 25 years, Berea College's Partners for Educational Excellence program has supported the educational success of 50,000 low-income students across Appalachian Kentucky and is considered a national model for rural youth.

The Middlebury College partnership with DeWitt Clinton High School in the Bronx is another example of a successful partnership. It has not only benefited students and faculty at both institutions, but spawned several other partnerships, including the UVM collaborative with Christopher Columbus High School, also in the Bronx, which has been recognized as one of the most successful comprehensive partnerships ever. While an urban collaboration, the principles underlying the Middlebury–DeWitt Clinton partnership can be easily adapted to rural communities. The success of this collaboration was shared in a monograph called *To Share a Dream*. Two months after the monograph was published, a symposium for college and school personnel sponsored by the Plan for Social Excellence, Inc., a foundation supported by financier Jim Kohlberg, took place in Mount Kisco, New York. The overwhelmingly positive response morphed into the creation of an organization called CEEP (Consortium for Educational Excellence through Partnerships) that spawned the creation of 120 school–college partnerships.

The Day College Teachers Became Believers

When faculty from Middlebury College first entered DeWitt Clinton High School in the Bronx, some had their doubts about what they were about to attempt, but the day's interaction between the two academic communities changed the culture of Middlebury, making the college more receptive to inner-city youth.

On a cold, windswept February day in the Bronx, eight Middlebury College faculty members walked up the marble steps, past the Corinthian columns and through the front doors of DeWitt Clinton High School to begin the first "Middlebury Day." Minutes later, as they entered the Principal's office, they were warmly greeted by David Fuchs. "Have a cup of coffee, a bagel," he told them.

When the clock struck 8:30 a.m., the Middlebury professors nervously trudged off with student hosts to eight different classrooms where they would teach their subject to urban kids. In Dan Kaplan's physics class, Prof. Bob Prigo explained how Newton's laws can help students swish basketballs. Then, just as the bell rang, with a drumroll behind him, Prigo demonstrated Newton's laws by breaking four pine boards with his fist to the delight of his physics class. This moment, accentuated by laughter and applause of the students, signaled: "YES! This partnership can work!" Fears about unreachable students and distant faculty vanished.

These eight faculty members returned to Middlebury with new images of the inner city. Rich Wolfson, a physics professor, recalled his day at Clinton: "I remember walking the halls between classes and peering into classrooms. After all one has heard about chaos in inner-city schools, I was surprised by the quiet and how studious looking each class was. It's been an education for us that things may not be as hopeless as the media make them seem."

The first Middlebury Day won the support of the Middlebury College community. The stereotype of the inner-city school had been broken for the visiting faculty. Provost John McCardell, who taught several history classes at DeWitt Clinton, reported to the President's cabinet in glowing terms. A few days later, Middlebury President Olin Robison pledged his support to the partnership (Dalton, 1990).

Partnerships Between College and High School Faculty: Teaching and Learning

College partnerships can involve advanced learning opportunities not only for high school students, but for their teachers as well. Here are some activities from a collaboration between rural schools and professors from Middlebury, Williams, and Amherst Colleges, funded by a grant from the Arthur Vining Davis Foundations. These activities can be adapted for different academic disciplines and communities.

- A Middlebury College professor, working with a Willsboro (NY) science teacher, visited the science lab at Willsboro and conducted DNA experiments with the students. In turn, the Willsboro students visited the professor's lab at Middlebury.
- Two Middlebury College professors, joined by 11 international students, visited Ticonderoga (NY). The college students were paired with the high school students to learn about American high schools. The two professors gave lectures to English classes and met with the Ticonderoga English teachers.
- A Bolton (NY) computer science teacher, joined by her students, visited a Williams College computer science professor and his students in the College's videography lab. Together they created a presentation, entitled "Introduction to Video Logic," that they edited using advanced technology. A few weeks later, the Williams professor visited classrooms at Bolton, where he showed the video and explained the technology. He also taught classes in mathematics and computer science.
- A science teacher at Ticonderoga, accompanied by five students, visited a chemistry professor at Williams College, where they conducted experiments in nanotechnology. The students met with admissions staff, toured the campus, and attended a Shakespeare play.
- A Willsboro science teacher teamed up with a Middlebury College biology professor to create a science-oriented blog, giving Willsboro students and teachers access to scientific resources not previously available and allowing them to communicate electronically with Middlebury students and faculty.

- Fifteen English teachers from Adirondack schools participated in an AP English workshop, led by two English professors from Middlebury College. The workshop helped Ticonderoga introduce AP English into its curriculum as part of a school-wide effort to revitalize its English and language arts courses. Building on its successful work, Ticonderoga is training teachers at other Adirondack schools on how to revamp curricula and strengthen teaching.

Building a College Partnership

Now that you've seen some of the many ways college partnerships can benefit rural schools and their students, here are some ways to make a partnership happen for your school or community:

1. Decide what you're looking for: College student mentors; a way to raise aspirations and build college knowledge; a summer program for students who want more exposure to STEM or want to enhance their music skills; or a way to help your teachers understand what has changed in the study of chemistry.
2. Start by Googling programs or partnerships to see what's already out there. Alternately, you might want to identify a particular college first. Then check out those programs. If you're interested in a summer program that provides health care exposure, you'll find lots of choices. Most will have a cost but some, like UVM's HealthStart or West Point's summer STEM program, are free.
3. Identify what you have that colleges want. It might be money: Syracuse University Project Advance, like other dual-enrollment programs, is always looking to sign up more students who will pay to participate. It might be students: Colleges need to recruit students to fill seats and beds, and they know that it's good business to expose high school or even middle school students to their campus and programs. In particular, some colleges are looking to increase their cohort of first-generation students. Also, college students might need a place to do service, and your school can provide a place for mentoring.
4. It's all about relationships. Successful partnerships depend on a rapport between the liaisons at the school and the college. They

don't need to become best friends, but they need to work well together; respond quickly to emails, phone calls, and texts; and each be committed to a flourishing partnership.

5. A good way to experience partnering firsthand with a college is to invite someone from that college to speak at your school. Consider a family program on financial aid or admissions.
6. Virtual connections open up limitless possibilities. You can find mentors, financial aid experts, or professors in STEM subjects who will hold Zoom sessions with your students; these connections can be from your state or region or several thousand miles away.
7. Acknowledge and appreciate. After you engage with a college, thank them.

If you and your colleagues want to create a comprehensive partnership, you'll need top leaders to buy in. The superintendent needs to believe in and support the partnership, as do key leaders at the college. The steps to follow are similar to the recommendations in Chapter 5 for business partnerships because both kinds of partnerships, whether big or small, depend on relationships. They require good communication, champions, and the support of a team.

- *Start small.* Pilot test with one activity. If it goes well, try another activity.
- *Schools should first identify their needs before approaching a prospective higher ed partner.* Examples of needs include exposing students to STEM careers and building interest in STEM.
- *Partnerships need champions,* and they must meet the needs of both the school and college. Partnerships need clear goals and agreed timelines.
- *Develop a team.* Partnerships that are led and implemented by one person don't survive. Individuals get burned out; individuals leave. A successful partnership requires significant resources to succeed, the most important of which is personnel time.
- Communication. Champions communicate well with their counterparts at the college. They return phone calls and emails within 24 hours. The partnership graveyard is littered with poor communicators.

The story of Christopher Columbus High School in the Bronx shows how a partnership grew from an idea into a robust, decades-long program involving hundreds of students, teachers, and university partners.

An Impactful Partnership for All (from Dalton, 1990)

Shortly after becoming the Principal at Christopher Columbus High School in the Bronx, Jerry Garfin told the President of CFES, Rick Dalton, "I want Columbus to regain its glory and become the best school in the Bronx. I went to this school. I love this place."

Garfin asked Dalton if CFES could help him find a college partner. "It's part of my vision," said Garfin. Through a former board member at UVM, Richard Tarrant, Dalton was able to get the attention of the UVM Provost, who asked his Admissions Director, Don Honeman, to attend a CFES workshop in Mount Kisco, New York.

At the workshop, Garfin and Honeman sketched out the first steps in a plan that would change the destinies of both institutions and ultimately hundreds of low-income students from the Bronx. JetBlue Airlines joined the partnership by providing 300 free round-trip tickets each year between New York and Burlington, Vermont. "That reduced the distance between us. Instead of five hours of travel, we were 60 minutes apart," said Garfin. This enabled students and staff to visit the UVM and allowed members of the UVM faculty and staff to visit the Columbus campus in the Bronx.

Over the last decade and a half, more than 400 young people from Columbus High School, and the two small schools that were created in the building after the partnership was established, Collegiate Institute for Math and Science and Pelham Preparatory Academy, have attended UVM. A staggering 80% of those students have attained UVM degrees or are on target to do so, and scholarships and support from UVM totals more than $30 million.

The partnership has been marked by myriad activities centered on college pathway knowledge, mentoring, Essential Skills, and academic enrichment. Columbus students in grades 9–12 receive extensive support in understanding college pathways from UVM admissions and financial aid officers, who meet with them in the Bronx and Vermont. There are summer internships for Columbus students at UVM, students from UVM teach at Columbus, UVM professors teach high school English and science, college and high school students perform service activities side-by-side, and the UVM choir and vocal groups perform for Columbus families and in the school's hallways.

Each year, according to Garfin, several hundred educators and students from both institutions participate in and benefit from the partnership.

How to Kill a Partnership

As beneficial as partnerships can be to both schools and colleges, most don't succeed. And very few succeed for the long haul, that is, five years or more. They take time to build, effort to nurture once established, and, above all, require focus and direction. Here are some surefire ways to kill a partnership, whether comprehensive or limited:

- poor communication—not returning emails or phone calls,
- lack of hospitality—making the representative wait in the reception area for several minutes,
- taking your partner for granted, and/or
- structuring the collaborative so that it benefits just one of the partners.

Conclusion

This chapter outlined a number of practical strategies for promoting college readiness. We started by defining college readiness and the skills and knowledge that comprise it, along with some tools developed by CFES to help students build their own college readiness. Another important theme emphasized here is that college preparation needs to start early—by middle school, students should start cultivating the skill set they'll eventually need to succeed in college. Most critically, however, students need allies and champions, and in rural communities in particular, college partners can play a critical role as advocates, role models, and information sources for college-bound students, their teachers, and their families. This chapter highlights successful partnerships between colleges and rural schools, showing high-impact examples of collaboration ranging from the one-time activities to comprehensive partnerships.

References

Dalton, R. (1990). *To share a dream: The Clinton-Middlebury partnership.* Plan for Social Excellence, Inc.

Gentry, D. (2020). *A model for partnership: How colleges can anchor rural schools and communities*. Berea College.

Gibson, L. (2020). Harvard credit for high-schoolers. *Harvard Magazine.* https://harvardmagazine.com/2020/03/jhj-harvard-credit-for-hs

McDermott, C. (2013). Researchers explore factors behind mismatched college choices. *The Chronicle of Higher Education.*

TBS Staff. (2020). Seven ways you can earn college credits while still In high school. The Best Schools. https://thebestschools.org/magazine/seven-ways-can-earn-college-credits-still-high-school/

Leveraging Technology

Expanding Rural Opportunities

Jon Reidel

A few days after schools closed due to the COVID-19 pandemic, a peculiar scene emerged across a rural section of Vermont near the Canadian border known as the Northeast Kingdom: Rectangular objects began to appear at the ends of driveways leading to the houses, trailers, and duplexes of students attending area schools. As it turns out, they were coolers, repurposed as places for teachers and school staff to drop off breakfast and lunch for their students, along with daily homework assignments.

"Most of our students qualify for free or reduced lunch and would have gone hungry without these meals," said Brighton Elementary science teacher Beth Rodondi, who helped deliver the meals. "In terms of homework, we needed to get it to them by any means necessary until we got up and running digitally."

The difficulties experienced by Rodondi and her colleagues when the pandemic hit were shared by educators across rural America and cast a spotlight on an already inequitable digital divide. By sheer will and ingenuity, they found ways to overcome the divide when faced with an unprecedented health care crisis. The Beekmantown Central School District in upstate New York deployed school buses equipped with Wi-Fi to nearby Peru, New York, so students could get within 300 feet of the buses' routers to gain internet access. It became another strange, pandemic-induced ritual: After a long day of work, parents would park their cars near the buses while their children did homework. These "digital parking lots" sprouted up across rural America outside grocery stores, gas stations, and libraries, serving as lifelines until better digital options emerged, if they did at all.

The Brighton and Peru examples are critical to helping students on the wrong side of the digital divide during times of crisis, but they were short-term fixes to larger, more complex issues facing rural schools from northern California to coastal Maine. With millions of young Americans attending virtual school from home during the pandemic, the long-standing gap between those who have reliable, affordable internet and those who don't has never been clearer. In some schools, teachers reported losing touch entirely with over half of their students, while their plugged-in classmates continued to learn and pull ahead even further academically.

Despite our country's digital divide, some rural schools have found ways to leverage technology to overcome cost, distance, and other obstacles. We know from Chapter 1 that youth in rural settings who live 50 miles or more from a college are significantly less likely to pursue higher education than their peers whose communities are near postsecondary institutions (Hillman & Weichman, 2016). Technology can shorten the distance between communities and colleges. This chapter will share ways that technology can be leveraged to ameliorate this situation and enhance college and career readiness. We will also show how technology has the power to build the economies of rural communities by allowing technology startups—and local college graduates wanting to return to their communities—to take root.

The Digital Divide: How Broad Is It?

The actual size of the digital divide has been an ongoing topic of debate since the term was first used over 25 years ago to highlight the gap between those who had access to information and communication technology and those who did not. Microsoft estimates that 157 million Americans—about half the population—lack relatively fast internet connections (McKinley, 2020). The Federal Communications Commission (2019), using different counting methods, says more than 21 million Americans, mostly in rural areas, lack access to fast internet.

Fortunately, the digital divide continues to narrow, despite debates about who should spearhead the effort to completely close it. As government and the private sector battle over who should subsidize the closing of the divide, many students remain on the wrong side of it. In fact, about 9.7 million students aren't connected to the Internet, according to data from EducationSuperHighway, a nonprofit focused on connectivity in public schools. Not surprisingly, the least connected states are rural— West Virginia, Louisiana, Kentucky, and Mississippi—at about 26–28% non-connectivity (Hobbs & Hawkins, 2020).

Microsoft's efforts to close the gap can be seen just outside the windows of the CFES (College for Every Student) Brilliant Pathways offices in the Adirondacks, illustrated in the following Microsoft blog post:

> Last year, a team of Amish-owned horses dragged a load up a ridge near Essex, New York. It was a normal scene for rural America—straight out of a Norman Rockwell painting—except that they were bearing telecommunications equipment to connect the local community to the Internet. Essex is barely 12 miles across the lake from Burlington, Vermont, but broadband is scarce. In our increasingly digital and interconnected world, broadband is as important as electricity or water. Rural communities without broadband face higher unemployment rates and see fewer educational and economic opportunities. For the woman overseeing the horses, Beth Schiller, CEO of CvWireless LLC, this is a solvable problem.
>
> (McKinley, 2020)

Despite these efforts, large swaths of rural America remain without connectivity. Part of the reason for what feels like a lack of urgency to close the digital divide is the way in which it has been framed. Rarely discussed is the fact that students without Internet access are being denied the right to an equal education. Students across America are promised access to equal educational opportunity regardless of race, ethnic background, religion, or sex, or whether they are rich or poor, citizen or non-citizen. If students are unable to access online classes because they live in rural communities, this right is clearly being denied. Politicians on both sides of the aisle agree, including former Governor George Pataki (Republican, New York) and United States Senator Bernie Sanders (Independent, Vermont), both supporters of CFES' efforts to level the playing field for students in underserved communities across America.

"Every student with the desire and ability should have the opportunity to attend college and postsecondary training programs," Senator Sanders said when CFES announced it was working with four new schools in the Green Mountain State. "I am pleased to learn that more Vermont students will have access to counseling and programs to help them make post-high school decisions. By helping young Vermonters explore educational and career opportunities, organizations like CFES Brilliant Pathways play a critical role in equipping our younger generations with the knowledge and skills they need for productive and fulfilling lives and careers."

Whatever the current measure of the digital divide, it remains a major obstacle for students, parents, and schools on the losing side of the divide. The disparity of the digital divide became clear during the COVID-19 crisis when students who attended rural schools fell even further behind their urban and suburban counterparts. The stark inequality was obvious even within the same rural school districts where students from more affluent families with Internet access completed online assignments, while their less-wealthy classmates who tended to live in remote areas struggled to even log on, according to teachers. COVID-19 challenged the notion that technology was the great educational equalizer for rural students, as some fell further behind while others thrived.

Can Online Learning Solve Problems Faced by Rural Schools?

It's undeniable that digital learning provides greater flexibility. Its potential as a solution to current educational challenges in rural areas, which are home to a quarter of all primary and secondary students in the United States, continues to emerge (DePaul, 2020). But rural schools face challenges unlike those of their urban and suburban counterparts. Some of these obstacles include:

- lack of computer and Internet access in homes,
- declining enrollments,
- no college campuses nearby,
- lack of a college-going culture,
- low teacher salaries,
- high instructor turnover,
- smaller budgets and less resources, and
- fewer high-level (Advanced Placement (AP)) courses

Many schools also lack advanced courses in math and science, challenging electives, and world language courses. A real gap exists between the variety of options that students experience in rural and urban districts. For instance, as population size decreases and distance to major urban areas increases, AP course options begin to disappear (The Foundation For Blended and Online Learning, 2018). This is another area where technology can close the gap: Rural schools are tapping into online AP courses so their students can take them and increase their chances of getting accepted into college.

Rural Schools That Are Leading the Digital Teaching and Learning Revolution

Hard work has always been a staple of rural America. Dwight D. Eisenhower once said that "farming looks mighty easy when your plow is a pencil and you're a thousand miles from the corn field" (Eisenhower, 1956). Despite farms disappearing and other rural jobs on the decline, some schools have found ways to continue the tradition of hard work and ingenuity through technology. New and effective virtual learning and teaching programs created out of necessity during COVID-19 have emerged at rural school districts and are advancing the college and career readiness goals of their students.

Beekmantown Central School, New York, is a prime example of how a rural school district with the dream of becoming a digital teaching and learning leader can change the life trajectories of students through technology.

The Rural School that Could: How Beekmantown Conquered the Education Crisis Created by COVID-19

In 2013, when Dan Mannix became Superintendent of Beekmantown Central School, he took a walk through the halls, peering into classrooms along the way. He didn't like what he saw: Rows of desks with textbooks on them.

"It looked like when I was in school, except it was the 21st century," recalls Mannix. "I knew we had to make some changes and get on the right side of digital teaching and learning or get left behind."

Lacking funds, Mannix started by forming a technology committee, changing the title of Director of Technology to Director of 21st Century Learning, and applying for three tech grants. "We didn't get any of them, but that didn't stop us," says Mannix. "If you want to be an agent for change, the change can't be 'I need more', it has to be that you make change with what you have at the time."

Mannix decided not to replace a retiring English teacher based on a decline in student enrollment, a potentially unpopular move that freed up $100,000 to launch a digital initiative pilot program. "We needed seed money to get things started, and then when we finally got grants, it was pedal to the metal," he says.

When 33 volunteers came forward to launch the pilot program, Mannix told them that they were allowed to fail. The acronym FAIL (First Attempt in Learning) cleared the way for early setbacks, which turned into victories. "The only thing I wanted in return was for them to share their journey."

The journey started with a trip to the Future of Educational Technology Conference in Florida, followed by Google trainings, and visits to schools that were already using Chromebooks and other technology. One student shared a story about how virtual learning allowed her to stay engaged with classmates and keep pace academically while she was out sick. Another student, who was in a special education program, said using technology finally made him feel like he was on a par with his classmates.

"That was all I needed to hear," says Mannix. "The kid was on the verge of tears, thanking Google for making him feel like everyone else."

Fast-forward five years and Beekmantown's digital teaching and learning program is the envy of the region. When COVID-19 hit, the school flipped a switch and everything went digital. Attendance was an astonishing 97% only a few days after students were sent home, compared to less than 75% among other schools in the region. The fact that teachers called parents on a daily basis if their child didn't log on probably helped the school get to this number.

Mannix's background as a deputy human resource director and labor-relations specialist at the Boards of Cooperative Educational Services was also helpful. He was heavily involved in pandemic planning scenarios during the H1N1 virus and started planning for COVID-19 in January 2020 when he first heard about it spreading in China.

"We met with faculty before there was a case in New York and told them straight up that we have to be ready to pivot to full digital teaching and learning," says Mannix. "We told them that maintaining connections with kids and getting regular feedback was most important."

The impact of virtual learning on students in Beekmantown during COVID-19 proves that low-income, rural schools can overcome seemingly insurmountable odds to become national models. But in some ways, the pandemic simply cast a light on the powerful influence that virtual learning was already having on students and teachers across the school system. Digital teaching and learning tools had been helping students who were out sick to keep pace academically years before the pandemic.

"When you have to post an assignment in a Google Classroom, you can't say, 'I did my homework, but the dog ate it,' " says Mannix. "Students who are absent are no longer checked out. They're plugged in—literally."

Ever the forward-thinker, Mannix is already looking to the next phase of virtual learning and teaching. He's convinced that the world has changed since COVID-19, prompting questions about critical aspects of education, such as how we will use brick and mortar schools going forward. "Fundamental change doesn't happen when you simply add on to what you are already doing," he says. "It happens when everyone is committed to actual change, driven by a desire to help students reach their postsecondary aspirations and become college and career ready."

Choosing the Right Online Platform for Students, Teachers, and Parents

One of the biggest decisions school systems have to make in creating an effective virtual learning and teaching platform is what system to adopt. The scientific literature devoted to distance education starts with the once cutting-edge practice of snail mailing video cassettes. By the mid-1990s, the revolutionary practice of "electronic mail" and the use of the World Wide Web was all the rage. It wasn't long before infusing Twitter and Facebook into curriculum became the most advanced pedagogical approach.

By 2014, Google was flooding classrooms with Chromebooks and laptops, followed by the explosion of Google Classroom, because it's simple to use, flexible, and free. It competes with dozens of other learning management systems, including Canvas and Edmodo, which let schools upload and track coursework. For most schools, the initial scramble to online teaching and learning is a mix of thrown-together resources ranging from home delivery of assignments to Zoom calls and higher-end management systems. In Vermont, Beth Rodondi says her school will fully adopt Canvas, a course management system that supports online learning and teaching by allowing teachers to post grades, information, and assignments online. The entire state of Vermont is considering adopting Canvas, so everyone, including parents, can be trained on the same system and can support each other.

There are pros and cons to adopting any virtual learning platform. Fraught as the choice might seem, however, the choice of platform plays only a minor role in the success of a virtual classroom experience. Far more important are the relationships between students and teachers; professional development in online pedagogy for teachers; strong, consistent Wi-Fi connectivity; clear guidance on grading and other online policies; and the adoption of a system that students, teachers, and parents understand and are trained to use, albeit on different levels.

Out of all these concerns, the needs of students and parents are paramount, and teachers hold the key to providing an enticing interactive virtual experience that parents can support. The Vermont Agency of Education took a major step in that direction when it signed an expanded agreement with the Vermont Virtual Learning Cooperative (VTVLC) to provide continuity of learning resources to Vermont schools and students. The partnership provided a virtual learning management system to support school districts and supervisory unions, career technical centers, and adult education centers. The system was free to districts, schools, and providers, and offered support to educators and schools as they served students for the remainder of the 2019–2020 school year. It is prepared to meet student needs in the coming year.

"Vermont Virtual Learning Cooperative has long been a great partner with schools and the Agency to provide online and blended learning opportunities," says Secretary of Education Dan French. "They are stepping up to help Vermont students during this difficult time, and their experience and expertise with online learning are greatly valued as we work to ensure continuity of learning in all Vermont schools."

VTVLC serves over 14,000 Vermont students through online courses and has partnership agreements with 25 schools across the state, building on the expertise of local Vermont educators. It also offers courses to individual students at multiple non-partner schools. Instructors like Rodondi, who are licensed Vermont educators and certified in online teaching, will provide training, professional learning, and mentorship to other Vermont educators as the system is scaled up. The expansion of Canvas, which is highly compatible with other platforms and used by other education institutions in Vermont, allows for seamless integration with dual-enrollment and early college pathways.

Rodondi's students were among 1.5 billion students—more than 90% of the world's learners—who were stuck at home due to school closures in about 190 countries at the beginning of COVID-19, according to estimates by the United Nations Educational, Scientific and Cultural Organization (UNESCO) (UNESCO, 2020). As we saw, educators scrambled to create online learning content and teach young people remotely. There was a steep learning curve for everyone: Educators learned critical lessons about teaching online as students attempted to navigate their digital classrooms. As time passed and teachers had time to reflect and learn more about online learning, some key takeaways were identified.

Perhaps the best way to illustrate those takeaways—and the struggles that led to them—is by sharing Rodondi's story of working with her students and parents in the Northeast Kingdom of Vermont.

Transforming the Rural Northeast Kingdom into a Virtual One

Located 15 miles from the Canadian border, Island Pond is known for fishing, hunting, hiking, skiing, maple syrup, and snowmobiles. It is rural and poor, with 25% of its 821 residents living below the poverty line. It has not been immune to the opioid crisis that placed Vermont among the top 20 states for opioid-related deaths in 2016 (Center for Disease Control and Prevention, 2020). It's one of the last places you would expect to find a tech-focused school.

Rodondi, a single mother of three, a full-time elementary school science teacher, an adjunct professor at a nearby college, and an active member of the community, has given her heart and soul to the region in which she grew up. In 2020, Rodondi started taking "Intro to Online Learning" through VTVLC. It included two courses on methods and an online practicum leading to a certification in online teaching from the Vermont Agency of Education. "It has been a godsend," says Rodondi, who became a licensed online instructor.

One of the reasons she took the course was a general feeling that she and other teachers were unprepared for online teaching when COVID-19 hit. "The biggest thing as a teacher I keep thinking about is how ill-prepared we were as a whole, and I think every teacher in the entire nation would say the same, except maybe a few," she says.

Rodondi's students also took a four-week introductory course on online learning and became proficient with the learning management system Canvas and its features, including how to submit assignments and access modules. "We will use Canvas going forward," says Rodondi. "I hope the state adopts it, because it would go a long way in connecting all schools."

Living on a dirt road with no broadband, Rodondi relies on dial-up to connect with her students. She struggled to engage students initially but improved remote attendance after taking a course on motivating online learners. She started hosting a virtual math class every morning not only for her regular students, but also for any students who needed help in math. "We had to pick assignments that didn't cause overload. I also did a lot of alternative assignments to ensure that they are getting outside. There can be too much technology and too much screen time. I wanted to help them find that balance."

Rodondi's expectations of what each student should submit for homework in an online course changed with the realization that some students had more parental support than others. "I have a student who completes everything," she says. "He's the poster child for pandemic learning. But not every student is like that, so you have to meet them where they are and set standards and expectations for each student."

As unprepared as teachers and students were for virtual learning, Rodondi says it's the parents and guardians who felt the most stress trying to adopt. She received a rush of calls from parents, many of whom were friends with college degrees, in a panic about how to help their child. "A friend of mine who is a doctor called me frantically to tell me that she'd never even heard of Google Classroom," says Rodondi. "I mean she's an MD and was really struggling. What really hit home for me was how ill-prepared parents were for online learning."

Another student with multiple learning disabilities was unable to receive help from his parents, who were essential workers during COVID-19. "The sheer desperation from the parents in the evening was heart-breaking," says Rodondi. "I'd get texts that said 'I just can't anymore' or 'I quit'. I told the mother that she was protecting us as an essential worker, and we're going to do right by your child, so don't you worry about it."

To help them cope, Rodondi met with parents every Saturday evening at 5 p.m. during the pandemic in a parking lot at a nearby state park for a social meet and a few cocktails.

"The first few meetings inevitably ended up being a complaint session about home schooling," she says with a laugh. "Then it went from 'we've got this' to 'we can't do it anymore' to 'I see the light at the end of tunnel'. There have been some real high points and some really low moments. I've had my own issues as a parent, trust me, but we've helped each other navigate this new world, and now we're in a position to make our school a leader in virtual learning and teaching."

Examples of advice that can be given to parents to foster online learning success are listed in Box 7.1.

Box 7.1 What Advice Can You Give to Parents?

CFES has learned a lot from educators like Rodondi, who believe that supporting and training parents is a primary driver of online learning success. The following tips for setting up an effective virtual learning home environment based on feedback from teachers, principals, superintendents, and the Vermont Agency of Education have proven effective for parents and caregivers in both rural and urban settings.

- **Create a learning space**: The goal here is to identify a quiet space away from potential distractions like televisions, cell phones, or gaming devices. Ideally located within sight of an adult, the "learning zone" should send the message that when students enter it, it's time to get down to business. That said, it should also be a fun, creative space where online learning is viewed as a positive experience.

- **Stick to a schedule**: Parents or guardians should develop a daily routine for consistent learning. This should include time for educational activities, meals, exercise, social activities, and even naps. In short, choose whatever routine works best for fostering maximum learning and a happy child.
- **Stay (non-academically) connected**: Isolation is not good. Parents, teachers, and students should meet regularly to talk about not just how they are doing in school, but also how they are feeling in general about life. In cases where teachers may not be receptive to non-academic discussions, an online mentor can be a powerful ally. Mentors can be anyone with a passion for helping students, including college students, coaches and local community members working in different professions. Mentor training helps, such as the college and career readiness trainings offered by CFES.
- **Celebrate success:** It can be hard to feel successful without a room full of classmates to celebrate a good grade or happy moment. Take the time to acknowledge that you are proud of your child for all that they are doing. This can go a long way in inspiring your child to work even harder.
- **Take it outside**: Rodondi is convinced that one of the best things a parent can do for their child is to get them off the computer and outside to play. She intentionally gives assignments that students must go outdoors to complete.
- **Cocktails and coffee**: Take a page from Rodondi's playbook and meet with other parents over coffee or cocktails to celebrate—and commiserate—the trials and triumphs of online learning.

Everyone Can Get Online. So Why Aren't They Logging On?

Let's pretend for a second that the digital divide no longer exists. Broadband has magically spread across America, and everyone has a computer. That should make online education equal for everyone in America regardless of their socioeconomic status or where they live, right? Nothing could be further from the truth. During COVID-19, if technology was the only issue, students from urban schools with high-speed internet would have logged on at a higher rate. See Box 7.2 for the story of ViAsia Bramblett, a student

Box 7.2 Why I Struggled to Log on During COVID-19: A Student's Perspective

ViAsia Bramblett is a senior at North Hardin High School in Radcliff, Kentucky, a rural town bordered to the north by Fort Knox. An A-student voted most likely to succeed, she struggled to participate in her online courses during COVID-19 after experiencing feelings of depression and anxiety.

"I'm a people person, so I fell into a deep depression and started slacking," she says. "I made lists of things I needed to do to get a certain grade but struggled to complete them. If my classes were in-person, I would have gotten all A's like usual, but I kept pushing things back. My mind was definitely not into the work."

Bramblett was not alone. She was among the thousands of students who struggled with virtual learning during the pandemic, based on findings from a major study by the Prichard Committee Student Voice Team (2020), an organization dedicated to moving Kentucky to the top tier for education excellence and equity for all children. More than 13,000 students responded to a survey as part of the "Coping with COVID Student-to-Student Study," showing why so many failed to maintain their academic performance.

In short, 47% of students reported feeling unmotivated; 39% felt more stress; 35% felt more anxious; the motivation to learn dropped from 75% to 31%; only 12% of students preferred online learning to in-person; and feelings of confidence about their future fell from 78% to 61%.

Bramblett said she tried to focus on ways to deal with her depression by hosting "little online mental health clinics" with her friends. She volunteered on Earth Day, got involved in social issues, shared motivational quotes, and worked on starting her own blog.

"I wasn't just lazy," she says. "I did mental checkups on my friends and wrote supportive letters and cards to my family and people who worked in the medical field, and things I thought could help people. I just wasn't in the right frame of mind to do homework."

Part of the reason she was less interested in doing online schoolwork was because the online material was boring and unengaging. "In one of my classes, it was mostly tests, but when COVID hit, the teacher started assigning a lot of papers without much notice, so it got more stressful, and my grades kind of slipped," says Bramblett, who is headed to the University of Kentucky in the fall. "It was 100% more work, and there was also very poor communication. I never had a grade check, so I didn't even know if I was passing."

Some of Bramblett's friends never even logged on during the last two months of school, due in part to depression and lack of Internet access. Her mother, who works in the school cafeteria, delivered homework assignments and food to students on school buses to help keep them engaged.

But in other cases, Bramblett says students who struggled with in-person learning actually thrived in the online setting. "My cousin actually did better online. She was nearly failing every class, and when they went online, she got pretty good grades. She has severe anxiety and doesn't like being around people and never asks teachers for help, so I think it was just easier for her to communicate with teachers online and do the work independently without being bothered."

who struggled to log on for reasons other than technological difficulties during the pandemic.

Chris Bishop, Assistant Headmaster at Jeremiah E. Burke High in Dorchester, Massachusetts, located in one of Boston's most impoverished areas, drove to the apartments of his students to see why they weren't logging on to complete homework assignments. Having grown up in the area, he knew that some students were home alone and didn't have parents to help. "You have to talk with them about why it's important to their future to complete online assignments," he says. "That's hard to do unless you already have a strong relationship with a student. They have to trust you first."

The Importance of Establishing a Pre-Existing Online Relationship

Dreama Gentry, Executive Director of Partners for Education in rural Appalachia, agrees with Bishop that it's extremely difficult to teach online effectively if you haven't already built a strong personal relationship with a student. "There is plenty of evidence showing the importance of building relationships with students so they can trust you online just as much as they do in person," she says. If a teacher can't meet a student prior to the start of an online course, building rapport through personal emails and video updates can improve grades and retention.

"We had the most success in engaging students online when they had already been actively connected to an adult because that relationship held the young person accountable," says Gentry. "If you have a strong relationship, they are going to pick up the phone and call you back. You also know their peers and family, and so even if the student is silent, you know other people you can nudge to get them to respond."

Gentry recommends that teachers try the following methods to connect with students they did not know well before an online course:

- **Get comfortable with technology:** "It's natural for young people to build community and connect with people they have never even met before," says Gentry. "I don't think adults over a certain age feel comfortable with that, and their anxiety comes across. An educator who is more comfortable with technology can use it to build community, and that's powerful."
- **Don't start from a position of power:** Teachers have a hard time building online relationships with students because they enter them from a position of power, which is a non-starter for most students.

"Students will be willing to do the work if we communicate with them in a way that opens up a relationship. You can stay role appropriate and share power," says Gentry. "Understanding group dynamics and power becomes more important if we're trying to build relationships using technology."

- **Take a look in the mirror:** During COVID-19, most of the discussion around poor online attendance focused on the students, but some of the blame should fall on those providing the online content, which is often unengaging and varies greatly by teacher and district. "I wonder if we're putting the blame on the wrong side," Gentry says. "The whole digital divide discussion has been all about how do we get devices to kids, but if teachers don't know how to deliver engaging content via technology, the kids are no better off."
- **Rural and urban districts struggle most:** Gentry says teachers in high-poverty rural and urban areas, where teachers are often hard to recruit and retain, struggle more with online content. "These districts get less-qualified teachers because they pay less, so they have trouble retaining excellent teachers," she says. "And I think the quality of educators transitions over to the online piece. All the discussion has been about how kids are not doing this or that or that they don't have capacity. Well, if you were selling them something to buy, kids will log on and find a way to connect."

Lessons from Higher Education

Findings from a special report by *The Chronicle of Higher Education* titled "Online 2.0: How to Lead a Large-Scale Transformation of Virtual Learning" offered some key findings that K–12 educators should consider (McMurtrie & Supiano 2020). It cited multiple studies showing that students in online courses perform about the same as their in-person counterparts. In a 2018 study, students in an online course had higher grades and reported being more satisfied than students taking in-person courses (McMurtrie & Supiano 2020). That was not the case during COVID-19, when hastily thrown together "emergency" courses were deemed inferior by both professors and students.

There is some evidence, however, that "blended" learning—classes that are offered partially online and partially in-person—might be better than either approach by itself. The blended or hybrid model offers the most flexibility, a key component for students succeeding in an online course, because it lets some students attend in person and others remotely. One version, known as HyFlex, has received major buzz for its ability to allow students to decide, week by week, which mode they prefer (McMurtrie and Supiano, 2020).

The hybrid model can be challenging for colleges from a scheduling standpoint, but according to the President of Assumption College Francesco Cesareo, it's an inevitable addition to the traditional college schedule. His advice on how to prepare for and succeed in a new college environment is contained in Box 7.3.

Box 7.3 How to Prepare for and Succeed in a New College Climate: Lessons from a College President

The earlier high school seniors can reimagine how they think about college both academically and socially, the easier the transition will be when they enter a hybrid world of virtual and in-person learning. That was the advice of the President of Assumption College Francesco Cesareo during a CFES Brilliant Pathways webinar titled "How Might Higher Education Change in the Post-Pandemic World?"

The longtime College President talked with CFES Board Chair J. Bart Morrison, Associate Professor of Management at Assumption, about the impact of the COVID-19 crisis on postsecondary institutions and how colleges are addressing it.

"As we look to the future of higher education, we have to imagine that regardless of what happens to residential living, there will be some form of remote learning taking place," said Cesareo. "Students have to begin to think about how learning occurs in different modalities ... to become independent learners guided by a faculty member in that learning process."

Students who enter college with Essential Skills™ such as agility and perseverance will have an advantage, Cesareo said, but only if they apply these skills to the new paradigm of virtual learning. "For students in CFES, I would say that you have an advantage in that environment because of the principles behind the Brilliant Pathways program," he said. "You are used to thinking 'How do I adapt by utilizing the Essential Skill of agility and put into practice all of the other competencies I've learned as a CFES Scholar moving forward?"

Cesareo refutes the criticism that online learning is not as effective as traditional in-class learning, arguing that each learning modality has advantages. "Education can take on many forms," he says. "My response is always that learning and teaching are taking place but in a very different manner and approach ... how much you embrace it makes a difference."

Professors who initially struggled with a virtual format are studying the pedagogy of online learning and re-designing their courses to increase student engagement, said Cesareo. "What we were doing was remote learning, not necessarily online learning, and there's a difference. Online learning is very different from what students experienced during the pandemic. That was remote learning, which didn't include interactive lessons and other pedagogically-based exercises."

Cesareo also talked about how colleges are working to ensure that the social and community-based aspects of higher education are preserved. He's considering clustering students into "households," so there's less contact with those outside the family unit, but still fostering that same strong community feel that comes from living, dining, and taking courses together.

"Taking care of your mental health is the single most important thing a student can do," said Cesareo.

The Pedagogy of Online Learning

There is a growing body of literature on the pedagogy of online learning and an increasing understanding of just how different it is from in-person teaching and learning. The online classroom is different enough from the traditional one that faculty members and adjuncts are creating courses for digital delivery that are substantially different from those they teach on campus.

The most critical component to creating successful online courses is ensuring they offer just as much or more student engagement than face-to-face models, which is something K–12 educators should consider when developing online lesson plans. Here are some effective ways to promote engagement in an online learning environment:

- **"Sage on the stage" no more:** Even teachers who are legendary for their captivating stage presence realize their lectures simply don't work in a virtual setting. So how can colleges and universities engage students virtually in a way that has them eagerly coming back to log on each week? The secret to holding students' attention online is focusing on active learning with a mixture of discussions, video and audio clips, and hands-on collaborative exercises.
- **Have a multimedia mindset:** Unlike many teachers, students are generally pretty comfortable with technology. In fact, many thrive on it, which is why teachers should give students the freedom to submit assignments in different formats such as PowerPoint, videos, podcasts, and other multimedia. This not only invigorates and motivates students, but in some cases, makes it easier and more enjoyable for teachers to grade.
- **Engage shy students:** In larger lecture halls, some students are intimidated to speak in front of 200 people, so they rarely participate. This is not so online where they might only see their professor even though hundreds of classmates are listening. The same applies to K–12 settings: A usually shy student might feel more comfortable offering opinions in an online setting, whether it be in a Google Classroom or by posting responses to prompts or exchanging ideas in a dialogue box.
- **Be present:** One of the most important pieces of advice given by veteran online college instructors is to be as mentally present in every class as in a regular classroom. Some instructors interpret that to mean they should talk a lot, but in fact, it means exactly the opposite: They should listen more and respond when appropriate. Asking students how they are doing outside the classroom is just as important as talking about an assignment.

Why Some Students Thrive Online While Others Fail—and How Teachers Can Help

As we saw from ViAsia Bramblett's story, not all students respond to the challenges of online learning in the same way, and even well-adjusted, academically strong students can struggle in virtual environments.

Katarina was another such student. She was among the smartest, most outgoing students in her rural Adirondack high school. The three-sport athlete voted most likely to succeed was an A-student with an eye on playing college sports at a top academic school. When COVID-19 hit, however, she became withdrawn when she couldn't practice with her teammates and participate in all of the other activities she thrived on in school. Her grades slipped as her attendance became sporadic, and she rarely completed online assignments. "She was the last person we thought would struggle," admits one of her teachers.

Less than 45 minutes away at a rival high school, Terrance was just hitting his academic stride. It was a new feeling of accomplishment for the normally reserved sophomore, whose struggles with anxiety in the classroom resulted in consistently poor grades. But when COVID-19 forced classes online, he felt as though he'd become a new person. He could post comments online during class without feeling anxious or judged. His grades improved, and he actually started interacting with more classmates than ever before. "We thought he might withdraw even further with online instruction, but it had the opposite effect," says one of his teachers.

Research on the psychological impact of online learning and why it impacts some students differently than others started to emerge in the wake of COVID-19. Best practices for how to help struggling students emerged from teachers' conversations with students about what would most help them move forward. Without question, a pre-existing in-person relationship established before an online learning experience was found to play the biggest role in successful online education.

In the absence of such relationships, educators in CFES schools across the country have found other practices to be similarly effective for building personal rapport and trust between teachers and students and thus improving student engagement.

In Beekmantown, for example, teachers were required to call the parents of students who weren't logging on and participating in online discussions. The calls played a key role in the 97% participation rate of students during the COVID-19 pandemic because it showed that teachers cared about their students and wanted to support the parents as well.

Other teachers agreed that the single most important practice for re-engaging students like Katarina and others who aren't engaging for a host of complex reasons is to call, text, or email students to check on their well-being. "They need to know you care," says Rodondi. "If the student and their parent(s) know you have their back, they will respond."

Once you have their buy-in, adds Gentry, you have to give them a reason to log on. "There's a reason some students thrive in an online setting and others struggle. It's not always about personality or because some students are more technologically inclined than others. It's often about the content the teacher is providing. No one ever says 'Oh, maybe the reason some kids don't participate is because the teacher doesn't understand online instruction and offers no engaging content.' " But recent findings by educators suggest such concerns should be top of mind for teachers.

CFES has also applied these tools for online learning and engagement to its extracurricular programs. For example, the primary concern when COVID-19 hit was initially ensuring seniors continued to pursue their postsecondary plans. CFES Fellows, who are recent college graduates themselves, joined high school seniors at schools near Lake Placid, New York, on virtual college tours via Zoom to help them navigate the tours and answer questions. As recent graduates, the fellows were not only relatable for the high school students but able to provide reality checks to the promotional videos, often stopping them at key points to interpret and explain what was being presented. Students followed up with more in-depth questions about housing, professors, scheduling, how to meet people if you are an introvert, majors, financial aid, studying abroad, and other topics. Students were encouraged to watch college tours with their parents, alumni, admission representatives, or other recent college graduates.

A Return to Rural: Students Coming Back Home to Live and Work

Broadband connections aren't a panacea for all that ails rural America. Simply plugging in an ethernet cable won't create jobs, increase farmers' yields, or provide a veteran with healthcare. Rural communities need resources beyond infrastructure to rebuild and lift themselves up (DePaul, 2012). Chief among those is human capital. Though the direction of migration has favored urban areas in recent years, due in large part to a need for high-paying jobs to pay off student loans, these patterns have shifted over time. Following decades of urbanization, net migration shifted toward rural areas in the 1970s and mostly remained that way through the 1990s (Rupasingha, Yongzheng, & Partridge, 2014). Migration overall slowed in the early 2000s and during the 2007–2009 recession but shifted toward urban areas in the post-recession period (Johnson, Curtis, & Egan-Robertson, 2016).

More recently, however, young people have expressed a desire to work remotely from more rural areas and for startups in small towns, assuming the price is right. Few people have worked harder on this issue than Matt Dunne, a former Google executive and founding Executive Director of the Center on Rural Innovation (CORI).

A Former Google Exec to Rural College Graduates: Come on Home

Matt Dunne has a message for new college graduates from rural America: You can come home (or go someplace like it) and still be successful. The Executive Director of CORI knows this because he did it himself and because he's led national campaigns to revive rural communities' willingness to invest in digital economies.

As Manager of Google's Community Affairs Division, Dunne's "Come on Home" campaign defies conventional thinking by staffing major data centers and tech startups in places like Lenoir, North Carolina, and Prior Creek, Oklahoma, with local talent and college graduates willing to move home. Contrary to popular perception, he says, young professionals are open to small town living with one caveat: They have to be able to afford to pay off student debt.

"The Google folks thought I was out of my mind, but we got more applicants than we knew what to do with," says Dunne, who led all United States philanthropy and engagement for Google, including its national fiber rollout. "The biggest barrier is that graduates don't think they can get a job that is aspirational and, secondly, can pay off their student debt. We helped create a view of what was possible and aspirational."

Dunne says the COVID-19 pandemic made a lot of people reconsider living more rurally, including some of his friends from New York City. "I was like a part-time realtor," he says. "We started seeing a run on homes across Vermont."

"It completely countertrends the breathtaking comments I hear from major foundations that everyone wants to move to the city," says Dunne. "I constantly hear that we are just pushing against the inevitable, when in fact the people in the study with the greatest agency chose to stay in rural areas, and I put myself in that category."

Dunne practiced what he now preaches when he returned home to rural Hartland, Vermont, in 1992 after graduating from Brown University to become one of the youngest state legislators in the United States. It was a bittersweet move that he felt fortunate to be in a position to make but that would have been unlikely if not for the tragic death of his father to undiagnosed melanoma when Matt was just 13.

"There was insurance [money], and my mom put all of it into making sure that my brother and I didn't have to pay for college," says Dunne. "I graduated without debt and couldn't have moved home to run for public office and work part-time for $8 an hour if I had $60,000 of debt sitting on my shoulders."

Instead, Dunne says he probably would have followed his classmates to a high-powered firm in the city to pay off debt, even though the cost differential would have evaporated any financial advantage within the first ten years. He moved away after seven years in the legislature when President Clinton tapped him to serve as director of AmeriCorps VISTA and oversee 6,000 full-time volunteers in the fight against poverty.

After returning to Vermont in 2002, Dunne was elected to the Vermont State Senate and served as Assistant Director of the Nelson A. Rockefeller Center for Public Policy at Dartmouth College, where he prepared young people for careers in public service and management of nonprofits. He also helped grow a Vermont-based software company to over 100 employees and $18 million in sales, served as Chair of the Vermont delegation to the New England Board of Higher Education, and still holds an appointment with the Massachusetts Institute of Technology (MIT) Media Lab.

During his travels, Dunne recalls hearing teachers telling high school students that they would need to move away to be successful. In one instance, the Head of the Gifted and Talented Program told students "not to get stuck here like me."

"I was with the Economic Development Director who was like, 'What is he talking about? We have a new tech startup downtown and are building a digital economy here'. All the kids were like, 'We're told every day that we're in this program so we can get out of here'."

It took time to change mindsets, but students in Prior Creek started winning state robotics championships and sending students to the likes of Duke and Brown Universities. "We had techs come and show them how to build servers that worked," says Dunne. "It showed them that they had agency and that they could do that and live in their hometown."

Back in Vermont, Dunne is hiring people at CORI who grew up in Hartland and went away to colleges and wanted to move back home. It's not always the case. "Some people need to get the hell out of hometowns that are tough places to live. When you have a high school of 275 kids convening each month because a parent died of an overdose, that's trauma each and every day. It's hard in many of these communities and understandable why some people might not want to move back."

In most cases, though, Dunne says the time has never been better for students to return to their rural roots to pursue careers in well-paying jobs like coding, computer science, and automation. "The move to automation is accelerating in fascinating ways with people not wanting to be at risk when another pandemic hits," he says. "You will have machines stocking shelves at Wal-Mart instead of associates and cheese-wheel turning robots instead of people at Vermont cheese companies."

Empowering the next generation with the tools to contribute in the development of automation is critical. "But you have to have the broadband and the curriculum that actually goes with it," he adds. "If you are living on Zoom, you can share these kinds of ideas and collaborate on Google Docs. That's how rural communities can proactively build digital economy ecosystems and young people can become aspirational in their career, work, and lifestyle."

Rural Brain Gain: A Young Entrepreneur Moves Home to Launch a Tech Startup

Entrepreneurship is key to rural revitalization and is often fueled by recent college graduates tapping into the digital capacity of small towns to create scalable tech solutions. The promise of rural entrepreneurship is embodied in young businesspeople like Sho Rust, who moved from Los Angeles back home to Cape Girardeau, Missouri, in 2018 to launch Sho.AI—a tech startup revolutionizing the face of digital branding from his parents' garage.

Rust says living in Japan, France, New York, and Los Angeles gave him experience and helped him realize that he wanted to build a company back home focused on AI-enabled software to help businesses scale through seamless brand management. "I have a lot of fondness for Los Angeles and New York too, but it just so happens that right now, for this startup and team, Cape Girardeau just makes a whole lot of sense," says Rust, adding that the cost of an office in Venice Beach would have been prohibitive.

The slow migration back to rural America was accelerated by COVID-19 when corporations realized employees were just as productive working remotely. Young entrepreneurs were emboldened to launch startups in small towns, which started offering more infrastructure and other technical support.

"There's a new center for media, a whole new Marquette Tech District, gigabit Internet everywhere, and coffee houses," says Rust of Cape Girardeau. "There's definitely a huge push. I would like to see more investors in the area, but I understand that for investors to be here, there also needs to be results, and we're looking to provide those."

One of the main issues facing startups in small towns is a lack of qualified employees. Attracting top talent to the middle of nowhere is still a tall order. Rust says there's more local talent than people realize in rural America, and that if you build it, they will come from nearby larger towns.

"What we've found is that good people exist here in different communities," he says. "There's this crazy kind of underground culture here that people aren't aware of; this kind of gamer-programmer type that is embedded here in Cape Girardeau, and they're crazy good. They don't understand their value just yet."

It remains to be seen if enough jobs will exist in the future for students from rural areas to live and work in places like where they grew up. Rust says it's a matter of convincing enough people to try rural living because once they do, they won't want to go back to the city. "There's more fulfillment, happiness, and bang for your buck when you go to a rural area," he says. "It's that simple. In places like Missouri, you will have the space to think and the space to meditate. It's valuable ... my big city friends come here all the time. That tells you something."

Conclusion

The effects of the COVID-19 pandemic on the American education system were profound and exposed how unprepared the vast majority of schools were to make the switch to virtual learning and online teaching platforms. The negative impacts of the digital divide on rural students proved far worse than expected and cast a light on the inequities between urban, suburban, and rural areas. Yet despite the unequal playing fields, a number of rural schools beat the odds and are now thriving as virtual learning centers.

In the end, it's not about how much money a school district spends on online teaching resources, but rather how invested teachers are in learning how to serve their students in the new world of virtual learning. Dan Mannix ensured that all his teachers were involved in the process of becoming a leading virtual learning and teaching school; Beth Rodondi kept students and parents engaged as best she could until she became trained in the pedagogy of online learning; the Vermont Agency of Education saw the importance of providing a free platform for all schools to use so they could work synergistically; and Dreama Gentry challenged teachers to look in the mirror and ask themselves why students weren't logging in to their classrooms.

Looking ahead, the role of technology in the classroom will only continue to increase. Staying on top of the latest online teaching platforms and related pedagogy is critical to the success of every school moving forward, but as we saw in the stories of educators guiding their students through the COVID-19 pandemic, the most important ingredient for student success continues to be the care and dedication that educators have for students whether in-person or in the new world of online learning.

References

Center for Disease Control and Prevention. (2020). Heroin overdose data. www.cdc.gov/drugoverdose/data/heroin.html

DePaul, K. (2020). Can online learning mitigate rural schools' biggest challenges? Getting Smart. www.gettingsmart.com/2020/02/can-online-learning-mitigate-rural-schools-biggest-challenges/

Eisenhoer, D. D. (1956). Address at Bradley University, Peoria, Illinois, on September 25, 1956.

Federal Communications Commission. (2019). Inquiry concerning deployment of advanced telecommunications capability to all Americans in a reasonable and timely fashion. Report No. FCC-19-44. https://docs.fcc.gov/public/attachments/FCC-19-44A1.pdf

The Foundation For Blended and Online Learning. (2018). *Digital learning strategies for rural America: A scan of policy and practice in K–12 education*. The Foundation For Blended and Online Learning and Evergreen Education Group. https://education.vermont.gov/sites/aoe/files/documents/edu-maintenance-of-learning-guidelines-for-educators.pdf

Hillman, N. & Weichman, T. (2016). Education deserts: The continued significance of "place" in the twenty-first century. Viewpoints: Voices from the Field. www.acenet.edu/Documents/Education-Deserts-The-Continued-Significance-of-Place-in-the-Twenty-First-Century.pdf

Hobbs, T. D., & Hawkins, L. (2020). The results are in for remote learning: It didn't work. The Wall Street Journal. www.wsj.com/articles/schools-coronavirus-remote-learning-lockdown-tech-11591375078

Johnson, K., Curtis, K. & Egan-Robertson, D. (2016). How the great recession changed U.S. migration patterns (Brief No. 01-16). Population Trends in Post-Recession Rural America. https://w3001.apl.wisc.edu/pdfs/b01_16.pdf

McKinley, S. (2020). Microsoft airband: An annual update on connecting rural America. Microsoft On the Issues. https://blogs.microsoft.com/on-the-issues/2020/03/05/update-connecting-rural-america/

McMurtrie, B., & Supiano, B. (2020). Online 2.0: How to lead a large scale transformation of virtual learning. The Chronicle of Higher Education.

Pritchard Committee Student Voice Team. (2020). *Coping with COVID student-to-student survey*. Pritchard Committee. [Manuscript in preparation]

Rupasingha, A., Yongzheng, L., & Partridge, M. (2014). Rural bound: Determinants of metro to non-metro migration in the U.S. *International Center for Public Policy Working Paper Series*. https://scholarworks.gsu.edu/icepp/6

UNESCO. (2020). Education: From disruption to recovery. United Nations Educational, Scientific and Cultural Organization. https://en.unesco.org/covid19/educationresponse

Vermont Agency of Education. (2020). *Maintenance of learning: Guidelines for educators*. https://education.vermont.gov/sites/aoe/files/documents/edu-maintenance-of-learning-guidelines-for-educators.pdf

Staying in College
Solving Rural America's Dropout Crisis

Putnam County, West Virginia, has overcome the obstacles that many rural places face in sending students to college; the local high school consistently sends almost two-thirds of its students to college, compared to about half statewide. But Putnam County has found that for many students, the struggle doesn't stop at getting to college: It's staying there. One of the most popular colleges for Putnam County students is West Virginia University, less than three hours away. The initial trip up Interstate 79 to Morgantown is a significant one for many students. Unfortunately, more than half of those students will make the same trip back home within 10 months, having dropped or failed out. Why do half of the students from Putnam County thrive in college, while the rest return home, often forced to work in low-wage jobs?

The stories of Jake and Caitlin, who grew up in the same neighborhood, may offer some insight. Both were high performing students in high school and played sports. For as long as they can recall, they envisioned themselves going to college.

Caitlin received a track scholarship to West Virginia University (WVU), but soon after she arrived on campus, she began to question her own abilities. "I don't think I'm as fast as coach thought," she worried. "I'm just not as smart as everybody else." She started missing classes, staying out too late and, before long, she was struggling academically. At the end of the year, she was asked to leave. Caitlin went back home, worked in a local restaurant, and had a child a year later.

Jake's start at WVU was similar to Caitlin's. He attended classes intermittently and took full advantage of the college social life.

"Then a light went off," he says. "It was do or die. I set some short-term goals. I met with every professor, and I stopped skipping classes."

By employing the Essential Skills™, Jake got off academic probation and remained at WVU. "But it was close. I was able to draw on goal setting, perseverance, and agility to turn it around," says Jake, who graduated from WVU in four years and is now in pharmacy school.

Jake and Caitlin are true to the national average for college retention: One left, the other stayed and graduated. Just over half of the students who start a four-year degree graduate within six years, but, unlike Caitlin, most drop out for financial reasons with academic causes being a close second (Matthiessen, 2017). Caitlin lost her confidence, which aligns with points made in Chapter 3 about rural youth being more susceptible to doubts about their intelligence and ability to compete in college (Striplin, 1999), even when they have the same level of high school preparation and achievement as their peers (Engle, 2007).

This chapter examines the next big hurdle on the college-going journey of rural students: Staying in college. Just getting admitted to college and enrolling is not a happy-ever-after ending for rural students. Once enrolled, they face a new and equally complex set of challenges, including cultural alienation and peer pressure from home, as well as the challenges of meeting higher academic standards and budgeting their time and money. For these reasons, rural students find it more challenging to stay in college than their urban or suburban peers. This chapter examines some of the obstacles rural college students face, as well as some of the innovative strategies that have been developed to help them.

The Challenge of Family Buy-In

Parents and caregivers in rural communities find it hard to support higher education when it takes their children away from their home and changes them. Those of us who are educators need to help families understand the journey their children are taking. The support rural college students feel from home is based, in part, on their parents' familiarity with higher education and how their parents and other family members view college.

Parents who haven't experienced college themselves are less likely to know how to encourage their children or help them through normal first-year doubts and jitters (Matthiessen, 2017). Two-thirds of rural dwellers question the value of a four-year degree, which is one of many reasons why rural families need to be engaged in the college-readiness process.

For all these reasons, it's critical that parents become informed and understand the value college can offer their children. There are many ways to involve families in the college journey. Natan Arrazate (Box 8.1) succeeded

Box 8.1 Natan's College Journey: A Family Affair

Natan Arrazate of Van Horn, Texas, describes his own college retention challenges and how he was able to successfully overcome obstacles and graduate from his second college because of family buy-in and affordability.

It was crucial for me to find a college close to home. In Hispanic culture, it is harder to be independent because it's expected that all of my decisions be made with family in mind. Before I selected a college, my mother and father, who would be supporting me financially, reminded me that I needed to take their advice in choosing a school close to home. The cost of the college played a huge role for my parents, but it was also a desire to have me nearby. I have three younger brothers whom I feel a responsibility to help. After a college search with little guidance, I chose New Mexico State University. It is only two hours from home, but after a semester there, we were unable to pay my tuition. I also struggled to adjust to the 25,000-student campus coming from a small town and a culture that emphasizes family values and support. The campus is sprawling, and my dorm was located on the edge of it, so it felt kind of isolating despite being on a huge campus. I definitely missed home and would visit whenever possible. In retrospect, I probably could have adjusted in my second year, but a combination of cost, homesickness, and a feeling of not really belonging led me to transfer.

The transfer process was challenging. I had little guidance, and I needed to make a quick decision as the new school year approached. We learned about Baptist University of the Americas (BUA) from a family friend, and it was a better fit, both financially and in terms of size with less than 1,000 students. It also has a religious background that was appealing and a history of serving Hispanic students.

The only part that was concerning was how far away it was from Van Horn. Although San Antonio is more than six hours from Van Horn, I chose Baptist University of the Americas because my parents felt at peace in their hearts and minds about the decision and the price. Searching for a college was a family decision. In our culture, we make decisions together, and we make sure whatever we do will benefit every member of the family. It worked out well for me and my brothers, all of whom attended BUA.

at Baptist University in large part because his parents felt comfortable with the cost and with Baptist University of America's values. Helping parents understand the process so that they feel comfortable endorsing the college their child will be attending significantly increases the student's chance of completing a degree. Some schools have special family send-offs when their children leave for college. Others invite parents back on alumni days to connect with and support other parents. Judy May (Box 8.2) takes families from her school on college visits.

Cultural Clash

The first weeks or months of college are intimidating for almost all students, but for rural students, the culture shock of their new community can be overwhelming. The values of higher education often conflict with those of rural communities and families.

College students encounter new perspectives in the classroom and they often feel they must choose between adopting new ideas from the dominant culture or refuting them (Crain, 2018). Dreama Gentry, who directs the Partners for Education program at Berea College, says that "conflicts [exist] between how Appalachian communities and colleges view issues like religion, abortion, and gender roles." Educational systems are often biased toward middle and upper class, urban and suburban populations (Crain, 2018). A recent study revealed that students from rural Appalachia,

Box 8.2 The Judy May Story: Whatever It Takes to Help Kids Succeed

Superintendent at Friendship Central District Judy May lives on the same farm in Wellsville, New York, where she grew up with her two sisters and brother. Her parents live in a different house on that same farm but in another state, Pennsylvania. It's a big farm with 800 acres. When Judy was growing up, it was a dairy farm. Today it's a commercial hog farm for 13,000 pigs, raised by Judy's husband.

May's trajectory from farmer's daughter to School District Superintendent was far from straightforward. She hated high school. She had a speech impediment and worked with a speech therapist until 9th grade. But she was also heavily involved in Future Farmers of America and 4-H and held leadership roles in both organizations.

At age 16, she enrolled at Alfred State College. She married at 18 and moved to Florida before settling back in Wellsville with her husband, where she became a meat cutter. She held that job for six years until a supermarket merger eliminated her job and forced her to reevaluate her professional goals.

"My sister talked me into pursuing special education. It made sense. All of my high school friends had disabilities," May said. After earning bachelor's and master's degrees and spending eight years as a special education teacher, she got a call from a neighboring school. That led to her becoming the Superintendent of two small rural districts, before deciding to focus on Friendship alone.

Judy May's core values center on ensuring that kids succeed as members of "one big family." She continually exposes her students to opportunities in higher education, driving one of the vans on regular field trips to Cornell University. She encourages parents to accompany their children when they tour the campus, meet with Cornell students, and stop along the way to visit a museum or two. Last year, every one of Friendship's 100 students in grades 9–12 visited at least two college campuses.

The impact of the Friendship approach is showing results. "Parents are buying in and our kids are applying to colleges all over the country. Something they never did before," said May.

To ensure that her students succeed, May brings her rising college freshmen back to the school in August to talk with them about building their network on campus, understanding their financial aid packages, and how to cut through any red tape they might encounter. Throughout the year, she sends cookies to her college-enrolled former students. "I understand what these gestures mean. My grandmother did that for me," she says. As a former rural student who'd struggled herself, May understands hard work and the circuitous route that so many rural students must take to reach their goals.

for example, faced power differentials in the classroom that manifested in grading and the professor-student relationships (Dees, 2006).

In addition, colleges push students away from their home communities in many ways. If a student takes out a loan to attain a four-year degree, it's hard to earn enough to pay off that loan living in rural America. That means a student must move to suburban or urban America where jobs pay well. Many students, including Kristin Thorpe, who we met in Chapters 3 and 6 go through a period where they feel they don't belong in either world, college or their hometown. They're struggling to fit into a new environment where cultural differences are testing their adherence to lifelong values. While rural communities are more likely to be culturally homogenous and share a cohesive set of beliefs, universities thrive on diverse ideas and populations (Dahill-Brown, 2018). This can cast students as outsiders in their college communities, at least during the adjustment phase. Natan Arrazate (Box 8.1) talks about the connection he and others from his hometown of Van Horn, Texas, feel to their town and community. "Students long to immerse themselves in experiencing new places and meeting new people and getting away from Van Horn, but deep down, there is something about Van Horn they cannot let go of," he explains. "It is easier to go to a college where you know most of your class is going because it is comfortable."

Falling into the Dropout Abyss

A greater portion of students in the United States drop out of college than in any other country in the world. And rural kids are more likely to leave college without a diploma than their urban and suburban peers. Over the last 20 years, more than 31 million students dropped out of college without receiving a degree. Students who don't complete degrees and still owe loans are at a terrible disadvantage. Fifty-six percent of the students who enter college complete four-year degrees within six years, while only 29% attain two-year degrees within three years (Matthiessen, 2017).

College Retention Starts in High School

Students need to develop the mindset and skills to persist in the challenging environment of college well before they enroll. High schools can play a critical role in both preparing students for college life and work, while supporting their recent alumni who are enrolled in college. For instance, Gerry Garfin, the Principal at Christopher Columbus High in the Bronx, visited the University of Vermont (UVM) three times a year to check on his grads studying there; this is one of the reasons 85% of the Columbus students at UVM attained degrees. Several rural schools, including Crown Point and Gilbertsville Mount Upton, bring back their alumni in early January to advise current students about getting ready for college. Research also suggests that college credit in high school positively impacts a student's likelihood of succeeding in and graduating from a postsecondary institution (Swisher, 2016). Simply put, it reduces cost and increases their preparation for college. In Chapter 4, we saw how Drew Malone picked up 30 credits in high school from a nearby community college, which allowed him to finish his bachelor's degree in three years.

Senior Survivors: Preparing for College Success

An example of a simple but effective rural program to prepare college-bound students for success is the Senior Survivor program at Keene Central School, New York. The Senior Survivor program was the brainchild of Superintendent Cynthia Ford Johnston and her colleagues. Keene, which graduates between 15 and 20 students annually, is located in the High Peaks region of the Adirondack Mountains. "More than half of our grads weren't making it through the first year of college," said Johnston.

The response was to deliver a series of seminars on topics related to surviving and excelling in college, such as money, red tape, and finding a mentor on campus. In year two, Keene took its program to two neighboring schools. The next iteration enrolled 80 students and added topics such as transportation, managing finances, health and wellness, time management, personal safety, and housekeeping.

Johnston sees this practical preparation as crucial to students managing the transition from school to college. Ninety-five percent of the first cohort of Keene grads succeeded in year one of college (Holmes & Dalton, 2005).

One reason Senior Survivor succeeds is that it effectively prepares students for the unfamiliar and sometimes uncomfortable terrain ahead. Students who expect, rather than fear, the new experiences that college offers are more likely to succeed. At Crown Point Central School, Principal Tara Spaulding says that of her students who enter four-year colleges, "two in ten drop out or transfer, mostly for social reasons. Their parents are more their friends and enablers and want them to stay home. It's really hard for their kids to leave because they have created a culture—good, bad or otherwise—that is very comfortable."

Natan Arrazate, who attended Van Horn High School in Texas and now works there as a college and career readiness (CCR) advisor, describes a similar dynamic at his small rural school, located 10 miles from the Mexican border. "Students tend to settle because their parents let them. Their parents would rather coddle and keep them from being exposed to failure. I believe our community should learn to embrace failure in order to really teach perseverance and other Essential Skills that will ultimately allow their children to be successful."

What Students Need to Know Before Getting to Campus

To successfully navigate the college experience, first-generation students need more than academic skills—they need financial literacy, self-knowledge, and enough practical knowledge about available options and resources to advocate for themselves. Much of this knowledge, however, will not come from their regular high school coursework (Box 8.3). Don

Box 8.3 What to Expect Once You Get to Campus: Preparing for Common Challenges (Lambert, 2011)

Transitioning to college is a challenge for most students. Whether it's the first time they've been away from home or the first time they've had the freedom to choose what and when to eat or what academic/career path to take, challenges both large and small loom.

Below are some of the challenges students face when they get to college. Educators, mentors, families, alumni, and advisors should speak openly to college-bound students about these common challenges so that they know how to better manage these scenarios and know where and how to find help if they arise (Lambert, 2011).

Money, Money, Money	Money problems are the number one reason why students drop out of college. Chapter 10 shows strategies college students can use to navigate financial aid and related issues.
Making the Grade	Many students struggle to adjust to academic life and are caught off guard by the rigor of college courses. Academic challenges are the number two reason why students drop out of college.
Homesickness	Homesickness plagues many students, usually at the beginning of the first semester. Being away from friends and family and adjusting to an unfamiliar routine leaves them longing for the comfort and familiarity of home.
Time Management and Organization	Balancing class schedules and academic responsibilities with extracurricular and social activities requires a delicate balancing act that eludes many first-year students. Their grades may suffer or they may burn out in a futile attempt to take on too many things at once.

Outing, who oversees retention for students at Lehigh University, believes that nonprofit organizations that work with all stakeholders, such as CFES (College for Every Student), are ideally positioned to help fix the dropout problem. We've identified several ways that students can increase their chances for college success:

- Ensure that students are **sophisticated consumers**. When students research or visit colleges, during their high or middle school years, they need to research dropout rates and ask specific questions about how a college is supporting rural students. They should be willing to ask why students drop out and what the college is doing to prevent this from happening.
- **Develop a success plan**. Before heading off to college, students need to create their own written personal success strategies, ideally developed with a CCR advisor (Chapter 4). Students should also find a mentor with whom they can share early triumphs and turn to for support when the inevitable bumps occur. Success plans should involve the following steps: Go to class; meet with your professors during the first week and at least monthly thereafter; get involved in extracurricular activities, such as intramural sports; and volunteer.
- **Get exposure**, **exposure, exposure**. To prepare its students for the wider world, Crown Point Central School exposes its students to colleges, urban culture, and a continual flood of speakers in its weekly assemblies. That's one of the reasons why 85% of its students who start college attain a degree on time.
- **Learn about money**. Students should review their financial aid packages with their mentors or CCR advisors before leaving for college. They should become familiar with the basic details of financial aid, scholarships, loans, credit cards, and credit ratings. They should also develop an expense sheet to identify how they will spend their money (transportation, books, etc.) and how those expenses will be covered.
- **Cut the red tape**. Before heading off to college, students need to learn strategies for dealing with the red tape they may encounter, such as renewing financial aid, securing a work-study job, registering for the right classes, purchasing books, and other steps that will be new to them.

- **Develop Essential Skills for college success**. We saw at the beginning of this chapter how Jake's mastery of the Essential Skills helped him overcome the obstacles he faced when starting his studies at WVU. The Essential Skills are critical for a successful transition to college.

Getting the Most out of Class (Lambert, 2011)

Another challenge for first-year students is the speed and intensity of college-level coursework, which often comes as a shock. New college students may find that study habits that worked for them in high school are no longer effective. To succeed in college, students need to know how to plan and prepare for class, and this requires organization and teamwork. The tips below may seem obvious, but for some students, mastery of these habits and organizational tips can make or break their academic experience. Students should thus be introduced to these strategies, encouraged to participate actively, and emboldened to ask questions in class early in their college career.

Note-Taking Basics

- Use a designated notebook for each class or organize your notes in folders on your laptop or other device.
- Stay organized.
- Listen/look for repeating ideas or concepts.
- Use a consistent note-taking format.
- Use abbreviations.
- Summarize key ideas.

Organization

- Color-coordinate classes. Keep a three-ring binder and notebook of the same color for **each** class or organize folders and documents on your laptop accordingly.
- Date notes, both written and electronic, each day you take them. Keep all notes, handouts, and homework arranged in chronological order in the appropriate section of your binder or saved in folders on your computer. Color-coordinate classes
- Keep a three-ring binder and notebook (of the same color) for **each** class or organize folders and documents on your laptop accordingly. Keep all notes, handouts, and homework arranged in chronological order in the appropriate section of your binder or saved in folders on your computer.
- Use a calendar/agenda to plan out your homework and study schedule.
- Have a designated study space in your dorm or library.
- Make sure there are no distractions such as loud music or video games in your study zone.
- When you finish your homework, check to be sure that each assignment is in your folder, ready to be turned in or attached to an email to your professor.
- Always keep all graded assignments and materials for class until after your final grade for the course is posted.

Active Listening

- Step 1: Focus

The first step in active listening is to **focus**. Give your full attention to the speaker.

- Step 2: Ask

While you listen, **ask yourself questions** about what the speaker is saying. Then try to answer your questions or see if the speaker answers them. Asking and answering questions in this way can help you make sense of the speaker's message.

- Step 3: Connect

Keep asking yourself why the speaker is saying what he/she is saying. Try to **connect the main ideas** with each other, as well as to any background knowledge you may have on the subject.

- Step 4 Try to Picture

Try to picture in your mind what the speaker is saying. Some people find that they can listen and remember better if they connect words with images.

Stay Engaged

- Track the speaker with your eyes as you listen (the speaker may be the professor or a classmate).
- Sit in the front of the class.
- Help create a positive learning atmosphere where everyone feels comfortable to participate.

Ask Questions

- When you ask a question, write it down or type it so that you can refer to it while reviewing your notes, or when studying for a test.
- Don't be afraid to ask questions. If you are wondering about it, chances are someone else is too.

Team Up

- Find a classmate or two with whom you can compare notes.
    - This is a great opportunity to make sure you don't miss a topic and a chance to review material.
    - When you are given the chance to share the material, it helps you remember it.

- Use Google Drive or another cloud-based platform to compare and share notes with others.

Students should also be introduced to the following strategies for staying on top of their course material between classes:

Smart Study Skills: Work Smarter, Not Harder

- Review material from your books and notes weekly or on an ongoing basis. Don't wait until the last minute.
- Save old assessments and use them to study for future tests. Even if the questions are different, the format/question style might be the same.
- Make study guides.
- Make your own note cards to practice vocabulary and key dates or terms.
- Study with friends. Compare your notes and discuss the key ideas from class.

Read Strategically

- Skim before you read in detail to get the overall gist. Connect this to what you already know about the topic.
- Use pictures and bold headings to preview important points of the text.
- Don't underline or highlight everything, only the important ideas and concepts.
- After each section, stop and think about what you just read.
- Jot down or type out the main idea and details of each paragraph/section of text as you read.
- Use clues from the context to decipher the meaning of unfamiliar words. If that doesn't work, look up the word online.

Time Management and Work–Life Balance: Another Set of Critical Skills (Lambert, 2011)

Learning how to study, manage time, and balance competing priorities are all skills needed for success in college. Here are some self-management strategies and practices students should learn and try to master early in their college career. They'll prove useful not just in college, but in their future professional lives as well.

Priority Setting and Time Management

New college students can sometimes feel they have more homework than hours in the day to do it. And worse, they may have no idea where to start. Here are some useful strategies for staying on track and in control:

- Develop a standard routine for studying and completing homework.
- Carefully review every assignment and note which ones have multiple parts. Schedule time to work on each part, and do not check off your list until each part is complete.
- Don't procrastinate!
- Eliminate any possible distractions.
- Never break your concentration in the middle of an assignment, go strong to the finish.
- Start working on the furthest deadline first. By the time the deadline approaches, you will have already gotten through a chunk of your work and will be less likely to procrastinate.
- Include short, planned breaks in your study time.
- Do the assignment for your favorite subject last.

Coping with Stress

Stress is an almost inevitable part of the college experience, even for well-prepared, academically strong students. Successful students know and expect this, and they use the strategies below to stay accountable to their goals and look after themselves physically and mentally.

- Set realistic goals and manage both your time and expectations for what you can accomplish during each study session.
- Pace yourself! Take small steps toward your goals when necessary.
- Focus on what you can control; avoid being bogged down by what you can't.
- Take time to celebrate small successes and the successes of your friends.
- Reach out and ask for help when you need it. You are not in this alone!
- Stay motivated. Continue to set goals for yourself and raise the bar.

Dropping Out: Where to Plug the Leak?

Who's best able to correct the retention problem: Colleges, students, families, or high schools? Let's look at higher education. College graduation rates in the United States range from 3 to 98%. We know that colleges typically have lower graduation rates when they enroll larger percentages of lower-income students, Black and Latinx students, men, older students, and students with low SAT or ACT scores (Leonhardt and Chinoy, 2019). There tends to be a great deal of finger-pointing about who's responsible for the dropout crisis. Students and their families blame colleges, while high schools blame families and colleges, and colleges tend to blame students, rather than themselves.

The common ground for colleges with high persistence rates is that they have been trying harder and longer to retain students, and they succeed in retaining at-risk students by deepening their connections to other people on campus. More than half the colleges in the country have no strategy or plan to improve retention for rural students or any group for that matter (Leonhardt & Chinoy, 2019). To ensure success, colleges need to understand, acknowledge, and address the unique character development needs of rural students on college campuses. See Box 8.4 for a list of the kind of support students need at different points during the year.

Box 8.4 The First Year of College: A Basic Road Map (Lambert, 2011)

June	Summer orientation
July	Registering for classes
August	Placement exams
	Packing for college
	Connecting with roommates
	Moving to campus
	Making new friends on campus
	Setting semester goals
	First week of classes
September	Purchasing books and class materials
	Balancing schedules and demands
	Add/drop period for classes
	Getting acquainted with support services (writing center, tutoring, etc.)
October	Studying for mid-term exams
	Getting involved in campus activities
	Long weekend break
	Reapplying for FAFSA (Free Application for Federal Student Aid)
November	Thanksgiving break
	Registering for next semester's classes
December	Studying for final exams
	Travel plans
	Winter break
	Paying all campus bills
	Planning for second semester
January	Setting goals for second semester
	Purchasing books and class materials
	Balancing schedules and demands
	Add/drop classes
February	Long weekend break
March	Planning next year's housing
April	Registering for next semester's classes
	Spring break
	Applying for a summer job

May	Studying for final exams Packing up and moving home Paying all campus bills Staying connected to college friends over the summer

Lehigh University, Berea College, and the University of Georgia are three higher education institutions that have made a commitment to enrolling and retaining rural students and have successful programs in place for doing so.

Lehigh University: Extra Help for First-Generation Students

Lehigh University has an entire division, the Center for Student Access and Success, that is committed to identifying, recruiting, enrolling, supporting, and graduating first-generation students from rural and urban communities. While Lehigh graduates 95% of its overall student population, that drops to 87% for first-generation students, a group that includes underserved rural populations.

Here are innovative ways that Lehigh supports rural and other at-risk populations:

- **Beyond graduation**: Lehigh's commitment to its first-generation cohort extends beyond degree attainment. "We're committed to economic mobility for our students and that means providing an education and a network that will transform a student's socioeconomic status," says Don Outing, Lehigh's Vice President for Equity and Community. Fifty-seven percent of the poorest students who attend Lehigh move into the top economic quintile, according to Outing. Lehigh recognizes that internships, research, and study abroad can lead to first jobs and graduate school, and they make these opportunities possible for all students.
- **Expanding financial aid**: The Student Emergency Fund expands the definition of financial aid to help students with unexpected

problems such as a broken-down car, a malfunctioning computer, or family illness. The fund covers the cost of a passport, attendance at a global day at the United Nations, a three-day trip to Montreal, study abroad scholarships, grant writing support and coaching, and career strengths assessment and coaching. Fellowships cover travel, housing, living, and incidental expenses that are part of study abroad and internships.

- **Connecting and deepening**: Lehigh provides rural and other underserved populations peer mentors who address transition challenges. A summer program immerses first-generation students in the Lehigh community with workshops on academic success strategies, financial literacy, health and wellness, and campus support services. Following this program, students meet with faculty and staff in all four years to focus on academic success strategies, career development, leadership training, internships, study abroad opportunities, and financial wellness.
- **Celebrating first-generation students**: Lehigh builds and strengthens relationships between first-generation students, faculty, and staff. Faculty and staff who themselves were first generation or low-income and want to offer special outreach to rural and other underserved students place a sticker on their office door (which reads "1st Generation Fan Club") so that students know there is someone who supports them at that location.

Berea College: Supporting Appalachian Youth

Almost every student at Kentucky's Berea College is from rural Appalachia, with 100% of the student body from low-income households. In fact, each student receives a Tuition Promise Scholarship, meaning no student pays tuition (Strong-Leek, 2018). Despite its low-income, rural student body, and other factors that predict a high dropout rate, Berea College has a strong retention record and is intentional in its efforts to support and retain rural students.

Two innovative programs are worth noting. The Appalachian Male Initiative (AMI) targets white males from rural communities, the Berea cohort least likely to graduate. Another program engages Berea's most at-risk families. Those families are identified during the admissions process, and Erin Connor, who leads the program, calls those families regularly.

The AMI targets male students from some of the nation's most economically distressed rural communities in central and southern Appalachia, which stretches across eight states. All of these male students take a first-semester course that supports their transition to college and their identity development. Outside of class, students are mentored by male faculty members.

According to Chris Green, Director of the Loyal Jones Appalachian Center at Berea, the most at-risk of the three cohorts is the white male cohort, most of whom come from Eastern Kentucky, with others from West Virginia, Tennessee, North Carolina, Virginia, Ohio, and Alabama. The program is designed to help these students feel connected to Berea College. Green explains the difficulty is that these students are from conservative regions of the country, and they can be distrustful of Berea's progressive mission. "Too often, they feel out of place," says Green.

"We help them build strength, develop community, and learn to value their own assets and the inherent beauty of their cultures," says Green. "The program helps the young men feel more at home at Berea, makes them more confident to ask questions in other classes, and gives them a deeper understanding of different perspectives." See Box 8.5 for an example of how a support program at Berea College helped one student stay on track.

Box 8.5 Staying on Track with the Appalachian Male Initiative

The following portrait of James, a participant in the Appalachian Male Initiative (AMI) at Berea College, was written by Richard Childers, a mentor and advocate in the AMI program.

> In 2017, James journeyed from his home in western North Carolina to Berea College. He was quiet but came into the class with strong academic abilities. He worked hard to keep up with his academic work and was certain of his choice to pursue higher education, but this did not

mean his college career would be without challenges. James started off strong. He stayed in contact with us and attended many of the evening events hosted in the Appalachian Center, right next door to where our Appalachian Studies class takes place. James eventually began to express just how important it was for him to have participated in the AMI course as well as this additional programming. Early on he wrote the following in his class journal: "I really miss home and my friends and all the good times we used to have." This is a recurring feeling among AMI students, which is why we focus so heavily on community and relationship-building in the program.

James was passionate about ensuring that the same assistance would be available for other Appalachian students who were making the transition from high school to college. James would later share how the AMI opened his eyes to what a unique place Appalachia was and how lucky he was to be from this region. He wanted others to be able to have that experience and appreciation for their home. James was even set to begin working with the AMI as a paid student mentor. That was prior to unforeseen family dynamics pulling him back home to North Carolina. James' mind was set on finishing his degree, and he assured us that he would not be leaving. But when the semester rolled around, he withdrew and returned home to be with his family just before the beginning of what would have been his junior year.

Back at home, James worked hard and never lost sight of his educational goals. James returned to Berea College, and he continued his studies in the spring of 2020, also continuing to participate and work with the AMI program.

He is just one unique example of the struggles these students face and the type of circumstances that impact their retention rate. One might look at James' academic records and assume that he could have pulled through, but his story shows how even the strongest students have multiple factors at play in their lives, all of which weave into their postsecondary experience in some fashion. The relationship we built kept us in communication with James from the moment he arrived on campus, throughout his decision to leave, and then as he reapplied and returned to school. If it had not been for our regular contact with James, he could have easily fallen through the cracks.

University of Georgia: Helping Rural Students Transition to College Life

The University of Georgia created the ALL Georgia Program to support its 4,000 rural students, about 15% of the student population. The program supports Georgia's rural students with a network of resources and common experiences. Specifically, the program offers a four-week residential, pre-enrollment summer experience, and a handful of credit-bearing courses designed to help rural students be successful in and out of the classroom. Additionally, ALL Georgia offers students what Thomas Chase Hagood, one of the leaders of the program, calls "wraparound services that include mentoring and connections with other students and professors."

These programs highlight the important work that is being done to help keep rural students in school.

Conclusion

There are encouraging signs with the work that is being done to retain rural students. Demographic trends and enrollment challenges are causing colleges throughout the country to look to rural schools and communities as a source of future college students (Pappano, 2017). And colleges know that healthy enrollments depend not just on recruiting but on retaining students. Lehigh University, Berea College and the University of Georgia are just two examples of higher education institutions that are making the commitment to ensure that rural students graduate. There are hundreds more.

Undergirding the importance of this work is the following troubling fact, introduced in Chapter 1: Just 29% of rural youth aged 18 to 24 are enrolled in college, compared to 49% of urban youth in that same age cohort (Krupnick, 2018). This staggering difference reflects rural dropout rates. This chapter has explored some of the unique reasons for rural dropout and provided strategies to fix the problem that can be implemented by higher education institutions, high schools, families, and rural students.

References

Crain, A. (2018). Serving rural students. National Association of Colleges and Employers. www.naceweb.org/career-development/special-populations/serving-rural-students/

Dahill-Brown, S., & Jochim, A. (2018). The power of place: rural identity and the politics of rural school reform. In McShane M. Q. & Smarick A. (Eds.), *No longer forgotten: The triumphs and struggles of rural education in America*. Rowan & Littlefield.

Dees, D. D. (2006). "How do I deal with these new ideas?": The social acculturation of rural students. *Southern Rural Sociology*.

Engle, J. (2007). Postsecondary access and success for first-generation college students. *American Academic, 3*(1), 25–48.

Holmes, D., & Dalton, R. (2005). Peak experiences: Raising aspirations and educational achievement of rural youth in Adirondack communities. Foundation for Excellent Schools.

Krupnick, M. (2018). The students who don't believe college is an option. The Atlantic. www.theatlantic.com/education/archive/2018/01/the-students-who-dont-believe-college-is-an-option/550715/

Lambert, T. (2011). College MAP: Mentoring for persistence guidebook. College For Every Student.

Leonhardt, D. & Chinoy, S. (2019). The college dropout crisis. The New York Times. www.nytimes.com/interactive/2019/05/23/opinion/sunday/college-graduation-rates-ranking.html

Matthiessen, C. (2017). Why are so many college students returning home? GreatSchools. www.greatschools.org/gk/articles/dropping-out-of-college-record-numbers/

Pappano, L. (2017). Colleges discover the rural student. The New York Times. www.nytimes.com/2017/01/31/education/edlife/colleges-discover-rural-student.html

Striplin, J. J. (1999). *Facilitating transfer for first-generation students: Undergraduates whose parents never enrolled in postsecondary education*. Retrieved from ERIC Digest, www.eric.ed.gov.

Strong-Leek, L., Green, C., & Carter, Y. (2018). College men from marginalized America: Male retention initiatives at Berea College. Association of American Colleges and Universities.

Swisher, A. (2016). Preparing rural students for college and career. Washington Monthly. https://washingtonmonthly.com/2016/08/05/preparing-rural-students-for-college-and-career/

Building STEM Interest, Awareness, and Readiness

The Future is Now

Sierra White's dream coming out of rural Willsboro Central School in northeastern New York was to become a doctor. She took that postsecondary aspiration across Lake Champlain to the University of Vermont (UVM), where she soon realized it wasn't going to happen.

It wasn't lack of ability—rather, she discovered another love. The CFES (College for Every Student) Scholar was thriving as a biology major and preparing for medical school when laboratory research caught her attention. She joined a research lab at her advisor's suggestion and began studying eye field migration and development, using zebrafish as a model organism.

"I developed a passion to learn about disease progression," says White. In her freshman year, she wrote a paper on cystic fibrosis, which had seriously impacted members of her own family. "Then I realized that I wanted to pursue a career in scientific research with an emphasis on lung disease development, progression, and treatment," she says.

White applied to the PhD program in Cellular, Molecular, and Biomedical Sciences at UVM. When she was not accepted, she turned to her mentor for advice. "She told me I absolutely should not give up and helped me get a job to advance my experience so I would have a better chance applying the second time around," says White.

After spending a year working for a science equipment development company, White re-applied. This time she was not denied. "The most valuable lesson I learned is that hard work, goal setting, and most important, perseverance, are keys to achieving your goals, especially in the sciences. In the sciences we must expect but never accept failure," says White. "All of this molded me into a promising scientist."

White continued to use these Essential Skills™ when she began studying allergic asthma, pulmonary fibrosis, influenza infection, and COVID-19. Her dissertation focuses on mechanisms behind pathogenesis of allergic asthma with the goal of finding new targets for better treatment.

"My advice to younger students is to not beat yourself up if you aren't 100% sure what you want to do with your life coming out of high school," she says. "Choose a major that interests you, but also take classes in other areas to get a feel for what might pique your interest. Be agile. You can always change your mind and still develop a successful career."

This chapter examines the challenges faced by promising students like Sierra: For numerous reasons, both cultural and structural, rural students are less likely than their urban and suburban counterparts to pursue careers in science, technology, engineering and math (STEM)—a troubling trend that leaves young rural adults and their communities locked out of opportunities in many growing industries. The chapter begins by examining the obstacles deterring rural students from STEM majors and careers, then shows practical, replicable steps that schools and communities can take to counteract these forces. The chapter ends by sharing the success stories of a diverse group of rural young adults who've beaten the odds and successfully pursued STEM careers.

Beating the Odds

Sierra White overcame two obstacles when she became a scientist with a PhD: Being female and being from a rural area. Beginning in high school, women often begin to sort themselves out of STEM academic pathways by choosing not to enroll in high-level math courses, for instance. By the time they get to college, they pursue STEM majors at lower rates than males (Kahn & Ginther, 2017). While rural high schoolers hold equal or greater interest in STEM careers compared to their urban and suburban peers (Crain & Webber, 2020), they are less likely to enroll in college and particularly unlikely to enroll in a research university (Koricich, Chen, & Hughes, 2018). Researchers have also found that traditional gender norms in rural areas may hinder students who are interested in certain career fields (e.g., male students going into nursing) (Ali & Saunders, 2008), a dynamic that could exacerbate barriers for females interested in STEM fields that remain dominated by men (Blickenstaff, 2005).

One of the primary challenges faced by rural students is limited exposure to STEM career paths and fewer community role models in engineering, technology, and scientific fields. In some cases, family members may also object to rural students pursuing STEM careers that will take them away from their local communities (Grimes, Arrastía-Chisholm, & Bright, 2019). Many studies also point to weak academic preparation in high school as a key obstacle to rural students' postsecondary success in STEM. Rural school districts are less likely to offer sufficient opportunities in Advanced Placement (AP) coursework (Gagnon & Mattingly, 2016), and rural students tend to graduate with less rigorous math preparation than their nonrural peers (Anderson & Chang, 2011). Brogan Morton, who grew up in a small town in northern New Hampshire, says, "Plenty of kids in my school were good in math and science but other things got in the way. You can't feel like you're the only one who's done it before."

Little Obstacles Multiply: Why STEM is a Hard Choice for Rural Students

As we saw in previous chapters, the pull of home and family is strong in rural communities, which makes venturing away from home for college or work an especially intimidating process for rural students. This is particularly true for those wanting to pursue STEM careers. "As an engineer, I had to leave home because there are no jobs in my profession," Morton says. "But if you grew up in suburbia, you don't have to make that leap. I could have stayed in New Hampshire if I'd lived in the southern part of the state, near Boston."

For this reason, geography plays an important role in the distribution of STEM workers (Xue & Larson, 2015), which in turn influences efforts in rural schools to develop the next generation of STEM talent. There's not only a shortage of STEM role models in rural locales, there's a dearth of STEM teachers as well (Harris & Hodges, 2018).

Even if rural school districts want to improve STEM learning opportunities for their students, complex bureaucratic hurdles make it more difficult for them to capitalize on funding opportunities (Yettick, Baker, Wickersham, & Hupfeld, 2014). All of these factors account for a gradual decline in the rural STEM pipeline that begins in high school and continues throughout the postsecondary pathway. In short, lots of little obstacles—limited exposure to STEM careers, geographic isolation from postsecondary institutions, lower college enrollment rates, and inadequate preparation for continued study in STEM—multiply to create a cumulative disadvantage for rural students trying to pursue STEM (Crain & Webber, 2020). "Every small thing is another grain of sand in the gears," Morton says.

Fewer Rural Medical Students = Fewer Rural Doctors

Trends for rural students in the medical school pipeline reflect the pattern we're seeing across STEM fields. While students from rural areas make up 20% of the population in schools across the country, they made up only 4.3% of medical students as of 2017, representing a 15-year decline in rural students going to medical school. The number of rural applications to medical school dropped by 18% between 2002 and 2017, while they increased by 59% from urban applicants (Finnegan, 2019).

These trends are troubling not just for would-be medical students but also for their communities. Rural populations have higher rates of chronic illnesses, get fewer preventive services, and have seen fewer gains in life expectancy than urban populations. The gap in access to physician care is contributing to increased rural mortality, and many medical schools across the United States have redoubled their efforts to recruit students willing to work in underserved rural communities (Gong et al., 2019).

Why STEM Matters for Rural Communities

In addition to considering the importance of fulfilling rural America's healthcare needs, it is important to consider the economic changes on the horizon that may impact rural communities. STEM fields are particularly important to this conversation, since many of these changes are driven by innovation in science and technology or shifting priorities in public policy.

For example, the increasing potential for America's knowledge workers to operate remotely—including professionals in information technology, computer science, or medicine—opens the door for rural locales to recruit new residents into their communities. Sweeping new legislative proposals such as the Green New Deal have the potential to transform rural America, especially if state and federal governments pour money into local renewable energy projects. And finally, exciting new developments in traditionally rural fields such as agriculture are creating a growing reliance on highly-trained talent in engineering, plant genomics, environmental science, and computer science. Some of these events may spur renewed interest in rural math and science education and drive an increased demand for STEM talent development in rural communities. The time to start preparing rural students to take advantage of these opportunities is now.

Cultivating STEM-Ready Students: What Works

Before rural students can embark on college-level STEM coursework and careers, it is imperative that we help them develop and maintain STEM awareness, interest, and competency throughout their K–12 education. The following key strategies and principles, along with examples of hands-on programs, can be used to spark interest in science and technology concepts and careers. At the end of this chapter, there is a resource section with hands-on activities that support STEM awareness, interest, and learning.

General Principles for Building STEM Awareness

Here are some strategies parents, teachers, and community supporters can use to help students become STEM ready:

- **Start young**: One of the hurdles that STEM educators face is trying to engage older students in STEM activities for the first time. It's never too early to start STEM education. Kids need to get excited about science early to inject imagination and creativity into the learning process (Earth Networks: Education, 2017). In northern New York, the CFES health care program involves students in grades 6–12 acting as peer mentors to share STEM knowledge with elementary school youth. CFES helps students as young as kindergarten approach STEM through our core practices.

- **Find partners**: As we saw in Chapters 5 and 6, business and higher education partners are invaluable resources for rural schools wanting to stay on top of current educational and economic trends and connect with the bigger world. Keeping up with the rapid evolution of STEM-related jobs is difficult for rural educators, but partners who are actively involved in this evolution can make this happen. Partnerships help students and teachers connect the dots between STEM courses and STEM professions (Cohen et al., 2013). For instance, utilizing hospitals as partners allows students exposure to careers in medical fields that they may not have known about and how these careers support overall patient care. They are also places where students can talk with experts about STEM careers and STEM study. Partners can provide STEM career exposure for students through job shadowing and internships, supporting curriculum development, and providing professional development for teachers. State and regional industry groups (e.g., biotechnology or agribusiness organizations) have a vested interest in expanding the STEM workforce and may be eager to serve as partners for rural schools or facilitate connections with individual companies.
- **Find a mentor**: Lack of awareness about possible STEM careers is problematic for the general student population and especially for rural students. They need to see STEM workers and scientists like Sierra White as real people. Through mentoring interactions, CFES exposes students to STEM role models, including local professionals.
- **Encourage STEM study**: Push students to take math and science courses in high school. Establishing math and science efficacy during high school years is a key driver in providing a foundation for continued learning in STEM disciplines (Maltese & Tai, 2011). Just as importantly, policymakers should help make it possible for more rural students to complete advanced coursework in STEM (Gagnon & Mattingly, 2016)—courses that will put them on a path to college and prepare them to succeed if they choose to continue in a STEM discipline.
- **Make STEM interesting**: Activities that spark curiosity and interest—including mentoring, project-based learning, college STEM tours, and meeting STEM professionals—help reinforce STEM pathways by providing ongoing exposure. Infusing STEM into other areas of learning helps build student interest and awareness. STEM activities can be incorporated into the CFES core practices (Mentoring, Essential Skills,

and Pathways to College and Career) to help students build interest and awareness.

- **Harness the Essential Skills**: Sierra White talked about the importance of setting goals and the value of other Essential Skills such as perseverance and agility. CFES helps students leverage Essential Skills to achieve STEM readiness through student-led service projects and through resources like the STEM Scholar Map (Box 9.2).

CFES STEM Resources

CFES has developed resources to help students gain awareness of STEM fields and careers and learn to see themselves as future STEM professionals. Here we present two of them, the CFES STEM activity chart (Box 9.1) and the STEM Scholar Map (Box 9.2).

Box 9.1 The CFES STEM Chart: Suggested Activities by Grade Level

The following chart lists activities by grade level for the three CFES practices (Mentoring, Essential Skills, and Pathways to College and Career) that engage students to become STEM ready.

Grade	Mentoring	Essential Skills	Pathways to College and Career
All	• All mentoring activities are school-based. • Mentoring programs engage multiple mentors with ties to STEM: teachers and staff, community members, college students, and older peers studying STEM.	• Participate in ongoing Essential Skills development through interactions with local STEM professionals, college students, older STEM Scholars, and CFES professional staff.	Through school – college and school – business partnerships, students: • participate in college visits • meet STEM professionals.

Grade	Mentoring	Essential Skills	Pathways to College and Career
	• Mentors/mentees consistently engage in Essential Skills and Pathways to College and Career activities together.	• Engage in at least two student-driven STEM-related service activities each year to apply Essential Skills to real life experiences.	
9–12	• Develop and teach STEM lesson/activity to younger students. • Interview a STEM professional about what they do and share the information with peers (through school news, or other means). • Facilitate completion of the CFES STEM Scholar Map for a group of younger students. • Tutor middle school students in math/science.	• Identify a STEM-related problem affecting your school/community and share strategies to overcome this problem with community leaders. • Identify local flora/fauna and create an interactive tour for younger students, visitors, and/or community groups. • Organize a technology fair for your school community.	Ask students to: • Attend STEM-specific summer opportunities at area colleges. • Research STEM- specific scholarship opportunities. • Participate in a STEM class and/or lab during a college visit. • Take part in internships and job shadowing with STEM professionals.

Grade	Mentoring	Essential Skills	Pathways to College and Career
	• Read a children's book with a STEM protagonist to an elementary class.	• Participate in an engineering project on a college campus and ask students to identify the Essential Skills that they used. • Organize a math/science competition for middle school students.	• Use the Brilliant Career Lab website to identify careers in STEM and learn about the degree re-quirements for those pathways.
6–8	• Research a famous STEM role model and create a presentation for younger peers on why that person inspires you. • Tutor elementary students in math/science to prepare them for middle school.	• Lead a team of peers to create an activity book that teaches STEM concepts to younger students. • Plan and participate in a service project focusing on the environment (e.g., beach cleanup, recycling program, community garden). • Teach senior citizens how to use technology (e.g., computers, calculators).	Ask students to: • Research STEM colleges and careers. • Participate in STEM-specific scavenger hunt on a college campus. • Attend a STEM class specifically designed for middle school students while on a college visit. • Complete the CFES STEM Scholar Map.

Grade	Mentoring	Essential Skills	Pathways to College and Career
3–5	• Guide younger mentees on a nature walk around the school, helping them identify different plants and bugs • Get a book from the library on STEM experiments for kids; get students to ask their mentor to do one of the activities with them.	Ask students to: • Work with a team to complete a STEM activity (science experiment, coding project). • Talk about the skills needed to work in different STEM fields (teamwork, agility, etc.).	• Watch videos about different STEM professions. • Take a guided virtual tour of a college's STEM facilities.
K–2	Ask students to: • Pick a STEM-inspired book to read with their reading buddy. • Draw a STEM professional at work, ask their peers to guess the job.	Get students to: • Engage in STEM learning activities that promote curiosity and problem-solving • Identify a person in their network with a STEM job.	• Hear from STEM guest speakers (college student or professional) about their job and education through classroom presentations or virtually through "Skype a Scientist." • Attend a science fair hosted by upper grades to see STEM in action.

Box 9.2 STEM Scholar Map

The STEM Scholar Map was developed by CFES Brilliant Pathways as a resource to help students in grades 6–11 see how the Essential Skills and Pathways to College and Career, two of three CFES practices, can build STEM readiness. The graphic organizer includes prompts that allow it to be completed independently or as part of a facilitated discussion. Facilitators may adjust the level of information included to be applicable to a range of grade levels.

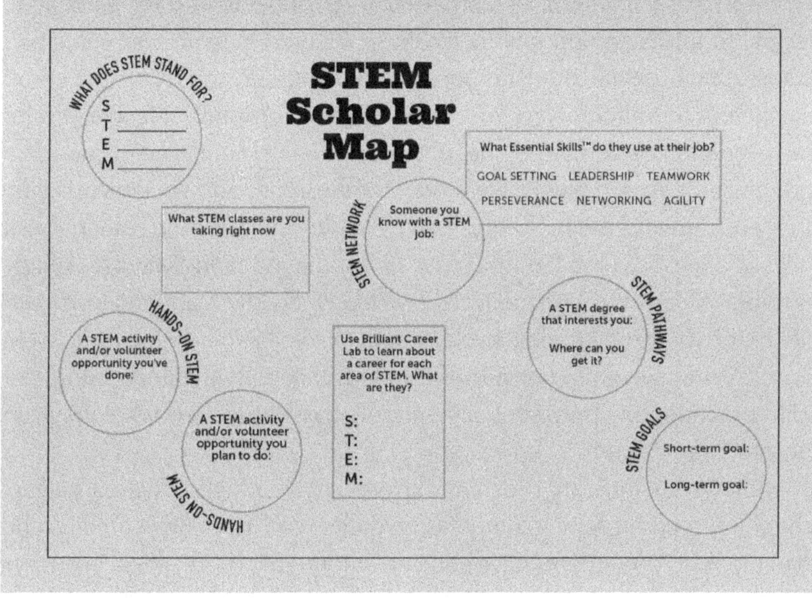

Bringing Science to Students

Introducing rural students to friendly STEM professionals and providing opportunities for them to see these professionals at work is an especially compelling way to inspire them to consider careers in science and technology. In the next few sections, we share a diverse variety of programs that have successfully engaged and educated rural students.

Launching Rural Careers in Engineering

In 2013, Dave Morell was presented a gift: Morell had been teaching high school math and college physics when he was asked to design an engineering program that would serve a dozen or so students annually from ten rural schools at the BOCES (Boards of Cooperative Educational Services) Center in Otsego, located in the rolling hills of central New York, a stone's throw from the Baseball Hall of Fame and surrounded by dairy farms.

"Most participating schools have 25–30 students in their graduating classes, so this is an opportunity for those talented in math and science to do something special. Students apply to the program, and those that enroll take the bus to Milford, New York, every day," says Morell. "I lead a physics and calculus class and an engineering project-based course every morning, and the students are taught literature, composition, and social studies by other educators in the building." Every couple of weeks, the students visit colleges and STEM-related industries in the Binghamton-Syracuse-Albany corridor. "When we visit colleges, we don't do the standard tour. Our kids meet with engineering students and professors and sit in on STEM classes. When we go to businesses, our kids talk with engineers and other STEM practitioners. They connect with role models and see what they can become," says Morell.

Morell's engineering program mirrors that of a high-powered magnet school in an urban setting. Students graduate with 18 college credits, and 98 of the first 100 students have gone on to four-year universities, including Cornell, Georgia Tech, Virginia Tech and Rochester Institute of Technology. Almost everyone does an internship along the way at places like SpaceX, Northrop Grumman, and Carnegie Robotics, LLC.

What do Morell's students do after earning four-year degrees? They become software, civil, computer, structural project, and mechanical engineers, as well as aquatic biologists, chemists, and financial consultants.

Morell says his kids are more than smart and successful. "They are athletes, scouts and musicians. They go home after school and work on family farms, mow the grass, take care of younger siblings. They care about their families and they make their communities better," he explains. Morell got a gift and gave it back: Opportunities through STEM for 100 (and counting) rural kids in central New York.

Building Health Care Interest and Awareness

One of the first things students want to hear about when Dr. John Fortune walks into their classroom is his most shocking cases as a trauma surgeon. By the end of class, all they want to hear about is the high-quality jobs in health care he just introduced to them.

Fortune, a professor of surgery at UVM's Larner College of Medicine, traverses the North Country with his interactive presentation as part of a careers program in STEM/health care sponsored by the Brooks and Joan Fortune Family Foundation in conjunction with CFES Brilliant Pathways.

Fortune's current work with CFES allows him to focus on the part of his 35-year career as a professor, researcher, and renowned trauma surgeon that he cherishes most: Educating young people.

"The one thing I really missed is teaching residents and medical students," says Fortune. "To watch a young man or woman progress through their educational pathways and develop the skills to work as a mature surgeon is pretty amazing. Talking to young kids through CFES and introducing them to careers in health care is similarly gratifying and really important to me."

One of Fortune's main goals is to ensure that students are aware of the wide variety of career opportunities in health care, which are increasing along with America's aging population. The need for respiratory therapists, radiology technologists, pharmacists, home health providers, and a host of new jobs is expected to increase for decades. It is estimated that demand for nurses alone will rise from 16 million to more than 22.5 million in the next five years.

Fortune has witnessed the evolution of the health care profession since entering medical school at Duke University, where he majored in English literature as an undergraduate. He grew up watching his father, a chemist for Eli Lilly and Company, conduct medical research, including the creation of the first colorimetric analysis test used to measure glucose levels in urine. That breakthrough paved the way to ensure the appropriate dose of insulin for the treatment of diabetes.

After medical school, Fortune worked on a National Institutes of Health Fellowship in lung physiology at University of California San Diego before moving to the Albany Medical Center, New York, where he finished his residency and became Director of Trauma. He later served as the Director of Trauma and Chief of General Surgery at the University of Arizona while also running a residency program. He became interested in simulation and surgical education at the Southern Illinois University before moving to Syracuse to lead the trauma program and burn unit and serve as Head of General Surgery.

"I've been fortunate to have worked at institutions on the cutting edge of research and practice," says Fortune, who came to the UVM Medical Center as a trauma, burn, and critical care surgeon. Subsequently, he was the Interim Medical Director of the Regional Transport System to develop a coordinated system to transfer critically ill patients between the hospitals in the vast, rural region of Vermont and northern New York.

"One of our proudest accomplishments was the initiation of a hospital-based aeromedical transport system to reduce the time for patients to get to definitive care," says Fortune. "This is going to save a lot of lives."

Six years ago, Fortune and his wife, Jan, moved to Essex, New York, where they had summered for over 30 years. He soon launched Sim*Vivo, a company that designs medical simulation modules for medical and nursing students to learn specific tasks. Ever the innovator, Fortune's company is developing an innovative chest tube with a United States Army grant meant to encourage small companies to solve major medical problems.

"When someone is injured and has blood in their chest, the tubes that are currently used frequently fail to remove all of it, resulting in residual blood clots that require additional surgery," says Fortune as he pulls a long clear tube with a gadget attached to it out of his bag. "We were funded to develop a tube like this prototype that you can place in the bottom of the chest where the blood goes. Is that cool or what?"

Fortune, working with CFES professionals, brings devices like these made by Sim*Vivo to schools across the Adirondacks. They tell students about the education required to access jobs and then demonstrate specific job tasks, such as how nurses measure oxygen saturation and heart rates, how phlebotomists draw blood (demonstrating on a surgical mannequin arm), and how surgeons and emergency room physicians tie sutures.

"Batman" Builds Interest in STEM

It doesn't take long for Brogan Morton to capture the attention of middle school students. After an energetic introduction, he dims the lights as images of flying bats appear on a screen behind him, while he makes a case for why the world's only flying mammal is worth saving.

A mechanical engineer and founder of Wildlife Imaging Systems LLC, a leading provider of advanced machine vision solutions to further the conservation of wildlife, Morton speaks from experience. As Senior Product Manager at NRG Systems in Hinesburg, Vermont, he guided the successful development and commercialization of their Bat Deterrent System using ultrasound to reduce bat mortality near wind turbines.

Morton shares his passion for STEM with CFES Scholars across the North Country by offering examples from the wind and solar industries and providing hands-on demonstrations of engineering and scientific principles.

During a recent trip to Moriah Central School, students peppered Morton with questions: "Do bats suck blood from livestock?," "Are they totally nocturnal?," "Can they see in the dark?" Morton had all the answers and then some, including the fact that bats only have one pup at a time, making it hard for their populations to recover after the devastation caused by white-nose syndrome, a disease caused by an invasive fungus that affects hibernating bats. This makes it incredibly difficult to get them off the endangered species list.

With his audience fully engaged, Morton adeptly pivots to more STEM-related topics. He relates the fact that bats can "see" in the dark by making noises and waiting for sound waves to bounce back to know if they can fly safely forward.

"I learned a lot from his presentation," says Moriah student Addison Nephew. "The information about bats made it really interesting and led into the science part and how the technology worked. I hope he comes back."

In his presentations, Morton also debunks the myth that engineers sit behind a desk all day. He gives examples from his fieldwork over the years at NRG Systems, his part in the development of aerospace systems at a small startup, and as technical lead for several projects run by the Department of Energy and the Small Business Innovation Research of the Department of Defense.

Annual STEM Week for Rural Students

In April of each year, CFES connects rural students to a series of learning experiences and career resources in STEM. CFES STEM Week offers opportunities for over 2,000 rural students from Adirondack K–12 schools to see what STEM careers are and hear how to pursue them.

CFES STEM Week in the Adirondacks features a broad range of interactive activities with health care professionals, business leaders, and student mentors. College and business representatives also discuss higher education and career options. Here is an example of the activities scheduled during STEM Week:

The week's activities started with a live chat from Saranac High School, where trauma surgeon Dr. John Fortune of the UVM Medical Center (introduced above) spoke with students about the array of career options in health care and what it takes to become a health care professional.

"It's going to be tough, but all of you in this room can do it," he tells the students, "because with commitment and with hard drive—with 'grit,' as they say at CFES—the challenges can be overcome, and you can enter this very gratifying health care profession."

Early in the week, a sense of accomplishment pervades the CFES Center in Essex as students from Adirondack schools gather for hands-on learning and problem-solving in robotics workshops led by faculty and cadets from the United States Military Academy at West Point. Students, collaborating with peers from different schools, applied engineering principles, current technology, and their math skills to create code and program robots. The day ended with a competition where students saw the results of their efforts as they directed their robots to navigate a preset path.

Health care specialists also interacted with CFES students at a college and career health care fair hosted in Plattsburgh by CFES and the UVM Health Network—Champlain Valley Physicians Hospital (CVPH). Demonstrations by EMTs from CVPH, the School of Radiology, the laboratory, and other hospital departments and services showed students how medical equipment works and the health conditions these professionals treat. In addition, representatives from North Country Community College, Clinton Community College, SUNY Plattsburgh, and Champlain Valley Technical Education and Careers Center (CV-TEC) offered information about STEM career options and pathways.

At a separate event, student mentors who were trained through the CFES program joined business leaders to conduct a series of STEM-learning activities at Ticonderoga Middle School. The Superintendent of the Schroon Lake Central School District opened the day with a fun physics exercise—balancing a chair on his chin. A representative from International Paper explained and demonstrated the workings of a standard pump in the paper-making process, and environmental educators from the Lake George Association demonstrated water filtration methods. Ticonderoga High School mentors led several STEM sessions, including one where students built freestanding structures, as tall as possible, with 20 pieces of spaghetti, one yard of masking tape, and one marshmallow which was to be placed on top.

Success Stories: Ten Rural Students Who Became STEM Professionals

Thousands of reports over the last decade provide different projections for STEM needs in the United States, but all agree that the nation must greatly increase its STEM talent pool and a failure to do so will affect our global economic competitiveness. The relative absence of rural students in STEM career pathways thus translates into lost human capital. That will affect not only the quality of individual lives but the economic vitality of rural regions for years to come (Crain & Webber, 2020).

Despite the obstacles they face, many rural students do successfully pursue STEM careers. Here we present profiles of ten such students, all now thriving in their chosen professions. Each story is a tale of what can be, with advice for how younger students can succeed on the STEM pathway.

Billy, Engineer

Billy grew up in a small town in northern Idaho. He didn't know what engineering was until 11th grade. That's when his high school guidance counselor told him, "You're really good at math and science. You should consider becoming an engineer." When Billy asked his counselor what engineers do, the counselor didn't really know. After checking with a friend, the counselor reported back to Billy, "they design sewer plants." Billy ended up attending Idaho State University. "I chose mechanical engineering because I love to build stuff," he said. "Plenty of kids are good in math and science, but other things get in the way. It's difficult when others see you as a nerd, but that changes over time. Smart people are perceived as being cooler as they get older." Today, Billy works on clean energy technologies at the Idaho National Laboratory in Idaho Falls.

 Chris, Engineer

As a 10th grader, Chris was suspended from school for hacking into the Superintendent's email. One of the provisions for his return to Peru Central School in northern New York was that Chris join CFES. This led him to tutor students in math after school and participate in Leadership Lunches with Principal Chris Mazzella. "Chris got his act together and became the first in his family to attend college," Mazzella said. Four years later, after service initiatives that included tutoring middle schoolers in coding and computer science programming and teaching adults digital literacy, Chris graduated from SUNY Plattsburgh. He now designs engineering parts for large aircrafts. His advice to younger students: "Find something you're passionate about. Don't just go through the motions."

 Clare, Nurse

Clare grew up on a large farm in the wheat fields of Illinois, three hours southwest of Chicago. After graduating from high school, she went on to pursue her associate degree in applied sciences at Heartland Community College. Twenty-four years later, after raising three children, Clare received an online bachelor's degree from Purdue University. Currently she's working in Iowa as a behavioral health nurse, helping patients deal with pain and stress. "Life is not a straight line," she says. Her advice is to be agile: "Life changes your perspective. Be ready."

 Dana, Mechanical Engineer

Dana is testament to the impact of Dave Morell's engineering class, discussed earlier in this chapter, which she calls "the most incredible learning experience ever." Four years after Dave's class, Dana is enrolled at Rochester Institute of Technology (RIT) where she will soon attain both a bachelor's and master's in mechanical engineering. As part of her RIT program, Dana has interned across the country at four high-tech corporations, including SpaceX in southern California where she was part of a vehicle engineering team that designed and developed test standards. Growing up in Garrattsville, New York, a town of 232 people, the challenge of being from a rural community hit home in high school when Dana was part of the robotics team at Edmeston Central School. Competing against other schools opened her eyes "to the disparity between rural and suburban schools." She's felt support throughout her STEM journey, which began in elementary school. As a young girl, Dana's parents nurtured her interest in all things mechanical. "My dad used to take me to car museums. My love for cars is only exceeded by my love for things that fly." At the BOCES engineering program, she says, "Dave facilitated the pursuit of passion."

Matt, Geologist

Matt grew up in Scotia, New York, and attended SUNY Plattsburgh to play lacrosse and study geology. Matt says he chose geology because he loves the outdoors. His high school earth science teacher influenced his STEM pursuit. "He made the curriculum interesting, and I loved the hands-on lab where we applied concepts to real world applications," he says. Currently working at CDM Smith, a national construction and engineering firm, Matt's advice for future geologists and others who pursue STEM professions is: "Incorporate what you like to do into your profession."

Pete, Fish Biologist

Pete grew up the youngest of nine children in Vergennes, Vermont, with a dream of becoming a pilot. He attended Embry-Riddle Aeronautical University and graduated with a bachelor's degree in aeronautical science. A love of fishing and the outdoors, however, inspired him to earn a second bachelor's degree, this time in environmental science, from Lyndon State College, before attending graduate school at the University of New Brunswick in Canada to study Atlantic salmon and habitat restoration. After doing some seasonal work for the Vermont Fish and Wildlife Department, he was offered a full-time job as a fisheries biologist with the department. "If you want a job, start by volunteering," says Pete, who has been in his current position since 2007 after volunteering for AmeriCorps. "Once people see that you're committed, you're there."

Phil, Math Teacher

Phil grew up in Berlin, New Hampshire, and attended University of New Hampshire (UNH), where he majored in kinesiology. After graduating from UNH, Phil practiced sports medicine at a middle school in Connecticut until he was coaxed into the classroom to teach math. "I always loved math," says Phil. "In elementary school, I would walk two blocks to the home of my fourth-grade teacher, Mrs. Gagnon, who would challenge me with math problems. I loved it." Phil has advice for aspiring STEM educators: "If you're interested in a particular subject, especially in STEM, find a teacher/mentor. Let them know you're passionate. They'll love it."

Sophie, Test Operations Engineer

Growing up in a small town in Kansas, Sophie was inspired to ask big questions about space while looking up at the beautiful evening sky. She soon discovered a love of physics and the study of the universe but struggled in class. With the support of teachers, friends, and mentors, she eventually graduated with degrees in physics and applied mathematics and statistics from Johns Hopkins University in 2018. She describes her STEM track as less of a pathway and "more of a bowling lane with the bumpers up," with many role models helping keep her on course. Now a proud member of the Blue Origin space mission team, Sophie says she found magic in stargazing, puzzles, design challenges, and deep discussions with friends and teachers, which she attributes to her success. "If STEM feels overwhelming, you are not alone," she says. "Don't be afraid to reach out to teachers, friends, parents, or even professionals for support. Many of life's biggest rewards result from its biggest challenges, and there are many mentors who want to help you reap those rewards. You can even be a mentor for other people like your siblings and fellow classmates."

Tara, Emergency Responder

Tara grew up in Hancock, a town of 600 in western Massachusetts. After completing 8th grade with two other students in her class, she headed off to the regional high school in Williamstown. Shortly thereafter, she joined the local fire department and followed her emergency medical services dream for the next several decades. Today, Tara heads the 911 line in Pittsfield, Massachusetts, having held various emergency services positions since high school. "Holding someone's hand when they're in danger and giving them comfort is one of the greatest gifts we can give a fellow human being. Now I do it virtually," says Tara. Her advice for others who want to follow her STEM path is: "Volunteer. Give back to your community. Those hours of service are valuable not only to yourself but [to] the people you are serving."

Yuki, Environmentalist

Yuki graduated from Kohala High School, located in the village of Kapa'au, on the northern tip of the big island of Hawaii. As you drive north to this sleepy town, vast lava fields turn into lush vegetation, and you pass signs that mark the crossing of wild donkeys. In high school, Yuki took a deep interest in environmental studies, taking on projects that involved mitigation of sediment deposits into the ocean. She continued to pursue environmental sciences at Harvard where she completed her bachelor's and stayed on to pursue graduate work in environmental studies. Her advice for younger peers is: "Follow your passion."

STEM Activities to Educate and Inspire

Some students motivate themselves; most, however, need to be encouraged to follow these paths. Teachers and mentors can use the STEM-centered activity below (Resource 9.1) to inspire students.

Resource 9.1 Adventures in Engineering: Creating a Rube Goldberg Machine

Introduction

A Rube Goldberg device is a machine built for a simple task in an overly complicated way. Imagine a machine that is designed to ring a bell, pour water into a glass, or pop a balloon. You can easily do these tasks manually, so making the process more complex is an exercise in creativity. Rube Goldberg machines rely on chain reactions to complete their goal. A well-known example is the board game Mousetrap.

Materials

- assorted materials from around the house:
  - students will need a variety of objects that can move in different ways (rolling, swinging, pushing, and falling, for instance), and
  - recycled materials. Paper towel rolls, cardboard boxes, cans, and bottles are great choices for making a machine.

Instructions

- Use the steps of the engineering design process (planning, testing, and improving) to build a Rube Goldberg machine to accomplish a simple task.
- Ask students to identify what task they want to accomplish with their design. For example, ask: What will your machine try to accomplish? What simple problem will it solve in a complex way? Offer some ideas: Pouring water into a glass, ringing a bell, turning on a light, watering a plant, shutting a door, popping a balloon, or opening a book.

- Have students brainstorm the series of steps that will make up the chain reaction in the machine that will be designed. Instruct them to find materials around their house or classroom that can be used. Remind them that they need a variety of objects that can move in different ways (swinging, rolling, pushing, or falling) and encourage them to think about recycled materials that can be used. Think about different simple machines, like pulleys, levers, and inclines, which can be used in the design process.
- Now that students have decided on the chain reaction for their machine, ask them to follow the steps below to bring their project to life:
  - **Plan**: Ask participants to draw out each part of their machine design. Ideally, the machine will cause a chain reaction, so remind students to think about how the steps will connect.
  - **Build**: Use materials to create a Rube Goldberg machine! It may be helpful to put it together one step at a time and test that part a few times to make sure it works the way they imagined.
  - **Test**: Test the machine from beginning to end. It may take a few tries to get each step to work and connect smoothly, but don't give up! They may also need to make adjustments and improvements as they go.
  - **Improve**: Once the machines have been tested, ask students to think about what improvements they would make.
    - What steps would you add?
    - How could you make it run more smoothly?
    - What improvements did you have to make as you were building and testing your machine?

Take it from Here

- Think of a problem that exists in the school or community and design a machine or piece of technology to solve that problem. It can be a simpler solution than a Rube Goldberg machine!

- Which Essential Skills were used to complete this activity?
- What was challenging about this activity? Did participants persevere?
- Would the activity be easier in teams?
- Why is agility an important skill for an engineer to have? How was the skill of agility used in this activity?

Conclusion

In the United States, low-income students are ten times less likely to attain STEM degrees than their high-income peers. Given that the majority of the new, high-paying jobs in our country will be in STEM, it's crucial that we fix this broken pipeline and include more low-income students, especially those from rural communities. A growing body of research suggests that rural students may face a cumulative disadvantage—a series of obstacles that add up to a major equity gap—when it comes to STEM career pathways.

One place rural schools can turn for STEM partner support is the health care industry. While 20% of new jobs will be in health care, industry experts predict a dire shortage of health care workers. This has motivated hospitals and other health care sectors to sponsor readiness programs for rural students. Other industry groups in fields such as biotechnology or agriculture may also be willing partners in building rural student awareness about STEM career fields and helping them to prepare.

This chapter outlined strategies for providing hands-on experiences for rural students to build STEM awareness, interest, and readiness. We shared stories of successful rural STEM events and programs and of STEM role models and their advice for rural students. We also shared tips and resources for building STEM readiness programs in rural schools.

References

Ali, S. R., & Saunders, J. L. (2008). The career aspirations of rural Appalachian high school students. *Journal of Career Assessment, 17*(2), 172–188.

Anderson, R., & Chang, B. (2011). Mathematics course-taking in rural high schools. *Journal of Research in Rural Education*, *26*(1), 1–10.

Blickenstaff, J. C. (2005). Women and science careers: Leaky pipeline or gender filter? *Gender and Education*, *17*(4), 369–386.

Cohen C., Patterson D. G., Kovarik D. N., & Chowning J. T. (2013). Fostering STEM career awareness: Emerging opportunities for teachers. *Washington State Kappan*, *7*(1), 12–17.

Crain, A., & Webber, K. (2020). *Across the urban divide: STEM pipeline engagement among non-metropolitan students* [Unpublished manuscript]. University of Georgia.

Earth Networks: Education. (2017). STEM Education: 4 Ways to inspire STEM learners. Earth Networks. www.earthnetworks.com/blog/inspire-stem-learners/

Finnegan, J. (2019). The rural healthcare crisis: Number of medical students from rural declined 28% over 15 years, study finds. FIERCE Healthcare. www.fiercehealthcare.com/practices/rural-health-crisis-number-medical-students-from-rural-backgrounds-declined-28-over-15

Gagnon, D. J., & Mattingly, M. J. (2016). Advanced placement and rural schools: Access, success, and exploring alternatives. *Journal of Advanced Academics*, *27*(4), 266–284.

Gong, G., Phillips, S. G., Hudson, C., Curti, D., & Philips, B. U. (2019). Higher US rural mortality rates linked to socioeconomic status, physician shortages, and lack of health insurance. *Health Affairs*, *38*(12), 2003–2010. https://doi.org/10.1377/hlthaff.2019.00722

Grimes, L. E., Arrastía-Chisholm, M. C., & Bright, S. B. (2019). How can they know what they don't know? The beliefs and experiences of rural school counselors about STEM career advising. *Theory & Practice in Rural Education*, *9*(1), 74–90.

Harris, R. S., & Hodges, C. B. (2018). STEM education in rural schools: Implications of untapped potential. *National Youth-At-Risk Journal*, *3*(1). https://doi.org/10.20429/nyarj.2018.030102

Kahn, S., & Ginther, D. (2017). Women and STEM [Working Paper 23525]. National Bureau of Economic Research. www.nber.org/papers/w23525.pdf

Koricich, A., Chen, X., & Hughes, R. P. (2018). Understanding the effects of rurality and socioeconomic status on college attendance and institutional choice in the United States. *The Review of Higher Education, 41*(2), 281–305.

Maltese, A. V., & Tai, R. H. (2011). Pipeline persistence: Examining the association of educational experiences with earned degrees in STEM among US students. *Science Education, 95*(5), 877–907. https://doi.org/10.1002/sce.20441

Xue, Y., & Larson, R. C. (2015). STEM crisis or STEM surplus? Yes and yes. *Monthly Labor Review*. United States Bureau of Labor Statistics. https://doi.org/10.21916/mlr.2015.14

Yettick, H., Baker, R., Wickersham, M., & Hupfeld, K. (2014). Rural districts left behind? Rural districts and the challenges of administering the Elementary and Secondary Education Act. *Journal of Research in Rural Education, 29*(13), 1–15.

Paying for College
There's Help Out There

Paying for college is burdensome and complex. Higher education in America is more expensive than in any other country in the world and is even more confusing because different colleges charge different rates to different people. But there's no getting around the importance of a college degree in America. In fact, "no other country rewards a college degree as richly as the United States, and few other countries punish people so relentlessly for not having one" (Ripley, 2018).

This chapter takes a deep dive into the complex world of financial aid and scholarships and the challenges rural students face in navigating this world and funding their education. We begin with profiles of four rural youth who were led down different pathways by the cost of college. Their stories illustrate how rural students grapple with their own journeys. We then discuss some of the challenges students and their families face in funding college education and then provide practical information and advice that counselors, teachers, and mentors should know and be ready to share with students and their families.

Four Students, Four Journeys, Four Lessons

Gerald grew up in Tulelake, California, on the Oregon border. His dad worked at a hardware store and his mother was disabled following an automobile accident. After graduating in the top fifth of his class in a small school in a community known for farming and hunting, Gerald went off to California State University, Chico, to study business. To pay for college,

Gerald received a financial aid package that included a loan and a grant from the college. He also obtained a $5,000 annual scholarship from a local family that supports youth in his community. The local scholarship, critical to his being able to afford college and its attendant costs, stipulated that he complete a report on his yearly progress by the middle of June each year. Following his freshman year, Gerald missed the deadline to write and submit the scholarship report, and he lost out on the $5,000 award. That forced him to scramble his plans and transfer to the local community college.

David grew up in northern Maine. He didn't attend college because of the cost. He felt that staying at home and getting a job would be more helpful to his family. His dad worked seasonally on a potato farm and did other agriculture-related jobs in Aroostook County, and his mom drove a school bus. His four older siblings all dropped out of school by the 11th grade, and every one of them struggled; two battled opioid addictions and spent time in jail. David's parents told him not to waste his time going to college even though David had a B average, making him far and away the best student in his family. After finishing high school, David moved from job to job. He did some landscaping, cooked at the local diner, and drove a snowplow in the winter. "Life's good, but I may have made the wrong decision by not considering college. Too many people told me I couldn't afford college and that college just wasn't worth it. The problem is, I let them define my future," says David.

Courtney grew up and graduated from high school in southeast Kentucky and went on to Berea College. She selected Berea in part because it cost significantly less than her other choice, another small, private college in Kentucky. Berea, as noted in Chapter 8, does not charge tuition, but she still had to assume a small loan and participate in the college's work program by helping out in the library and later assisting the psychology department to secure speakers. Courtney and her husband, also a Berea grad, completed their four-year degrees with a debt of $5,000 combined. With no financial barriers to graduate school, Courtney was able to enter the University of Kentucky's PhD program in epidemiology and biostatistics.

Stephanie grew up in rural Texas, 40 miles west of El Paso. Her parents, Mexican immigrants, constantly reminded her about the importance of a college education, but they didn't understand the process, so she had to figure out financial aid on her own. She was "completely overwhelmed" when she had to fill out the Free Application for Federal Student Aid (FAFSA). Luckily, a college student volunteering at her school stepped in to help her complete the FAFSA and became her college and career readiness (CCR) advisor. But more obstacles lay ahead. "The FAFSA was the least of my struggles," Stephanie recalls. Because of cost, she began her postsecondary study at El Paso Community College. "I didn't know how to manage my own money," she says. "As with many low-income, first-gen rural students, my transition to college was difficult. After a bumpy first year of college, I realized that I needed to qualify for financial aid and that meant that I had to become independent." The federal definition for independence is a student not supported by family, and this required Stephanie to seek out resources on her own.

She wasn't the only student experiencing this struggle. Stephanie joined a community of peers in similar situations, and together they worked their way through the financial aid maze. They attended campus workshops that explained the process in detail and participated in financial literacy classes that taught them how to manage money. In her financial aid journey, Stephanie found that, "from careless mistakes, and with support, I was able to bounce back and become the first in my family to graduate with a bachelor's degree."

Like many other rural students, cost determined Gerald, David, Courtney, and Stephanie's postsecondary plans. David says he did not attend college because he wanted to make money instead of spending it on education—a myopic economic decision. He would likely have earned two or three times as much with a degree, although that would have meant leaving Aroostook County. Missing a deadline caused Gerald to leave the four-year college he was attending to transfer to a community college, and because Courtney paid very little for her bachelor's degree, she could enroll in a PhD program. Stephanie became an independent student according to the definition by the United States Department of Education, which allowed her to access scholarship support that would not have been available otherwise. This in turn paved the way for her to earn a bachelor's degree from the University of Texas at El Paso.

Rural students move down thousands of postsecondary pathways determined by college costs and financial aid. Most students graduate with loan debt, currently averaging more than $30,000, and the worst-case scenario is a large debt and no degree (Dickler, 2020). All of this speaks to the importance of becoming an informed education consumer.

Cost: Moving in the Wrong Direction

It can be difficult selling the prospect of college to rural students and families because of cost. David is a good example of this. Instead of pursuing the University of Maine at Presque Isle, 20 miles from his home, he was advised by friends and family to get a job out of high school. Since then, he's been pursuing a string of low-paying jobs. Courtney was able to attend Berea College without financial support from her family; she was grateful for that option, as she says her family "wasn't supportive of college at the time."

High college costs are a deterrent for many rural youth and scare many students and families, like David's, from considering college as an option. Controlling for inflation, tuition costs have doubled since 1970. Since 2005, student loan debt has grown almost fourfold, from $400 billion to almost $1.5 trillion (Federal Reserve Bank of New York Research and Statistics Group, 2020). Families from the lowest economic bracket pay 84% of their earnings, on average, to send a child to college. While college costs have soared, aid to families in need has stagnated. Need-based financial aid has steadily decreased, while merit aid has increased. Merit aid—generally awarded for test scores, resumes, and grades—tends to correlate with family income. Rural youth have less access to supports such as college counselors, test prep courses, and after-school activities, so it's no surprise that merit aid goes disproportionately to kids in suburban and urban communities, often from wealthy households (Dalton, 2017).

Educating Students on Paying for College

Students need to become familiar and comfortable with not just the idea of college but the details of funding their education years before they enroll. As college costs escalate, students need to put themselves in the best position to receive financial support for college. Here are some steps students should take both before enrolling and upon enrolling. CCR advisors or other mentors can help their students complete these critical tasks:

- **Find someone who is an expert on paying for college**. This may be the toughest task of all because disruption in higher education has changed the financial aid landscape, and it's difficult for advisors to stay up to date. CFES (College for Every Student) provides ongoing training for its CCR advisors on college and job trends and changes, and our *Ask Manny* column, which is available online, shares current information on financial aid, scholarships, loans, and other components of college readiness with students, educators, business leaders, and other partners. This is one instance in which students may *not* want to listen to their parents; David's family and friends, for instance, gave him bad information, encouraging him to get a job rather than a degree. Stephanie, however, found a CCR advisor at her school who was able to guide her through the FAFSA process, and later she tapped into a support network of friends and experts at her community college to help her become an independent student and qualify for federal aid.

- **Become an expert yourself**. Stephanie realized that she needed to become financially literate to fully understand the financial aid process and ultimately meet her higher education goals. To begin, students should understand how colleges award financial aid, where to find scholarships, how loans work, and the meaning of financial aid terms. All of this can be found later in this chapter. Federal loans, for example, tend to have the lowest interest rates and offer payment flexibility. Students can access these after applying for the FAFSA and should make sure they have taken full advantage of grants and federal loans available to them before considering higher-interest private loans.
- **Start early**. You can't start early enough. Don't wait until grade 12 to learn about paying for college and to start your scholarship search. Ask people you know who went to college how they paid for their education. Keep track of and stay ahead of deadlines because simply meeting a deadline may not be enough: Last year, more than 900,000 low-income students who applied for and were eligible for financial aid for college never received it, because their states had run out of money (Kolodner, 2018). Students will have plenty of deadlines throughout the process, so they need to check their emails to make sure that they are meeting all the requirements. Remember Gerald's cautionary tale: He lost his $5,000 local scholarship because he didn't send in his report on time, which forced him to transfer.
- **Fill out the FAFSA**. Almost all forms of higher education, state, and federal aid for college require students to complete and submit the FAFSA. Applications go live on October 1 of every year. The three

information items that students need are household income, size of household, and how many family members currently attend school. Parents'/guardians' tax information is also needed for the FAFSA. Resources for FAFSA completion can be found at: https://studentaid.gov/fafsa. The FAFSA also requires that students create a Federal Student Aid Identification (FSA ID), which creates an e-signature that is used for the FAFSA submission. For dependent students, one parent must also create an FSA ID and use it to co-sign the FAFSA. Students use this ID throughout their college years.

- **Make friends with your financial aid office** even before you get to campus. If you have questions after you receive your aid package from a college, contact the financial aid office. They are there to help! All colleges have a financial aid office (sometimes called the bursar's office or the office of student accounts).

  The financial aid office manages all things related to financial aid, although they may also handle other campus billing. Students should introduce themselves to the financial aid person who oversees their award and set up a time to meet with this individual, at least once a semester, to review their account details. Periodic check-ins will help students understand the requirements and learn of upcoming deadlines, while also maintaining a clear picture of their current financial standing. Students should see the financial aid staff as problem-solving partners who are there to help and support them. Students should be encouraged to ask questions and seek clarification about terms, deadlines, and other details. This proactive approach helps students understand their responsibilities and can prevent last-minute financial emergencies, such as an account deficit that might prevent a student from continuing to attend classes until the account balance is rectified.

  Here are the kinds of questions students should ask (if they don't already know the answers):

  - What is the current status of my account?
  - Are there late fees if bills are not paid on time?
  - Are there guidelines for any of my grants and scholarships (e.g., a specific grade point average (GPA) or specific major/minor)?

  - Will any of my scholarships or grants run out soon or decrease next year?
  - Are there deadlines I should be aware of? (Scholars can—and should—check the federal and state deadlines for the FAFSA in addition to deadlines the college may have.)
  - How does work-study fit into my financial aid picture?

- **Watch out for deals that seem too good to be true!** Students should be aware that some organizations fraudulently raise millions of dollars each year by preying on students whose families are new to the college search process. Some pressure and lure students and their families with success stories and promises of large scholarships. Others contact students about scholarships they never applied for, which is another red flag to avoid. When in doubt about an offer, call the financial aid office at a nearby college (Kerr, 2019). Students should also be wary of for-profit colleges, which often overstate their program quality and graduates' employment prospects. These schools have astronomically high dropout rates.
- **Also watch for deals that seem too good to be true.** On the other side of the coin, some deals that seem too good to be true may very well be true and worth pursuing. Students need to know that the sticker price may not be what they will need to pay. Institutions such as Harvard, for example, charge more than $70,000 a year, but thanks to their large endowments, and their commitment to supporting talented low- and middle-income students, students and their families might not have to pay anything. The service academies—West Point, the United States Naval Academy, and the United States Air Force Academy—are free to all students they enroll. Berea College charges no tuition, but all its students must be from low-income households in the Appalachian region. There are also local scholarships throughout the country that pay students from certain regions several thousand dollars toward college costs; in addition to receiving scholarships for being a resident of a certain geographic region, students are also selected for their grades and other criteria. Free college tuition programs are also offered in the state of Tennessee and the city of Kalamazoo, Michigan.

The Clark Scholarship and the Ticonderoga Alumni Association are among many programs dedicated to help cover college costs for students in their regions. They exist simply to make their communities better places by helping to increase the number of students who attend and graduate from college.

The Clark Scholarship: A Gift to Central New York

CFES works with 13 school districts in and around Cooperstown, New York, that are supported by the Clark Foundation. Students in those schools are eligible for the Clark Scholarship, which is awarded to a total of about 800 young people annually. Clark scholarships support college-related expenses incurred by students in the Leatherstocking region. Awards range from $5,000 to $8,000 and are given to undergrads for all types of postsecondary study and to graduate students who pursue degrees in health care and other critical areas.

Gary Kuch, a former teacher, principal, and superintendent in the Leatherstocking region, heads the Clark Scholarship Program. "It's an incentive for kids to attend and to stay in college," Kuch says of the phenomenal impact the scholarship program has had on this rural region in central New York. Indeed, 98% of recipients of the Clark Scholarship complete their college degrees on time! That's particularly impressive, when you recall from Chapter 8, that more than half of all college students drop out or fail out.

A Rural Community Invests in Its College Students

A dozen years ago, CFES Program Director Carol Cathey shared with educators from Ticonderoga, New York, the story of a program created in her Florida hometown, the Port St. Joe Scholarship Program, which has helped pay for college for several hundred youth over the past two decades.

Cathey's story inspired the creation of the Ticonderoga Alumni Association, which, since its inception in 2006, has made almost a quarter of a million dollars available to 574 students who were applying to college, technical school, or an approved apprentice program. The amount of the individual award is based upon points earned for grades, attendance, good behavior, extracurricular activities, community service, and family involvement in the school. The average award, entirely donated by Ticonderoga alumni, was $770 for members of the Class of 2019.

College Savings and Investment Strategies for Students and Families: Advice from Someone Who's Been There

Yanely Espinal learned some difficult financial lessons growing up with nine siblings and as a first-generation college student at Brown University. Now the Director of Educational Outreach at Next Gen Personal Finance, Espinal offers suggestions on how to avoid making the same mistakes she did, along with some valuable financial advice.

"When I was applying to college and I was offered money, I had no idea that some of that money might not be free," says Espinal. "Apply for scholarships and grants as early as possible, and when you do get a financial aid letter from a college, look at it with a microscope. Make sure you understand exactly what it says and how much you are responsible for paying."

Once in college, Espinal urges students to be frugal and to avoid accumulating credit card debt and other forms of debt with high interest rates. After graduation, students should create a debt payback plan, which will help build credit and allow for some initial investments at their first job, such as a 401(k) plan.

"A debt repayment plan is number one," says Espinal. "Pull up a debt repayment calculator and plug in some numbers, and it will tell you exactly how long repayment will take. Secondly, you should build up your savings account so you have a cushion in case something unexpected happens. Once you have those two in place, then you can invest. If your first job offers a 401(k) or 403(b), take advantage of it."

Financial Aid Myths and Reality: What Students (and Their Supporters) Need to Know

There's lots of confusion about how to pay for college and another pitfall to avoid is the plethora of misconceptions and bad advice often shared by well-intentioned people. Here are some common myths and facts that students and their families need to be educated about:

1. MYTH: Only students with the best grades qualify for financial aid.

   FACT: Some scholarships are "merit-based" and awarded based on a student's academic performance. However, most financial aid, including grants and loans, is "need-based," or awarded based on a family's ability to pay for college.

2. MYTH: Since my family hasn't saved anything for college, even if I might want to go to a four-year college or university, community college is the only option.

   FACT: While it helps to have savings set aside for college, there are other ways to pay for a college education. Families with lower incomes who have not been able to save will likely find that their expected contribution will be quite modest. And remember, low-interest loans are available to families and to students. Also, most colleges and universities offer tuition-payment plans as well. Rural students are the group most likely to undermatch in their college choice. That means even when they qualify, they don't pursue highly selective colleges (places like Lehigh and Harvard) where they might receive full tuition and money for incidentals like internships and study abroad programs. So, go to a community college if you feel that is the best choice to prepare you for your future, but not because you think you can't afford to attend a four-year college or university.

3. MYTH: I shouldn't even consider my first-choice school because it costs too much. Only rich kids go to elite schools.

   FACT: The rule of thumb is that the higher the total cost, the easier it is to demonstrate eligibility for financial aid. In fact, several national studies show that the family incomes of students in private colleges are, on average, lower than the family incomes of students in large state universities. Remember, the stated costs at a school can be deceiving, and aid is often available to offset some of those costs. Students should apply and then evaluate the financial award letter when it arrives.

4. MYTH: Only students from low-income families qualify for financial aid.

   FACT: While it is true that significant amounts of aid are reserved for families in need, there are forms of assistance available to help many families meet their expected contribution, including low-interest loans that are available to parents and students. All families are encouraged to apply for aid, whether they think they qualify or not. Many are surprised to find they are eligible.

5. MYTH: Millions of scholarship dollars go unclaimed every year. I just need to pay a service to help find them.

   FACT: Don't be fooled by such services! Professional scholarship-search services would like students and families to believe this so that they can turn a profit. There are many ways for students and families to do the same research on the Internet or with help from CCR advisors and the financial aid officers at colleges and universities.

6. MYTH: Who needs a college degree? I can park cars or wait tables and make good money right now! The cost of a college education just isn't worth it.

   FACT: The truth is that people with a college degree earn almost twice that of those with just a high school diploma. Over a lifetime, the gap in earnings potential between a high school diploma and a college degree is more than $1 million! Remember, unlike most items that depreciate or lose value over time (like a car or smartphone), a college degree will increase in value. Remember, no other country rewards a college education as richly as the United States.

7. MYTH: I've heard that college tuition and living expenses could be more than $75,000 a year. Are all schools this expensive?

   FACT: Only some are as expensive as that. True, there are private colleges where tuition costs that much. But remember Fact #3 above: Financial aid is largely proportional to the college's costs. Use the net price calculator on college websites to determine the true cost of attending each school.

8. MYTH: I am going to be the only student at my school on financial aid.

   FACT: Actually, more than 60% of full-time students at four-year colleges and universities receive some kind of financial aid. At private colleges and universities, 75% of the students receive financial aid (McFarland, 2019).

9. MYTH: I thought all debt was bad. I can't possibly take out thousands of dollars of student loans and not get into huge financial trouble later on.

   FACT: Excessive debt is bad and defaulting on any loan—including student loans—can be disastrous, but studies show that the financial benefits of a college degree compensate for the burden of student debt. A degree will translate into higher earnings, making the loans easier to repay. Also, students have a grace period for six months after graduation before beginning to repay the loan. There also are many options for monthly payments. For students who go on to graduate or professional school, repayment on undergraduate loans can be deferred. What's more, the interest on student loans is always lower than credit card debt, for example. It's best to think about a college education as an investment that will result in high returns, making borrowing worthwhile.

10. MYTH: As a star athlete, I will get an athletic scholarship.

    FACT: Fewer than two percent of high school athletes receive some form of athletic scholarship. Most student aid is awarded on the basis of financial need, not athletic talent.

Crunching the Numbers: Deciphering Financial Aid Awards

So, your favorite student has followed all your advice and has been accepted into a handful of colleges and all are offering financial aid. Congratulations!

Now comes the hard part: Figuring out exactly what's in those financial aid packages and what they mean in practical terms for your student and his or her family. Financial aid awards can be confusing since there is no standard way of organizing awards, and students and families are often left having to decipher what the numbers mean. This can be especially perplexing for those without a CCR advisor who can translate the language of loans, work study, grants, and other components of financial aid. In the following sections, we take a deep dive into the details of financial aid, including the anatomy of a financial aid package, financial aid terminology, and how to interpret and compare financial aid offers. It's essential for counselors, mentors, and others supporting college-bound rural students to educate themselves on these topics so they can offer students and families the guidance they need to make smart choices.

One challenge is that financial aid award letters do not always mention the college's cost of attendance and many fail to list all college costs. Instead, students and parents have to go to the college's website and dig for this number. What costs can we expect to see in these award letters? Some show tuition, fees, and room and board (for those who live on campus), which are paid to the college and are often referred to as direct costs. Other associated costs, such as textbooks and supplies, transportation, computers, student health insurance, dependent care and other living expenses, are deemed indirect costs. When we combine both indirect and direct costs, we start to see the total cost of attendance for students. Students should not expect this final number to be readily available in one place. They'll have to do the detective work themselves.

Why do we care about this? The expected family contribution—despite its name—does not fully cover the difference between the grants/scholarships offered and the actual cost of attending college. This is usually referred to as "the gap."

Why is that the case? Many financial aid packages will include loans and often leave the student with unmet financial need. This is because institutions don't have unlimited amounts of funds to give out in the form of grants and scholarships. When looking at loans, expect to see the name of the loan and the amount. However, aid packages don't show loan terms and conditions (such as interest rates, monthly payments, and total payments). This information can and should be found, but it will require some digging on the financial aid website.

Before going deeper into these details, however, students and their families need to familiarize themselves with the basic terminology of financial aid.

 A Glossary of Financial Aid Terms

The first step in managing financial aid is understanding some key terms. The following list represents a sampling of the terms that can be found at: https://studentaid.gov/help-center/answers/topic/glossary/articles#Grant. It'll be useful to introduce students to these terms and what they mean for their personal financial situations before they set off for college:

Award letter: An offer from a college that states the type and amount of financial aid the institution is willing to provide if a student accepts admission and registers to take classes at that institution.

Award year: The academic year for which financial aid is used to fund a student's education.

Cost of attendance (COA): The total amount it will cost for a student to attend college. This is usually stated as a yearly figure. COA includes tuition and fees; room and board (or a housing and food allowance); and allowances for books, supplies, transportation, loan fees, and dependent care. It also includes miscellaneous and personal expenses, such as an allowance for the rental or purchase of a personal computer; costs related to a disability; and reasonable costs for eligible study-abroad programs. For students attending less than half time, the COA includes tuition and fees and an allowance for books, supplies, transportation, and dependent care expenses, and can also include room and board for up to three semesters or the equivalent at the institution. However, no more than two of those semesters, or the equivalent, may be consecutive. Students should contact the financial aid administrator at the college they plan to attend if they have any unusual expenses that might affect the COA.

Disbursement: Payment of the loan funds to the borrower by the college. Students generally receive their federal student loan in two or more disbursements.

Financial Aid Office: The office at a college that is responsible for preparing and communicating information on financial aid. This office helps students apply for and receive student loans, grants, scholarships, and other types of financial aid.

Financial aid package: The total amount of financial aid (federal and nonfederal) a student is offered by a college. The college's financial aid staff combines various forms of aid into a "package" to help meet a student's education costs.

Grant: Financial aid, often based on financial need, that does not need to be repaid (unless, for example, a student withdraws from college and owes a refund).

Merit-based: Aid based on a student's skill or ability, such as a scholarship that is awarded based on a student's high grades.

Need-based: Aid based on a student's financial need, such as a grant awarded based on a student's low income.

Pell Grants: Federally funded and available to undergraduate and graduate students who are in a teaching credential program. Does not need to be repaid.

Scholarship: Money awarded to a student based on academic or other achievements to help pay for education expenses. Scholarships generally do not have to be repaid.

Stafford Loan: Federal student loans that must be repaid. These funds are available to both undergraduate and graduate students. There are two types of loans:

subsidized: the government pays the interest while you are in school, during grace periods or deferment, and

unsubsidized: students are responsible for paying principal and interest that accrues at any point in time.

Work-study: A federal student aid program that provides part-time employment while a student is enrolled in college to help pay education expenses.

Components of the Financial Aid Package

Financial aid packages include a combination of scholarships, work-study money, loans, and grants (Box 10.1). Colleges often refer to scholarships and grants as "gift aid." This is money that doesn't need to be repaid, but students and parents should be aware of the necessary requirements for maintaining those.

Box 10.1 Components of the Financial Aid Package

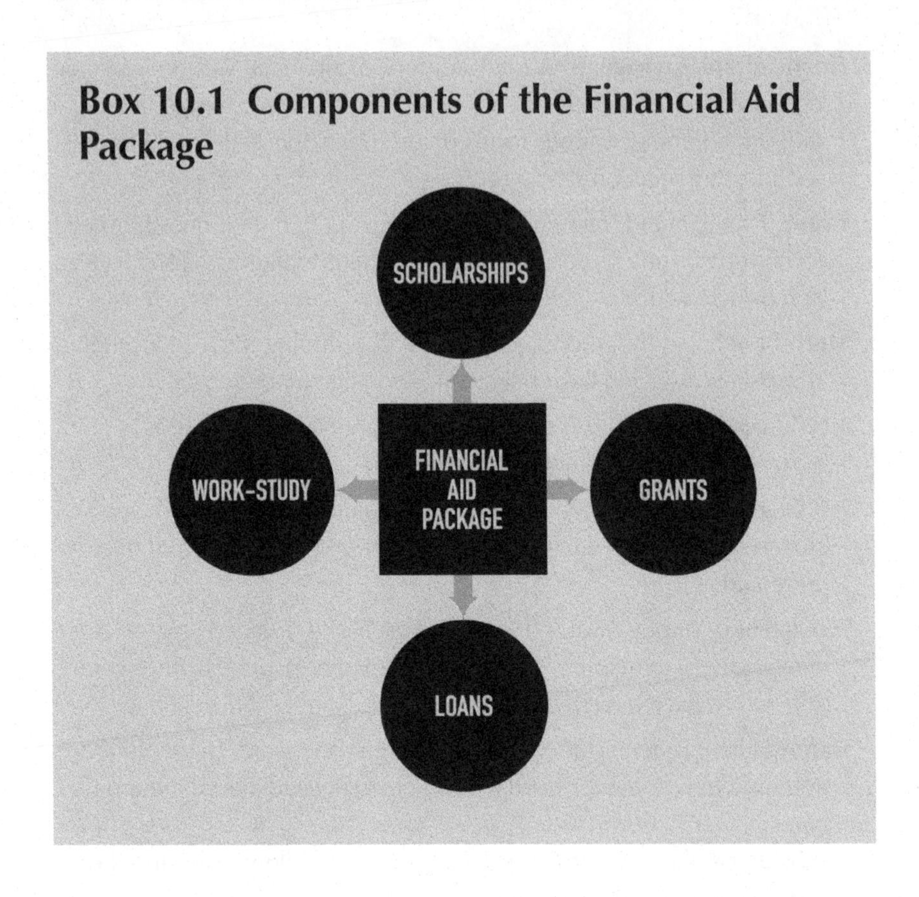

Gift aid may be merit-based and tied to academic performance. Loans can come in a variety of forms, from those subsidized by the Federal Government or unsubsidized private loans. While in school, the Federal Government covers the interest that those loans are accruing. There is also a Parent Loan for Undergraduate Students (PLUS) loan whose interest can be deferred until the student graduates. Finally, work-study is embedded in the financial aid package. For example, Courtney, introduced earlier in this chapter, worked in the Library and the Psychology Department as part of her work-study.

How to Read a Financial Aid Package

Students comparing different financial aid packages should gather all their numbers and paste them into a table like Table 10.1. They should also

Table 10.1 Comparison Results of Financial Aid Awards for Two Residential Colleges

	Cost of attendance	*Gift aid*	*Loans*	*Net cost*	*Net price*
College 1 Residential	$62,366	$34,815	$26,850	$701	**$27,551**
College 2 Residential	$53,170	$27,715	$5,500	$19,955	**$25,455**
College 3 Commuter	$28,652	$17,922	$10,694	$36	**$10,730**

remember, the cost of attendance is not always listed on the financial aid package, but it can be found on the college website.

To calculate the net price, which is what students and their families will need to provide to meet all expenses, subtract the gift aid (scholarship + grant), as seen in the formula below:

The logical question is how the net price gets covered. We find that this is where the biggest difference between aid packages comes from. It's important for students to understand how much of it will be met by loans and parental contributions and how much remains as the student's responsibility to cover (the gap). Below is a simple formula illustrating this:

Deciphering and Comparing Financial Aid Offers

To illustrate the process college-going students and their families will need to follow to compare aid packages, we will walk through several examples. We will separate these offers into residential (living on campus) and commuter (living at home and commuting to campus) examples and simplify things even further by referring to the sample colleges as Colleges 1–4. The first two documents we'll examine are letters containing information about what the financial aid includes. Remember, not all details are included in letters, so it's necessary to put all the puzzle pieces together. Students need to know they can ask for help if they have questions.

From the first two examples: College 1 does a good job showcasing the details between the different types of aid. It uses "gift aid" to describe grants and scholarships. It uses simple language to show the loans. In contrast to College 2, it combines all the sources of aid into one list and provides a total amount of financial aid. It's important for students to pay attention, especially when calculating their net price: They will need to take out the loans to cover the actual expenses involved.

For the 2020-21 Award Year

The Financial Aid Office is pleased to provide this official offer of financial assistance for the 2020-2021 academic year. Our entire staff looks forward to assisting you during your enrollment at **College #1**. To accept or decline these awards, please log into your Portal. A step by step guide can also be found on the portal.

GIFT AID	**FALL**	**SPRING**	**TOTAL**
INCENTIVE AWARD	$11,000.00	$11,000.00	$22,000.00
GRANT	$3,500.00	$3,500.00	$7,000.00
PELL GRANT	$2,908.00	$2,907.00	$5,815.00
TOTAL GIFT AID	**$17,408.00**	**$17,407.00**	**$34,815.00**

You are eligible for these other aid programs (Loans and Work Study) to assist in covering your out of pocket costs:

LOANS AND WORK-STUDY)	**FALL**	**SPRING**	**TOTAL**
DIRECT SUB STAFFORD LOAN	$1,750.00	$1,750.00	$3,500.00
DIRECT UNSUB STAFFORD LOAN	$1,000.00	$1,000.00	$2,000.00
DIRECT PLUS (PARENT) LOAN	$10,675.00	$10,675.00	$21,350.00
TOTAL OTHER AID	**$13,425.00**	**$13,425.00**	**$26,850.00**

To help you understand how these awards will assist you in paying for your education, please consider the following information. Your **Cost of Attendance (COA)** consists of the following Direct and Indirect expenses and is based on your status as a Resident student. (Not that costs may be estimated or averaged.)

Direct Expenses	(Paid to School)
Tuition:	$41,120.00
Fees:	$1,902.00
Room:	$12,016.00
Board (meal plan):	$3,600.00
Total Direct Expenses:	**$58,638.00**

Indirect Expenses	(Estimated personal)
Books & Supplies:	$800.00
Transportation:	$600.00
Personal Expenses:	$1,628.00
Living Allowance:	$700.00
Total Indirect Expenses	**$3,728.00**
Total Cost of Attendance	**$62,366.00**

Your Out of Pocket Cost (Cost of Attendance minus (-) total Gift Aid) is $27,551 for the 2020-2021 Academic year. Your expected enrollment is 12 or more credits per semester. Additional information, including estimated Cost of Attendance for additional years can be found on our website.

2020–21 Award Year
FINANCIAL AID AWARD

Dear Student,

Congratulations on being admitted to College #2! We are pleased to present you with your 2020–2021 financial aid award. Your award has been calculated based upon the information you provided on your Free Application for Federal Student Aid and on the expected cost of attendance and the estimated family contribution for the upcoming academic year, please log in to your Portal. A step-by-step guide can also be found on the portal.

Source	Fall	Spring	Total
College Scholarship	$7,500.00	$7,500.00	$15,000.00
College Grant	$2,600.00	$2,600.00	$5,200.00
State Grant	$850.00	$850.00	$1,700.00
Pell Grant	$2,908.00	$2,907.00	$5,815.00
Direct Sub Stafford Loan	$1,750.00	$1,750.00	$3,500.00
Direct Unsub Stafford Loan	$1,000.00	$1,000.00	$2,000.00
Total			**$33,215.00**

In addition, College #2 administers both federal work-study and the College #2 work student employment programs. The average earnings are approximately $1,500 per academic year. These have not been included in your award, but more information about them is available on our website.

Direct Expenses	**(Paid to School)**
Tuition & Fees:	$38,825.00
Room & Board:	$14,345.00
Total Direct Expenses:	**$53,170.00**
Aid:	$33,215.00
Net Direct Costs:	**$19,955.00**

Options to pay or finance the 2020–2021 net direct costs (e.g.: Expected Family Contribution and/or other family resources, payment plans, PLUS loans, and alternative loans), along with information about your above award and our financial aid policies, can be found online in our financial aid guide.

Please note that scholarships and grants offered by College #2 are funded in part by generous donations from alumni and friends of the College. If your college aid is funded by a donor, we will notify you of the source of this funding during the academic year.

In addition to outlining the scholarships and grants, College 1 does a good job illustrating the difference between direct and indirect expenses. College 2 is less transparent. It doesn't share the indirect costs in its letter. To compare both offers, put all the numbers in a table (see Table 10.2 below). Note that while they may have a similar net price of $25,000–$27,000 range, this doesn't include the additional costs a student may incur. More importantly, on a percentage basis, College 1 has a higher sticker price but is more affordable than College 2.

For comparison, we'll now look at a couple of commuter schools, a popular option for students with a college nearby, since living at home means saving on room and board. As we saw from the examples above, the average room and board fee is about $15,000/year. From the two examples below, we can see how well College 3 lists its gift aid, self-help aid, and expenses. On the other hand, College 4 leads with its direct costs, which may be more transparent.

Table 10.2 Comparison Results of Financial Aid Awards for Two Commuter Colleges

	Cost of attendance	*Gift aid*	*Loans*	*Net cost*	*Net price*
College 1 Residential	$62,366	$34,815	$26,850	$701	**$27,551**
College 2 Residential	$53,170	$27,715	$5,500	$19,955	**$25,455**

Financial Aid Award 2020–2021

The Financial Aid Office is pleased to provide this official offer of financial assistance for the 2020–2021 academic year. Our entire staff looks forward to assisting you during your enrollment at **College #3**. To accept or decline these awards, please log in to your Portal. A step-by-step guide can also be found on the portal.

Gift Aid	Fall	Spring	Total
Federal Pell Grant	$2,908.00	$2,907.00	$5,815.00
Grant A	$4,148.00	$4,148.00	$8,296.00
Bobcat Grant	$3,008.00	$3,008.00	$6,016.00
Total Gift Aid	$10,064.00	$10,063.00	$20,127.00

You are eligible for these other aid programs (loans and work-study) to assist in covering your out-of-pocket costs:

Self-Help Aid	Fall	Spring	Total
Direct Sub Stafford Loan	$1,750.00	$1,750.00	$3,500.00
Direct Unsub Stafford Loan	$1,000.00	$1,000.00	$2,000.00
Fed Work Study	$1,380.00	$1,380.00	$2,760.00
Total Other Aid	$4,130.00	$4,130.00	$8,260.00

To accept or decline these awards, you must log in to MyFinancialAid (http://my.college3.edu).

Your award was determined in part on the following information:

Expenses	
Tuition & Fees:	$23,262.00
Personal Expenses:	$1,893.00
Average Transportation:	$1,196.00
Average Healthcare:	$2,452.00
Total Expenses:	**$28,803.00**

We look forward to welcoming you to College#3,

The financial aid team!

Financial Aid Award 2020–2021

Dear Student,

We are pleased to provide you with your financial aid award for the 2020–2021 academic year. To accept or decline these awards, please log in to your Academic Portal. A step-by-step guide can also be found on the portal.

Below is an example of costs and awards based on 2020–21 estimates for a new undergraduate taking 15 credits/semester. If your financial aid is not enough to pay your student account bill, you are responsible for paying the remaining balance.

Expenses	Fall	Spring	Total
Tuition:	$13,641.00	$13,641.00	$27,282.00
Fees:	$685.00	$685.00	$1,370.00
Total:	**$14,326.00**	**$14,326.00**	**$28,652.00**

Your financial aid award is as follows. Keep in mind that financial aid for an academic year is applied in two payments: half for the fall semester and the other half for the spring semester.

Grants & Scholarships	Fall	Spring	Total
Green Scholarships	$1,000.00	$1,000.00	$2,000.00
Pell Grant	$3,098.00	$3,097.00	$6,195.00
Tuition Pledge	$4,863.00	$4,864.00	$9,727.00
Total Gift Aid	**$8,961.00**	**$8,961.00**	**$17,922.00**

You are eligible for these other aid programs (loans and work-study) to assist in covering your out-of-pocket costs:

Federal Student Loans	Fall	Spring	Total
Direct Sub Stafford Loan	$1,731.00	$1,731.00	$3,462.00
Direct Unsub Stafford Loan	$989.00	$989.00	$1,978.00
Federal Parent Plus Loan	$2,627.00	$2,627.00	$5,254.00
Total Other Aid	**$5,347.00**	**$5,347.00**	**$10,694.00**

Maintaining financial aid eligibility is an annual process. Not only must you reapply for financial aid every year, but our office is required to monitor your eligibility throughout each year.

The Financial Aid Team

Table 10.3 Comparison Results of Financial Aid Awards from Three Colleges

	Cost of attendance	*Gift aid*	*Loans*	*Net cost*	*Net price*
College 3 Commuter	$28,803	$20,127	$5,500	$3,176	**$8,676**
College 4 Commuter	$28,652	$17,922	$10,694	$36	**$10,730**

As we did with the residential college offers, we start our comparison of the commuter college offers by creating a table that directly compares their offerings (Table 10.3). Both Colleges 3 and 4 explain the different components of their overall financial aid award. College 4 is the only one that mentions student ability to maintain financial eligibility. These are the items that students and families need to learn about and stay aware of, as not all eligibilities are created equal.

Financial Aid Comparison Calculator

What follows is a calculator to help students and families compare colleges with different costs of attendance and amounts of aid. We filled it in with the four example colleges used earlier.

As you can see, the gap at College 1 is very low at $701, but we would need to take out over $26,000 in loans each year. Meanwhile, College 3 has the second-lowest cost of attendance and costs $8,676: $5,500 in loans plus a $3,176 gap that students and parents would need to figure out how to pay.

Reach out to the financial aid office for options of different ways to pay. Some options may include installments. For students who are not in a good financial position, relying on the net cost might be a bigger factor in their decision about where they attend college. Doing this activity helps students and their families understand how different the sticker price can be from the cost that students are required to pay after aid.

Manny's Journey: From First-Generation Student to Financial Aid Expert

Manny Tejeda's story brings us full circle: He shares how he struggled as a first-generation student to navigate the complexities of the financial aid world that we just explored, but he successfully earned a degree that would launch his professional trajectory as a financial aid expert helping the next generation of students.

Manny grew up in the lush rural foothills of the Dominican Republic before moving to the United States. As part of the CFES partnership at his school, Pelham Preparatory Academy in the Bronx (mentioned in Chapter 6), Manny attended the University of Vermont (UVM). Shortly after attaining his bachelor's, he became a director in the UVM Admissions Office, where he worked for ten years before joining the team at CFES Brilliant Pathways. Although Manny became a financial aid expert through his work at UVM and CFES, as an 18-year old, he struggled to navigate how to pay for college. Manny shares the story of how he learned how to pay for college, as he offers advice to rural students and the adults who support them.

A Long Road to College and Learning How to Pay for It: As Told by Manny Tejeda

"How many of you have been to a college campus?" asked the college recruiter, who spoke to our economics class during my senior year of high school. It was early September when I started thinking about the possibility of attending college. In the back of my mind, I knew it was something I wanted to do, but I didn't know where to start. After some of my peers asked savvy questions about majors, campus life, and how to pay for college, I realized how far behind I was in the process. There wasn't as much chatter about affordability and rising college costs then, even though the cost of many colleges had increased by 50% in the previous ten years. It helped being naïve.

- *Lesson: It helped that I didn't know much about the cost of college until later on in the process because I would have limited my choices to those places with the lowest sticker price, and I might not have even considered college as an option.*

I started doing research online about what I wanted to study and how those programs could lead to a high-paying job that would set me on a path to financial success. I only knew about high-earning careers in engineering, medicine, law, and accounting. Little did I know that there was a lot more to college and success than a major. I have three older siblings who didn't choose the college route, so I couldn't rely on them for guidance. I borrowed one of those "Best Lists of Colleges" books and started applying to colleges and universities without much strategy. I applied to a total of nine higher-ed institutions, including City University of New York (CUNY), private schools, technical schools, and an out-of-state public university.

- *Lesson: Looking for information on your own can be overwhelming. Focus your research with a set of guiding questions.*

I began to learn different terms: Deposit fees, campus housing, dining plan, and tuition. In the midst of waiting for acceptance letters, I decided to graduate high school early because I had credits from my school back in the Dominican Republic. At the time, I thought it was a great idea. It wasn't because that's when I needed to be in school the most. That would have allowed me to stay in touch with my peers who knew more about the process, and, of course, I missed the pure joy of being a high school senior.

- *Lesson: Develop and appreciate your network and tap into your mentors for guidance and listen to their stories.*

I lived at home with parents who didn't go to college and older siblings who had chosen to join the workforce, but I was still surrounded by people who wanted to help me find my postsecondary path. I decided that I needed to tap into resources and people who knew the process, and what better way to do that than my new network of friends who were already in college? Acceptance letters started coming that included invitations to visit campuses and financial aid award letters. It felt good to be invited to all these colleges, but it was shocking to look at some of the price tags.

- *Lesson: Basic financial knowledge is important in starting to understand all the financial aid lingo. Continue on the financial literacy spectrum so that you can be financially stable later on.*

I remember trying to complete my FAFSA and feeling overwhelmed. I didn't know how much money my parents made, yet I was required to answer all these questions. All I knew was that my parents were small business owners who spent too much time working. Thankfully, for my siblings and me, it meant we didn't have to worry about our next meal, having a roof over our head, or clothes to wear. I pressed on. One of my mom's friends from work took it upon herself to mentor me and helped me come up with a plan. She was an expert on paying for college and became my CCR advisor. We came up with a list of documents and information that I needed to fill out the FAFSA. After working on the FAFSA for a few days, I hit "submit" and notified the colleges that had accepted me.

- *Lesson: Filling out the FAFSA felt like such an achievement because of the multitude of items needed. Life is a lot easier if you are working with people who have experience.*

I felt proud when I submitted the FAFSA, but little did I know there would be more challenges to come. A few weeks later, I started to receive school-specific scholarships, grants, and finally, financial aid packages. My CCR advisor helped me sort through the letters and offers I received. There was no consistency to these financial aid packages or the way they were presented. My CCR advisor knew the difference between a good financial aid package and a bad one, so that was incredibly helpful. This allowed me to cross off colleges that were not a good financial fit. The whole process was overwhelming for me, but remember, it didn't take much to overwhelm me since I had very limited exposure to anything to do with college costs.

- *Lesson: We have to be more understanding with students who lack exposure to the financial aid world because their context is limited. In retrospect, it would have been a good time for me to know about the average yearly cost of college and the additional expenses that I would incur, such as books, supplies, travel, and room and board.*

I needed someone with experience to sit down with me and explain all the different components of financial aid awards. My CCR advisor was that person. She helped me gain a basic understanding of how loans worked, how interest is deferred until six months out of college, the best way to earn work-study funds, and the value of scholarships and grants.

- *Lesson: Use resources to your advantage. You don't need to know it all, but you need to tap into people around you who do know, and that knowledge is powerful when you are at the crossroads of making life-changing decisions like going to college.*

With this information, I narrowed down my choices from nine to three schools. Two of the schools were ten minutes away, and the other one was 300 miles from home. The three award packages couldn't have been more different. When I met with my CCR advisor, we talked about options. She asked me questions that helped me think about my opportunities. As I reflect back, it was the first time, aside from my parents, that someone was talking with me about major life decisions without influencing what they thought was best for me. This allowed me to weigh the pros and cons of each school. I can't imagine how I would have made it through the financial aid process alone. Would I have made it to college? I'm not sure.

- *Lesson: Embrace new opportunities in your life and adapt to new environments. That's where real learning happens.*

At this point, I had developed a network of older peers who were enrolled at each of my three college options, who also had backgrounds similar to mine. The more I asked them about their experiences, the more I learned. Once I got a feel for the student body, I went back to the numbers and listed the positives and negatives and the value I thought it would provide me. I gave high ratings to programs that emphasized practical experiences for students, cared for their development, and invested in their success. This may not be the best route for everyone else, but it was helpful for me. In the end, I decided to take out loans, since the support from my parents wouldn't cover the full amount that I owed. This included additional expenses like books, transportation, and a computer. I also got a summer job so I could save money and cover social expenses like dining out.

- *Lesson: Don't make your decisions solely on cost. It could be detrimental to your college experience. Remember there are over 4,000 colleges that you could attend and many would be a great option financially.*

Conclusion

Cost is the number one reason rural youth choose not to attend college and also why they drop out of college. While a low-income urban student will more often see college as an opportunity to climb out of poverty, young people from rural communities too often view higher education as a place to accrue debt. Rural students need to become paying-for-college experts, they need to be informed, and they need to make smart financial decisions and know how to beat deadlines.

What paying-for-college lessons can we learn from David, Gerald, Courtney, and Stephanie? David was advised to avoid college and he took the quick financial fix. Unless he finds college at a later date, he's destined to earn, over his lifetime, a fraction of what he might have made otherwise. Gerald lost out on several thousand dollars by not paying attention to a deadline. Courtney strategically selected her undergraduate college, which meant that she accrued minimal debt and could afford to enter a PhD program. Stephanie not only found a paying-for-college expert to mentor her but became a paying-for-college expert herself, which allowed her to attain her bachelor's degree.

Students need to harness the Essential Skill of networking, as Manny and Stephanie did, and build a support system of friends and mentors to find answers and resources. They need to network and find a CCR advisor and get to know people at the financial aid office. They need to learn the paying-for-college lexicon. When students own the paying-for-college process, they truly become college ready.

References

Dalton, R. (2017). A college wake-up call: Committing to economically disadvantaged students. Adirondack Daily Enterprise. www.adirondackdailyenterprise.com/opinion/guest-commentary/2017/11/a-college-wake-up-call/.

Dickler, J. (2020). More than half of students probably can't afford college due to Covid-19. CNBC. www.cnbc.com/2020/06/04/more-than-half-of-students-probably-cant-afford-college-due-to-covid-19.html

Federal Reserve Bank of New York Research and Statistics Group. (2020). Quarterly Report on Household Debt and Credit 2019. Federal Reserve Bank of New York. www.newyorkfed.org/medialibrary/interactives/householdcredit/data/pdf/hhdc_2019q4.pdf

Kerr, E. (2019). How to avoid scholarship scams. U.S. News & World Report. www.usnews.com/education/best-colleges/paying-for-college/articles/2019-04-01/how-to-avoid-scholarship-scams

Kolodner, M. (2018). Eligible for financial aid, nearly a million students never get it. The Hechinger Report. https://hechingerreport.org/eligible-for-financial-aid-almost-one-third-of-students-never-get-it/

McFarland, J. (2019). Conditions of Education 2018. United States Department of Education, National Center for Education Statistics. https://nces.ed.gov/pubsearch/pubsinfo.asp?pubid=2018144

Ripley, A. (2018). Why is college in America so expensive? The Atlantic. www.theatlantic.com/education/archive/2018/09/why-is-college-so-expensive-in-america/569884/

Conclusion
The Way Forward

Rural America is a land in crisis—but it's also a land of vast potential, given the grit and work ethic of its people and the growing interest among urban and suburban Americans in migrating to rural areas. The key to unlocking the potential of rural America is educating its youth for the careers of the future, and this means preparing them for college and supporting them as they pursue higher education.

However, as we've seen, the relationship between rural America and higher education has grown fraught in recent years. Rural parents are wary of the high cost of college and often discourage their children from considering it. Those who do manage to persist and attain degrees often leave their communities for good, seeking careers and opportunities not available close to home. This leads to a vicious cycle: Educated, ambitious young adults with the skills to revive their communities and serve as role models for youth disappear, leaving their already-impoverished communities with fewer resources than before. Oftentimes, the adults who are left, fearful of losing more of their children, pressure those remaining to stay, where they end up in dead-end jobs in dying industries. As a result, college-going rates in rural America are disturbingly low—only 29% of rural Americans between 18 and 24 are in college, compared to 49% for their cohorts from urban areas (Krupnick, 2018).

Still, there is cause for hope. The COVID-19 pandemic—and the growing acceptance and effectiveness of telecommuting and online education—has strengthened connections between rural and urban America in numerous ways, from rural schools and students tapping into online resources offered by larger institutions, to young adults from rural areas returning home after college to build tech careers and businesses. Technology can thus build bridges, connecting rural America to the knowledge and resources of the rest of the world.

And within rural communities, educators are taking matters into their own hands to give their students a better shot at the future. Schools such as Crown Point Central in rural New York State turned themselves around—from nearly failing to reaching the top tier in the state—through the development of a common vision and mission that all teachers and students strive for.

In addition, CFES (College for Every Student) and its many rural partners have identified a number of proven strategies to prepare and motivate rural students to pursue higher education and promising careers. These are not quick fixes—they all require teamwork, planning, and long-term commitment—but their effectiveness is indisputable:

- To succeed in college and their future careers, students must master the Essential Skills™—perseverance, leadership, networking, goal setting, agility, and teamwork. These can be introduced and cultivated through extracurricular activities, such as clubs and community work, and be incorporated into classroom learning as well.
- Business partners are an effective way for rural schools to tap into resources and networks otherwise unavailable to them. Besides providing funding, business partners can provide career training, mentoring, and useful contacts for both teachers and students. Businesses also benefit from these partnerships by cultivating future members of their workforce and gaining extra visibility in the community.
- Applying to college is a complex process, and for rural students who know few college graduates, it can seem confusing and intimidating. CCR advisors—volunteers from the community trained in the latest college admissions and financial aid trends—can play a critical role in demystifying the process for students and helping them stay accountable to their goals.
- Rural students tend to shy away from STEM careers, in part because of the limited availability of advanced STEM coursework in rural schools and the lack of local role models in STEM professions. This is an urgent problem, given the current and projected growth of technology-based industries and careers. It is thus crucial to start sparking interest and

familiarity with science and technology while students are still young. This is another area where business and higher-education partners can play a major role.

- Cost can appear as a hurdle to attending college for rural students is cost. Students and their families need to be educated in the first years of high school or before about the college-paying process and how to navigate it. Families may be pleasantly surprised to learn of the resources, such as grants, scholarships, and work-study that can make college affordable to low-income families.

When promising rural students opt out of the college pipeline, it's not just a loss for them as individuals, it's a loss for their communities, who've missed the opportunity to gain a future leader or role model for younger residents. And it's a loss for the rest of us when the gifts of a potential physician, inventor, or researcher go unrealized. But with commitment and effort, we can ensure that rural students get the opportunity to reach their full potential.

Reference

Krupnick, M. (2018). The students who don't believe college is an option. The Atlantic. www.theatlantic.com/education/archive/2018/01/the-students-who-dont-believe-college-is-an-option/550715/

Index